DATE DUE

DEMCO 38-296

Frank Martin

FRANK MARTIN

A Bio-Bibliography

Compiled by
Charles W. King

Bio-Bibliographies in Music, Number 26
Donald L. Hixon, Series Adviser

Greenwood Press
New York • Westport, Connecticut • London

Library of Congress Cataloging-in-Publication Data

King, Charles W.
    Frank Martin : a bio-bibliography / compiled by Charles W. King.
        p.   cm.—(Bio-bibliographies in music, ISSN 0742-6968 ; no.
26)
    Includes bibliographical references.
    Discography: p.
    ISBN 0-313-25418-4 (lib. bdg. : alk. paper)
    1. Martin, Frank, 1890-1974—Bibliography.   2. Martin, Frank,
1890-1974—Discography.   I. Title.   II. Series.
    ML134.M436K5   1990
    016.78'092—dc20   89-78255

British Library Cataloguing in Publication Data is available.

Library of Congress Catalog Card Number: 89-78255
ISBN: 0-313-25418-4
ISSN: 0742-6968

First published in 1990

Greenwood Press, 88 Post Road West, Westport, CT 06881
An imprint of Greenwood Publishing Group, Inc.

Printed in the United States of America

The paper used in this book complies with the
Permanent Paper Standard issued by the National
Information Standards Organization (Z39.48-1984).

10 9 8 7 6 5 4 3 2 1

To Maria Martin

Contents

Preface   ix

Acknowledgments   xi

Biography   3

Works and Performances   9

Discography   35

Writings by Martin   71

Bibliography   91
    General   92
    Titles   135

Appendix I: Alphabetical List of Compositions   223

Appendix II: Classified List of Compositions   228

Index   235

Preface

The decision to undertake a volume for the Bio-Bibliographies in Music series was based on the strong conviction that critical substantive writing about Frank Martin's music is sadly lacking in both quantity and quality. In addition, it seems that what has been written is not always readily at hand or immediately accessible to the general reader or even the researcher. Further investigation has revealed that there is, in fact, a great deal of material, not the least of which is the considerable body of writing by the composer himself. Many of the most important of these writings derived from articles, lectures, letters, program notes and interviews are now collected into several monographs in French with some parts in English and German. For the English speaking reader the problem remains; there is no monograph in English and for the most part the reader has necessarily relied on music encyclopedias.

This volume, then, concerns itself with bringing to the interested reader's attention as many sources as space will permit and providing the most comprehensive coverage to articles in English, while using this opportunity to call attention to the excellent work that has been done in the German, French, Dutch, and Italian languages. German articles by Bernard Billeter, Kurt von Fischer, Rudolf Klein, Willi Schuh, and Willy Tappolet are represented here. In French, there are articles by Ernest Ansermet, Edmond Appia, Robert-Aloys Mooser, Albert Paychère, Jean Claude Piquet, and Constantin Regamey. In the Dutch language, Wouter Paap, Hermann Sabbe, and Simon Vestdijk are among those represented. In Italian there is Roman Vlad. Any summary necessarily omits names of others who have made a valuable contribution.

I would not wish to conclude on a pessimistic note. Already one volume of Martin's important essays has been translated and is being prepared for publication. The likelihood of more to come is very promising. The over twenty-five formal papers in various languages, including some subsequently published dissertations, reflect the strong interest of students in this composer.

It is hoped that this volume of annotations may assist future researchers and stimulate the interest and curiosity of others to learn more of this composer's life and work.

Throughout this volume "See" entries refer to entries in the several sections, with preceding mnemonic letters: W = Works and Performances, D = Discography, B = Bibliography, M = Writings by Martin, which appear in similar fashion in the appendices and index.

Acknowledgments

Many individuals and some institutions have generously contributed to the preparation of this volume.

I should like to extend a special word of thanks to the following:

Maria Martin, Frank Martin Foundation, Naarden, Holland.
Dorman Smith, Music Librarian, University of Arizona, Tucson.
Max Schubel, Opus One Records, Greenville, Maine.
Dr. Janet Tupper, Denver, Colorado.
Reference and Inter Library Loan staff, University of Arizona.
National Sound Archive, London.

Technical assistance: Serena Baker, Spencer Hunter, University of Arizona Music Collection.

Proofreading and editorial assistance: Fenita and Charles King.

TRANSLATORS

Dutch: Nannette Bevelander, Sandra Chavarria, Margaret Gilmore, Johan van der Merwe, Ilse-Mari van Wyk.

French: Marcelle Bersin, Dr. Jean-Paul Bierny, Laurel Cooper, Terry Fahy, Colette Gariépy, Irene de Poukliakoff, Louis Haber, Mirene Hazebrouck, Lionel Lythgoe, Louis Pelosi, Manon Prizgintas.

German: Hans and Dorothy Bart, Oda Berg, Andrea Förderreuther, Helen Goetz, Milton Harmelink, Helga Kolosick, Eva Kremp, Beatrix Schneider, Stephanie Seymour.

Italian: Octavio Armendáriz, Dr. John Boe.

Russian: Marcia Aksman-Platt.

Spanish: Mona and Michel Frontain.

Frank Martin

Biography

"Osons donc employer ce beau mot de création, non pas pour enfler notre orgeil et nous mettre sur le plan même du créateur, mais avec humilité, avec prudence, pour ne pas laisser s'endormir en nous cet élément essentiel de notre vitalité. Il nous est donné à tous de creer..."

"Let us therefore dare to use this beautiful word creation, not to puff up our pride or to try to stand on the same level with the creator. Rather in all meekness and caution, in order not to let this important component of our vital power go to sleep. For it is given to all of us to create..."

The Swiss composer Frank Martin, whose creative life spans nearly three quarters of the twentieth century, remains to this day, for English-speaking musical audiences at least, something of an enigma.

It is not easy to explain satisfactorily why a composer of a large catalog of works (see Works and Performances section) of recognized high quality, embracing almost all forms and genre from folk-song arrangements lasting under two minutes to orchestral works, oratorio, and opera on a grand scale; a composer whose works have been heard on every continent and that have been performed by artists of world class status; a composer who has consistently been more kindly received by critics than most twentieth-century composers, and who has received many academic and musical honors during his lifetime, has somehow failed to attract the attention of subsequent generations of conductors and performers and ultimately a larger body of listeners. While it is beyond the scope of this essay to attempt an answer to this question, perhaps some of the answer derives from Martin's lifestyle and in the music itself.

Frank Martin was born the last of ten children in the Suisse Romande (French-speaking) area of Switzerland on September 15, 1890 which makes him a contemporary of Martinu, Prokofiev and Ibert among European composers of this period. Martin was the son of a prominent Calvinist minister whose French ancestors had fled the Huguenot persecutions and settled in Geneva where Frank Martin not only grew up, but spent a major portion of his adult life.

From letters, articles, and interviews we learn that Martin came from a happy home in which all of the children played musical instruments, but in which there were no professional musicians and no interest in having one. Young Frank demonstrated early his unusual gift in music and in particular his interest in the craft of writing music. Subsequently he wisely chose the piano as his instrument and developed considerable proficiency as evidenced by his own recording of the Huit préludes (see D105) and other works.

It was decided that Frank should pursue a regular academic curriculum in both secondary school and at the university, and his musical training was entrusted to private studies with Joseph Lauber, a composer and teacher of strong conservative convictions from whom the young Martin learned much through a solid foundation in the basics of music. In addition to Lauber, Hans Huber and Frederic Klose, two other musicians associated with the Geneva Conservatory of equally conservative and Germanic cast, took the young composer under their wing. As Roman Vlad points out in his article (see B110) the influences on young Martin's life included religious and cultural instruction, as well as artistic development--a combination which instilled in the young musician a profound respect for tradition and equally, a suspicion of anything that suggested modernism in music. From our present day point of view, we find it quite incredible to discover the young composer from a French speaking environment "deaf to the music of Debussy"; so strong was the German musical influence that dominated the city and area at that time.

The musical development of Frank Martin, like many of the earlier masters, divides into three distinct periods. The early formative period was largely shaped by the three above mentioned musicians to whom we can add a fourth, Ernest Ansermet, founder and conductor of the Orchestre de la Suisse Romande, who not only introduced Martin to the mainstream of new directions that European music was experiencing, but proved to be a lifelong friend, confidant, and, finally, the most important advocate of his music. Frank Martin's career as a composer was launched through the annual festival of the Association of Swiss Musicians which premiered many of his earliest works beginning in 1911 with the Trois poèmes païens for baritone and orchestra, and continued through 1921. During this time the Suite for Orchestra (1913), the First Violin Sonata (1915), Les Dithyrambes (1918), the Piano Quintet (1919), and the Pavane couleur du temps (1920) were introduced. All of these works demonstrate not only a determined preference for the works of Bach but equally an assimilation of the harmonies of Wagner and a stylistic affinity for the music of Franck and Fauré.

The decisive step which led Martin into the middle or experimental period was his escape temporarily from the environment of Geneva during which time he went first to Zürich in 1919 and 1920, then to Rome in 1921, and finally to Paris for two years in 1923, where he at last came into direct contact with the mainstream of European development that had been taking place in the early years of the twentieth century.

The first fruit of this new environment was the Quatre sonnets à Cassandre (1921) for mezzo-soprano, flute, viola, and cello on a text by Ronsard in which the music suggests middle period Ravel.

It was also during this period that Martin turned his attention to composing sacred music only to withdraw from it almost immediately due to his inability to resolve a personal conflict between what he considered subjective artistic expression in art music and the objective strictly ecclesiastical needs of music for congregational worship. It was during this period and possibly as a response to his experience of living in Rome that the composer began his Messe pour double choeur a cappella. Although completed in 1926, the Mass remained unperformed and unpublished until the mid-sixties. This, together with a never-completed Christmas Cantata, were the only sacred works composed until this impasse was resolved at the end of World War II when Martin received a commission from Radio Geneva to produce a work to be performed on the day that peace was declared. The composer believed that only a biblical text on the theme of forgiveness would fulfill this need and composed his In terra pax to fulfill the commission. This proved to be the first of several important large choral works using sacred texts.

By now Martin was already into his mid-thirties, married to Odette Micheli, and the father of the first of six children. Although little has been written about the Paris years, they proved to be extremely difficult and austere for the young musician trying to sustain himself and his family on the meager earnings derived from performances and commissions. Soon after, this marriage collapsed, and Martin returned to Geneva to reestablish himself in his native city.

A lifelong interest in rhythmic experimentation attracted Martin to the Jacques Dalcroze Institute in Geneva where in 1926 he was enrolled first as a student in order to complete the requirements to become a certified instructor in Eurhythmics, and afterwards was appointed as an instructor in harmony and improvisation. This intense interest in rhythm produced his piano trio, Trio sur des melodies populaires irlandaises (1925), and the orchestral work Rythmes (1926), both of which reflect this phase of the composer's development. During this same period Martin was establishing himself as a keyboard player in chamber music and in 1925 formed the Société de Musique de Chambre in which he played both piano and harpsichord. It was from this experience that he became familiar with the late piano music of Debussy that was to become an important influence in his future compositions.

By the end of the twenties Martin had become well established professionally and was appointed Professor of Chamber Music at the Geneva Conservatory. In 1933 Martin was invited to become director and Professor of composition, harmony and improvisation at the Technicum Moderne de Musique, a new private music school in Geneva, a post which he held until the school closed in 1940 due to financial and other difficulties.

Despite the fact that Martin now received more commissions for his work than in the lean Paris days, he was more and more experiencing a need for a new style and direction in his composing that would satisfy an inner need for personal expression and that would be expressed in a voice that would be uniquely his own. This growing need, coupled with an attraction to chromaticism, led the composer to undertake a serious study of the twelve-tone system of Arnold Schoenberg. Martin found himself drawn to the concept by the new freedoms it afforded, especially the idea of setting aside the limitations of the traditional cadence and the diatonic scale, while at the same time he rejected the concept of atonality as a form of musical anarchy. During this time Martin wrote the Quatre pièces brèves (1933) for guitar, Concerto no. 1 (1933-34) for piano, the string quintet Rhapsodie (1935), Danse de la peur (1935) for 2 pianos and orchestra, Trio à cordes (1936), and finally the Symphonie (1936-37) in which he applied the Schoenberg system to his own compositions as a means of mastering the craft of dodecaphony.

Then followed in 1938 the pivotal work Le Vin herbé, an oratorio based on Joseph Bédier's novel Roman de Tristan et Iseult, in which the composer was finally able to reconcile in just the right balance the new freedoms of the twelve-tone system with his need to retain a feeling of a tonal base. Thus is ushered in the final or mature period which Martin continually refined, but which was to become his stylistic trademark producing what we can now call the unique Martin sound. Following this initial success, there followed in 1944-45 his greatest success, the Petite symphonie concertante, a work for solo harp, harpsichord, and piano with double string orchestra, which was performed around the world and established Martin as a composer of international repute. As if further confirmation was needed, the Concerto pour sept instruments à vent, timbales, batterie et orchestre à cordes appeared in 1949. In 1950 the Violin Concerto was performed by Joseph Szigeti in Paris, with subsequent performances the following year in London and America. The long twenty-five-year apprenticeship was now finished.

At the end of the hostilities of the Second World War in 1945, Frank Martin then aged 55, remarried and widowed, moved to Amsterdam, home of his third wife, flutist Maria Boeke, for a trial period of living in a new environment. The composer explained that he knew too many people in Switzerland, and that there were too many demands on his time to properly devote himself to the discipline and hard work of composing. In the Netherlands another ten years were to pass before the Martins could withdraw from teaching and performing. In 1956 they obtained a home in the quiet suburb of Naarden where the composer lived for the remainder of his long life and where he could finally devote his full time and creative energy to composing. This he did up to and including the last days of his life.

During the final five or six years Frank Martin experienced a creative surge that allowed him to compose more and at a faster pace than ever before. His only explanation of this phenomena was that achieving into old age was a family trait most recently demonstrated by his father who was productive to the age of 92.

In his final years Frank Martin was besieged with commissions, most of which had to be declined and even among those accepted, some were never begun. It is intriguing to speculate on what may have come from a request for a piece for wind ensemble for the American bicentennial. Likewise, he received a request for a new piece for guitarist Julien Bream at a time when the composer was intensely interested in the rhythmic elements of flamenco music.

In the final decade came a succession of mature works beginning with Les Quatre éléments (1963-64) for Ernest Ansermet, the Cello Concerto (1965-66) for Pierre Fournier, a String Quartet (1966-67), the Second Piano Concerto (1968) for Paul Badura-Skoda, Maria-Triptychon (1968), for voice, solo violin, and orchestra commissioned by Irmgard Seefried and Wolfgang Schneiderhan. Next followed Erasmi monumentum (1969) for organ and orchestra, Trois danses (1970) for oboe, harp, and string orchestra for Heinz and Ursula Holliger, Poèmes de la mort for three male voices and three electric guitars for Lincoln Center (1971), Requiem (1971-72), and Viola Ballade (1972). During the final year of 1973-74 there was yet to follow Polyptyque for Yehudi Menuhin, Fantaisie sur des rythmes flamenco for Badura-Skoda and Martin's daughter Teresa, and the final work, Et la vie l'emporta.

Returning to possible reasons why Martin has not achieved the popular success of, for instance, Prokofiev, Bartók or Stravinsky, perhaps a part of the answer has been stated by Joseph Sagmaster writing in the <u>Program Notes</u> for the Cincinnati Symphony (4-7-8-1972). "One of the problems which Martin poses for the first time listener is the difficulty of classifying his music. He has been called a romanticist, a neo-romanticist, a neo-classicist, an eclectic, and a part-time follower of the twelve-tone or dodecaphonic school founded by Schoenberg. The only safe generalization seems to be that Martin wrote music for connoisseurs."

In retrospect, the music of Frank Martin is not experimental, trendy or locked in a dead end, but rather it is clearly in the main stream of the evolution of European art music. Just as Frank Martin learned patience in the slow and careful development of his art, so the gradual acceptance of his music by a larger audience worldwide awaits the patient passage of the years. Despite his music being out of fashion and the composer no longer here to provide "world premieres," time is on the side of Frank Martin.

Works and Performances

"Le rythme est un élément de liason
entre notre esprit et notre corps."

"Rhythm is an element of
connection between our spirit and
our body."

The underscored dates represent the year or years in which the work
was written.

1899

W1.   Tête de Linotte
       Song with piano accompaniment; 3 min.
       First extant composition written at age 9.
       Manuscript.

1910

W2.   Trois poèmes païens
       Baritone and large orchestra; 20 min.
       Text: Leconte de Lisle.
       Premiere: May 20, 1911, Vevey: Festival of the Association of Swiss
           Musicians, Louis de la Cruz-Froelich, baritone, Joseph Lauber,
           conductor.
       Geneva: Editions Henn.

1912

W3.   Ode et sonnet
3 treble voices a cappella with cello ad libitum; 3 min.
Text: Pierre de Ronsard.
Geneva: Editions Henn. See: D137

1913

W4.   Suite pour orchestre
15 min.
Premiere: June 14, 1913, Saint-Gall: Festival of the Association of
Swiss Musicians, Frank Martin, conductor.
Geneva: Editions Henn.

W5.   Sonate I pour violon et piano
18 min.
Premiere: July 10, 1915, Thoune: Festival of the Association of Swiss
Musicians: Maggy Breitmeyer, violin, and Joseph Lauber, piano.
Zürich: Hug. See: D205

1915

W6.   Symphonie pour orchestre burlesque
11 min.
Premiere: February, 1916, Geneva: Pierre Secretan, conductor.
Geneva: Editions Henn. See: D208

1915-1918

W7.   Les Dithyrambes
4 soloists, mixed choir, children's choir, and orchestra; 60 min.
Text: Pierre Martin.
Premiere: June 16, 1918, Lausanne: Festival of the Association of
Swiss Musicians: soloists M.-L. Debogis-Bohy, B. Cellérier, A.
Fleury, and E. Barblan; Ernest Ansermet, conductor.

1916

W8.   Le Roy a fait battre tambour
Alto voice and chamber orchestra; 5 min.
Text: popular folk text.
Manuscript. See: D191

<u>1919</u>

W9.   <u>Quintette</u>
Piano and string quartet; 23 min.
Premiere: 1919, Zürich: Frank Martin, pianist; Quartet de Boer.
Geneva: Editions Henn. <u>See</u>: D187

<u>1920</u>

W10.   <u>Chantons, je vous en prie</u>
Choruses based on old French noels.
Text: derived from <u>Mystère de la passion</u> by Arnoul Gréban.
Music arranged for a Nativity play by Pauline Martin.
Premiere: October, 1920, Geneva: Eglise de la Madeleine.

W11.   <u>Esquisse</u>
Orchestra; 15 min.
Premiere: October 30, 1920, Geneva: Ernest Ansermet, conductor.
Geneva: Editions Henn.

W12.   <u>Pavane couleur du temps</u>
String quintet; 7:30 min.
Alternate versions: piano 4-hands; chamber orchestra.
Geneva: Editions Henn. <u>See</u>: D151; W100

<u>1921</u>

W13.   <u>Quatre sonnets à Cassandre</u>
Mezzo-soprano, flute, viola, and cello; 12 min.
Text: Pierre de Ronsard.
Premiere: April 7, 1923, Geneva: Festival of the Association of Swiss
    Musicians: Colette Wyss, mezzo-soprano; directed by Frank Martin.
    <u>See</u>: B302; D183-D185

<u>1922</u>

W14.   <u>Oedipe-Roi</u>
Choruses and incidental music; 29 min.
Text from Sophocles and Jules Lacroix.
Choir of men, choir of women with instrumental ensemble.
Premiere: November 21, 1922, Geneva: Comedie se Genève directed
    by Frank Martin.

1922 & 1926

W15.   Messe pour double choeur a cappella
       26 min.
       Premiere: November 2, 1963, Hamburg: Bugenhagen-Kantorei; Franz
         W. Brunnert, conductor.
       Kassel: Bärenreiter. See: B220-B225; D125-D135

1923

W16.   Chanson du Mezzetin
       Soprano and mandoline, or oboe, violin, and cello; 3 min.
       Text: Paul Verlaine.
       Manuscript.

W17.   Oedipe à Colone
       Choruses and incidental music, soprano and baritone soloists, with
         chamber choir and chamber orchestra; 28 min.
       Text : Sophicles and André Secretan.
       Premiere: 1923, Geneva: Comedie de Genève directed by Frank
         Martin.
       Geneva: Editions Henn.

W18.   Armide
       135 min.
       Opera by Jean-Baptiste Lully, with a realization of the continuo
         transposed down a whole step and with the meter signatures
         reduced so that all of the recitative will move at a steady quarter-
         note beat.
       Premiere: December, 1939, Geneva: directed by Albert Paychère.
       Geneva: Editions Henn.

1924

W19.   Ouverture et foxtrot
       Two pianos; 8:30 min.
       Alternate versions: Concert pour instruments à vent et piano; Entr'acte
         pour grand orchestre; Chamber Fox Trot.
       Entr'acte was written for the Russian Marionnette Theatre of Madame
         Sazonova in Paris. Frank Martin arranged the Chamber Fox Trot
         for concert presentation in Boston on December 20, 1927,
         conducted by Nicolas Slonimsky, brother of Madame Sazonova.
       New York: G. Schirmer
       Manuscript: Entr'acte and Chamber Fox Trot. See: D139-D140

1925

W20.   Trio sur des mélodies populaires irlandaises
Trio for violin, cello, and piano; 18 min.
Premiere: April, 1926, Paris: the composer playing the piano part.
Zürich: Hug. See: B342; D210-D216

1926

W21.   Rythmes
3 symphonic movements for large orchestra; 18 min.
Premiere: March 12, 1927, Geneva: Ernest Ansermet, conductor.
Vienna: Universal Ed. See: B317

1928

W22.   Le Divorce
Incidental music for the play by Regnard.
Flute, saxophone, percussion, and piano.
Premiere: April, 1928, Geneva: Studio d'arts dramatique.
Manuscript.

1928-1931

W23.   La Nique à Satan
Soprano and baritone solo, choruses of men, women, and children
with accompanying ensemble of wind instruments, percussion, and
piano; 180 min.
Musical spectacle with a text by Albert Rudhardt.
Premiere: February 25, 1933, Geneva: Frank Martin, conductor.
Geneva: Editions Henn. See: B257-B260

W24.   18 Chansons
Songs for voice and piano derived from La Nique à Satan.
Geneva: Editions Henn. See: D45

1929

W25.   Roméo et Juliette
Incidental music to Shakespeare's play with additional text by René
Morax. Choruses with instrumental ensemble; 30 min.
Premiere: June 1, 1929, Mézières (Switzerland): directed by Frank
Martin.
Geneva: Editions Henn. See: B316

W26. Cantate sur la Nativité
Incompleted Christmas cantata for mixed choir, strings, and organ on a text by Arnoul Gréban. Some material from this manuscript was later incorporated into In terra pax. See: W68
Manuscript.

W27. Jeux du Rhône
Marches and choruses from Fêtes du Rhône for mixed chorus and harmony.
Text: René-Louis Piachaud.
Premiere: July 6, 1929, Geneva: directed by Frank Martin.

1930

W28. Sonate en la majeur. Sonata en mi mineur by Henrico Albicastro.
Violin and piano; 10 min.
Realization of the figured bass.
Geneva: Editions Henn.

W29. Sonate en mi mineur by Gaspard Fritz
Flute or violin and piano; 10 min.
Realization of the figured bass.
Geneva: Editions Henn.

W30. Chanson
Chorus for 4 treble voices; 3 min.
Text: C.F. Ramuz from his Le Petit village.
Geneva: Editions Henn. See: D42

W31. Le Coucou
Canon for 7 female voices; 3 min.
Text: J.-P. Toulet. Written for students during the period when Martin was a member of the faculty at the Institut Jacques Dalcroze.
Geneva: Editions Henn. See: D48

W32. Chanson en canon
Canon for mixed chorus; 3 min.
Text: C.F. Ramuz from his Le Petit village.
Composed for the Girls Middle School in Geneva.
Geneva: Editions Henn. See: D43-D44

1931-1932

W33. Sonate II pour violon et piano
16 min.
Premiere: October 7, 1932, Geneva: Jean Goering, violin, and Frank Martin, piano.
Vienna: Universal Ed. See: D206

1933

W34.   Quatre pièces brèves pour guitare
        8 min.
        Solo pieces for guitar written for Andrés Segovia.
        Alternate versions: solo piano (1933) and full orchestra (1934).
        Premiere: November 21, 1934, Geneva: [orchestral version] Ernest
            Ansermet, conductor.
        Vienna: Universal Ed. See: B299-B301; D168-D182

1933-1934

W35.   Concerto I pour piano et orchestre
        21 min.
        Premiere: January 22, 1936, Geneva: Walter Gieseking, pianist, Ernest
            Ansermet, conductor.
        Other performances: April 22, 1936, Barcelona: International Society of
            Contemporary Music (ISCM) Festival: soloist Walter Frey; Ernest
            Ansermet, conductor.
        Vienna: Universal Ed. See: B125-B126; D51

1935

W36.   Es ist ein Schnitter heisst der Tod
        German folk-song arranged for mixed chorus a cappella; 2 min.
        The specific purpose and occasion of this arrangement is unknown.
        Manuscript. See: D75

W37.   Rhapsodie
        Quintet for 2 violins, 2 violas, and double bass; 14 min.
        Premiere: March 10, 1936, Geneva: Suzanne Bornand and Leon
            Cherechewski, violins, Willy Kunz-Aubert and Jean Goering, violas,
            with Hans Fryba, double bass; Awarded first place in Concours de
            composition in "Carillon."
        Vienna: Universal Ed.

W38.   Die blaue Blume
        75 min.
        Ballet music which won first place in a competition but was never
            performed. The piano score was never orchestrated.
        Manuscript.

W39.   Danse de la peur
        Two pianos and chamber orchestra; 15 min.
        Music derived from the ballet music Die blaue Blume.
        Premiere: June 28, 1944, Geneva: Dinu and Madeleine Lipatti;
            orchestra conducted by Edmond Appia.
        Vienna: Universal Ed.

1936

W40.   Trio à cordes
       String trio for violin, viola, and cello; 16 min.
       Premiere: May 2 1936, Brussels: Trio Röntgen: Joachim Röntgen,
           Oskar Kromer, and Antonio Tusa.
       First U.S. performance: July 5, 1967, Dartmouth College, Hanover,
           New Hampshire: Stuart Canin, violin, Ralph Hersh, viola, and Paul
           Olefsky, cello.
       Vienna: Universal Ed. See: D209

1936-1937

W41.   Symphonie pour grand orchestre
       27 min.
       Premiere: March 7, 1938, Lausanne: Ernest Ansermet, conductor.
       Vienna: Universal Ed. See: B338-B340

1937

W42.   Petite marche blanche et trio noir les grenouilles, le rossignol
       Two easy pieces for 2 pianos; 2 min.
       Vienna: Universal Ed. See: D153

W43.   Ballade pour saxophone
       Alto saxophone and string orchestra; 13 min.
       Commissioned by Sigurd Rascher.
       Premiere: Autumn of 1938, Sidney: Sigurd Rascher.
       Vienna: Universal Ed. See: B120; D27-D28

1938

W44.   Le Vin herbé
       Secular oratorio in 3 parts.
       Commissioned by Robert Blum for his Züricher Madrigalchor.
       Premiere: April 16, 1940, Zürich: (1st part) Robert Blum conducting his
           Madrigal Choir. Complete 3 part work had its first performance on
           March 28, 1942 in Zürich by the same participants.
       Vienna: Universal Ed. See: B349-B375; D229-D230; M8, W50

W45.   Sonata da chiesa
        Viola d'amore and organ; 14 min.
        Commissioned by Hans Balmer.
        Premiere: December 8, 1939, Bâle: Gertrud Flügel and Hans Balmer.
        First U.K. performance: March 30, 1954: Harry Danks, viola d'amore
            and James Lockhart, organ.
        First U.S. performance: March 28, 1954, Wakefield, (Boston)
            Massachusetts: Anne Gombosi, viola d'amore.
        Alternate versions: See: W51, W96
        Vienna: Universal Ed.   See: B322; D198-D204

1939

W46.   Du Rhône au Rhin
        March for band; 4:30 min.
        Official march of the Swiss National Exposition, Zürich 1939.
        Premiere: May 6, 1939, Zürich: directed by Volkmar Andreae.
        New York: G. Schirmer.   See: D72-D74

W47.   Ballade pour flûte
        Flute and piano; 8 min.
        Commissioned by the Concours International d'Exécution Musicale.
        Alternate version: Flute and large orchestra with an orchestration by
            Ernest Ansermet.
        Premiere: November 27, 1939, Lausanne & November 29, 1939,
            Geneva: André Pépin, flute; Ernest Ansermet, conductor.
        Alternate version: See: W52
        Vienna: Universal Ed.   See: B118; D4-D24

W48.   Ballade pour piano et orchestre
        15 min.
        Composed on the island of Oléron.
        Premiere: February 1, 1944, Zürich: Walter Frey, pianist; Ernest
            Ansermet, conductor.
        First U.S. performance: April 28, 1970, Macomb, Illinois: Lee Luvisi,
            pianist; Chicago Symphony Orchestra; Irwin Hoffman, conductor.
        Vienna: Universal Ed.   See: B119; D25-D26, M10

1940

W49.   Ballade pour trombone
        Trombone and piano; 7 min.
        Commissioned for the Concours National Suisse d'Exécution Musicale.
        Premiere: September, 1940, Geneva.
        Alternate version: See: W53
        Vienna: Universal Ed.   See: D29-D34

1940-1941

W50.   Le Vin herbé (parts 2 & 3)
90 min. (complete)
Premiere: March 28, 1942: Zürich Madrigal Choir, Robert Blum, conductor.
Staged premiere: August 15, 1948: German language version as Der Zaubertrank at the Saltzburg Festival: Ferenc Fricsay, conductor.
First U.S. performance: February 26, 1961, New York: Schola Cantorum; Hugh Ross, conductor.
First U.S. staged version: August 23, 1968, Aptos, California: Cabrillo Festival, presented in English translation.
Vienna: Universal Ed. See: W44

1941

W51.   Sonata da chiesa
Version for flute and organ; 14 min.
Premiere: June 11, 1942, Lausanne: Maria Martin and Charles Faller.
Alternate versions: See: W45, W96, W111
Vienna: Universal Ed. See: B322; D198-D204

W52.   Ballade pour flûte
Version for flute, string orchestra, and piano.
Premiere: November 28, 1941, Bâle: Joseph Bopp, flutist; Paul Sacher, conductor.
Alternate version: See: W47
Vienna: Universal Ed. See: B118; D19-D23

W53.   Ballade pour trombone
Version for trombone and chamber orchestra.
Premiere: January 26, 1942, Geneva: Thomas Morley, trombone; Ernest Ansermet, conductor.
Vienna: Universal Ed. See: D31-D32; W49

W54.   Cantate pour le 1er août
Secular cantata for mixed chorus and piano or organ; 4 min.
Premiere: August 1, 1941, Geneva: Radio Genève.
Geneva: Editions Henn. See: D39

W55.   Das Märchen vom Aschenbrödel
Ballet on Cinderella after the Grimm brothers for soprano, mezzo-soprano, alto, and tenor soloists with chamber orchestra.
Choreographer: Marie-Eve Kreis.
Premiere: March 12, 1942, Bâle: soloists Marguerite Gradmann-Lüscher, Hélène Suter-Moser, Pauline Widmer-Hoch, and Max Meili; directed by Paul Sacher.
Kassel: Bärenreiter.

W56. Petite Complainte
Oboe and piano; 3:30 min.
Music derived from Das Märchen vom Aschenbrödel for the Concours
National Suisse d'Exécution Musicale.
Premiere: September, 1941, Geneva.
Zürich: Hug.

W57. Danse Grave
Piano.
Music from Das Märchen vom Aschenbrödel.
Manuscript. See: W55

1942

W58. La Voix des siècles
Incidental music, choruses and marches for the bimillenium of Geneva.
Premiere: July 4, 1942, Geneva: directed by Roger Vuataz.
Manuscript.

W59. Marche des 22 Cantons. Marche de Genava
Marches derived from La Voix des Siècles.
Geneva: Editions Henn.

1942-1943

W60. Der Cornet
Song cycle for alto voice and chamber orchestra; 58 min.
Text: Rainer Maria Rilke. Musical setting of his Die Weise von Liebe
und Tod des Cornets Christoph Rilke.
Premiere: February 9, 1945, Bâle: Elsa Cavelti, contralto; directed by
Paul Sacher.
Vienna: Universal Ed. See: B156-B162, D63-D65; M5

1943

W61. Ein Totentanz zu Basel im Jahre 1943
Outdoor dance spectacle for chorus, string orchestra, and jazz
ensemble; 120 min.
Premiere: May 27, 1943, Bâle.
Manuscript. See: B341

W62. Janeton
Men's chorus a cappella; 2 min.
Text: Roland Stähli.
Berne: Société des Chanteurs Bernois.

W63.   Si Charlotte avait voulu
       Men's chorus a cappella; 2 min.
       Text: Roland Stähli.
       Berne: Société des Chanteurs Bernois.

1943-1944

W64.   Sechs Monologe aus Jedermann
       Song cycle for baritone voice and piano; 17 min.
       Text: Hugo von Hofmannsthal.
       Commissioned by Max Christmann.
       Premiere: August 6, 1944, Gstaad: Max Christmann, baritone, and
          Frank Martin, piano.
       First U.K. performance: February 29, 1952, Wigmore Hall, London:
          Elsa Cavelti and Frank Martin.
       First U.S. performance: Spring, 1956: Gerard Souzay.
       Alternate version: See: W89
       Vienna: Universal Ed. See: B318-B321; D192-D195; M4

1944

W65.   Petite eglise
       Chorus of men or women's voices a cappella; 2 min.
       Text: Henri Devain.
       Berne: Société des Chanteurs Bernois.

W66.   Canon pour Werner Reinhart
       Chorus for 8 voices a cappella; 2 min.
       Text: Pierre de Ronsard.
       Manuscript.

W67.   Passacaille pour orgue
       13 min.
       Composed for Kurt Wolfgang Senn.
       Premiere: September 26, 1944, Bern: Kurt Wolfgang Senn, organist.
       Alternate versions: See: W97, W117
       Vienna: Universal Ed. See: B262-B270; D141-D148

W68.   In terra pax
       Oratorio breve for 5 soloists, 2 mixed choirs, and orchestra; 43 min.
       Text drawn from the Old and New Testaments.
       Commissioned by Radio Genève to be broadcast on the armistice day
          of World War II.
       Premiere: May 7, 1945, Geneva: [radio broadcast].
       First public performance: May 31, 1945, Geneva: soloists Madeleine
          Dubuis, Nelly Grétillat, Ernst Haefliger, Paul Sandoz, and Fernando
          Corena; Ernest Ansermet, conductor.
       Vienna: Universal Ed. See: B207-B213; D120-D123; M23

W69. Notre Père
       Unison choir and organ; 2 min.
       Fribourg: Edition de la Procure Romande.

W70. Ma belle; Le Mai; Eho! eho!; Chanson satirique; Noël de Praetorius;
          Psaume 42; Psaume 104; O Nuit, heureuse nuit
       Arrangements and harmonizations for men's chorus a cappella.
       Berne: Société des Chanteurs Bernois.

W71. Campagnarde; Joli tambour; Trimousette
       Folk-song arrangements for chorus.
       Berne: Librairie d'Etat.

W72. En revenant d'auvergne; C'etait Anne de Bretagne
       Arrangements for girls chorus a cappella from "Chantons."
       Berne: Libraire d'Etat.

W73. So Wünsch Ich Ihr eine gute Nacht; Wach Auf, Wach Auf
       Harmonizations for mixed chorus a cappella from "Berner Liederheft."
       Berne: Müller & Schade.

W74. Meine Stimme klinge; Wer jetzig Zeiten Leben will; Wohl Auf Wer Bass
          will Wandern
       Harmonizations for children's chorus a cappella from "Singbuch für die
          Oberstufe der Volksschule."

W75. L'Amour de moy s'y est enclose
       French folksong; 3 min.
       Arrangement for soprano, 2 flutes, and piano or for medium voices.
       Manuscript. See: D1

1944-1945

W76. Petite symphonie concertante
       Solo harp, harpsichord, and piano with double string orchestra; 22
          min.
       Commissioned by Paul Sacher for his Basle Chamber Orchestra and
          Zürich Collegium Musicum.
       Premiere: May 17, 1946, Zürich: Corina Blaser, harp, Hans Andreae,
          harpsichord, and Rudolf am Bach, piano; Zürich Collegium
          Musicum; Paul Sacher, conductor.
       First U.S. performance: January 17, 1948: NBC Symphony broadcast;
          Ernest Ansermet, conductor.
       First public performance: February 19, 1948: Chicago Symphony
          Orchestra; Ernest Ansermet, conductor.
       Alternate version: See: W81
       Vienna: Universal Ed. See: B271-B285; D154-D163; M28

1945

W77.   A la Foire d'amour
Text: Francis Bourquin; 3:30 min.
Chanson des Jours de pluie
Text: Roland Stähli; 2:30 min.
A la Fontaine (set to the same music as previous entry).
Men's chorus a cappella.

W78.   Dédicace
Tenor and piano; 3 min.
Text: Pierre De Ronsard.
Composed for the 80th birthday of Emile Jacques Dalcroze.
Premiere: July 6, 1945, Geneva: Hugues Cuenod, tenor, and Frank
   Martin, piano.
Kassel: Bärenreiter. See: D66

W79.   Petite fanfare
2 trumpets, 2 horns, and 2 trombones; 3 min.
Premiere: Autumn, 1945, Lausanne.
Manuscript.

1945-1948

W80.   Golgotha
Passion oratorio for 5 soloists, mixed choir, organ, and orchestra; 90
   min.
Text from the gospel narratives and from writings of St. Augustine.
Premiere: April 29, 1949, Geneva: soloists Renée Defraiteur, Nelly
   Grétillat, Ernst Haefliger, H.B. Etcheverry, and Heinz Rehfuss;
   Société de Chant Sacré; Samuel Baud-Bovy, conductor.
First U.S. performance: January 18, 1952, Carnegie Hall, New York:
   Dessoff Choirs; Paul Boepple, conductor.
First U.K. performance: November 9, 1955: BBC Chorus and
Orchestra; Winthrop Sargent, conductor.
Vienna: Universal Ed. See: B177-B200; D95-D96; M22

1946

W81.   Symphonie concertante
Version for full orchestra of the Petite symphonie concertante. See:
   W76
Premiere: August 16, 1947, Lucerne: conducted by Ernest Ansermet
   during International Music Week.
Vienna: Universal Ed.

W82. Athalie
       Incidental music and choruses, alto voice, and 2 choirs of girls with
          chamber orchestra.
       Text: Racine.
       Premiere: May 7, 1947, Geneva: Girls Secondary School chorus;
          directed by Albert Paychère.
       Manuscript.

W83. Ouverture pour Athalie
       Orchestra; 9 min.
       Music derived from Athalie. See: W82
       Vienna: Universal Ed.

1947

W84. Quant n'ont assez fait do-do
       Song for tenor, guitar, and piano 4-hands; 2:30 min.
       Text: Charles d'Orleans.
       Premiere: October 9, 1947, Lauren: Hugues Cuenod, tenor, Hermann
          Leeb, guitar, Madeleine Lipatti, and Frank Martin, piano.
       Manuscript. See: D167

W85. Trois chants de Noël
       Soprano, flute, and piano; 6 min.
       Text: Albert Rudhardt.
       Christmas songs composed for private use by the composer's family.
       Premiere: Christmas, 1947, Amsterdam: Françoise, Maria, and Frank
          Martin.
       Vienna: Universal Ed. See: D217-D224

1947-1948

W86. Huit préludes pour le piano
       21 min.
       Composed for Dinu Lipatti.
       Premiere: March 22, 1950, Lausanne: [radio broadcast].
       First public performance: July 2, 1950, Leysin: Denise Bidal, pianist.
       Vienna: Universal Ed. See: B201-B206; D101-D119

1949

W87. Ballade pour violoncelle
       Cello and piano; 16 min.
       Alternate version: cello with chamber orchestra.
       Premiere: November 17, 1950, Zürich: August Wenziger, cellist;
          Collegium Musicum, Zürich; Paul Sacher, conductor.
       First U.S. performance: November 24, 1952: Paul Tortelier, cellist; Little
          Orchestra Society of New York; Thomas Scherman, conductor.
       Vienna: Universal Ed. See: B121-B122; D35-D38

W88. Concerto pour sept instruments à vent, timbales, batterie et orchestre à cordes
22 min.
Premiere: October 25, 1949, Bern: Luc Balmer, conductor.
First U.S. performance: December 28, 1950, Carnegie Hall, New York: New York Philharmonic; George Szell, conductor.
Vienna: Universal Ed. See: B135-B139; D55-D58; M13

W89. Sechs Monologe aus Jedermann
Version for baritone or alto voice with orchestra. See: W64
Premiere: September 9, 1949, Venice: Elsa Cavelti, contralto; Rafael Kubilik, conductor.
First U.S. performance: November 5, 1956, Town Hall, New York: Dietrich Fischer-Dieskau, baritone; Little Orchestra Society; Thomas Scherman, conductor.
Vienna: Universal Ed. See: B318-B321; D196-D197; M5

W90. Chanson des métamorphoses
Song with piano accompaniment; 4 min.
Chanson populaire savoyarde.
Manuscript. See: D41

W91. Il Faut partir pour l'Angleterre
Song with piano accompaniment; 2 min.
Chanson populaire Valaisanne)
Manuscript. See: D90

1950

W92. Five Ariel Songs
Mixed chorus a cappella; 13 min.
Text: Ariel's songs from Shakespeare's Tempest.
Premiere: March 7, 1953, Amsterdam: Nederlands Kamerkoor; Felix de Nobel, conductor.
Vienna: Universal Ed. See: B175-B176; D91-D94

1950-1951

W93. Concerto pour violon et orchestre
30 min.
Premiere: January 24, 1952, Bâle: Hanheinz Schneeberger, violin; Paul Sacher, conductor.
First U.S. performance: November 13, 1952: Joseph Szigeti, violinist; New York Philharmonic; Dimitri Mitropoulos, conductor.
Vienna: Universal Ed. See: B140-B149; D59-D61; M3

1951-1952

W94.   Concert pour clavecin et petit orchestra
       20 min.
       Commissioned by Isabel Nef.
       Premiere: September 14, 1952, Venice: Festival of the SIMC; Isabel
           Nef, harpsichord; Fernando Previtali, conductor.
       First U.K. performance: March 8, 1955: George Malcolm,
           harpsichordist; Leppard Orchestra; Raymond Leppard, conductor.
       Vienna: Universal Ed. See: B123-B124; D49-D50

1952

W95.   Clair de lune
       Piano; 3 min.
       Written for inclusion in an anthology of easy 20th century piano pieces
           called Les Contemporains.
       Paris: Pierre Noël. See: D46-D47

W96.   Sonata da chiesa
       Version for Viola d'amore and string orchestra; 14 min. See: W45
       Premiere: April 29, 1953, Turin: soloist Aurelio Arcidiacono; orchestra
           conducted by Virgilio Brun.
       Vienna: Universal Ed. See: D204

W97.   Passacaille
       Version for string orchestra.
       Premiere: October 16, 1953, Frankfurt: Karl Münchinger, conductor.
       Alternate versions: See: W67, W117
       Vienna: Universal Ed. See: B262-B270; D149

1952-1955

W98.   Der Sturm (La Tempête)
       Opera in 3 acts; 150 min.
       Text: Shakespeare's Tempest in the German translation by Wilhelm
           von Schlegel.
       Premiere: June 17 1956, Vienna: Ernest Ansermet, conductor.
       First U.S. performance: October 11, 1956: New York City Center
           Opera; Erich Leinsdorf, conductor.
       Vienna: Universal Ed. See: B323-B337

W99.   Drei Fragmente aus "Der Sturm"
       Overture and 2 airs of Prospero; 25 min.
       Premiere: March 6, 1961, Lausanne & March 8, 1961, Geneva: Dietrich
           Fischer-Dieskau, baritone; Ernest Ansermet, conductor.
       Vienna: Universal Ed. See: D207

1954

W100. Pavane couleur du temps
Version for chamber orchestra; 7:30 min.
Geneva: Editions Henn.

1955

W101. Au clair de la lune
3 variations for piano 4-hands; 5 min.
Universal Ed.

1955-1956

W102. Etudes pour orchestre à cordes
String orchestra; 20 min.
Commissioned by Paul Sacher.
Premiere: November 23, 1956, Bâle: Paul Sacher, conductor.
First U.S. performance: December 18, 1959: Pittsburgh Symphony
Orchestra; William Steinberg, conductor.
Alternate version: See: W104
Vienna: Universal Ed. See: B169-B173; D83-D85; M17

1956

W103. Ouverture en hommage à Mozart
Premiere: December 10, 1956, Geneva: [radio broadcast] Ernest
Ansermet, conductor.
Vienna: Universal Ed.

1957

W104. Etudes pour deux pianos
Alternate version of Etudes pour orchestra à cordes. See: W101
Premiere: October 28, 1957, Staatliche Hochschule für Musik,
Cologne: Alexander Meyer von Bremen and Frank Martin, pianists.
Vienna: Universal Ed. See: D86-D87

W105. Chaconne
Cello and piano; 9 min.
Transcription of the 2nd movement of the 2nd Violin Sonata.
Vienna: Universal Ed. See: D40

<u>1957 & 1959</u>

W106. <u>Le Mystère de la Nativité</u>
Christmas oratorio for 9 soloists, mixed chamber choir, men's choir, large mixed chorus, and orchestra 105 min.
Text: Arnoul Gréban.
Premiere: December 23, 1959, Geneva: Ernest Ansermet, conductor.
Staged premiere: December 16, 1962, Saltzburg: Heinz Wallberg, conductor.
First U.K. performance: December 13, 1960, Royal Festival Hall: London Philharmonic Orchestra and Chorus; Jaroslav Krombholc, conductor.
First U.S. performance: December 16, 1962, Carnegie Hall, New York: Harvard Glee Club and Radcliffe Choral Society and Harvard Orchestra; Henry Swoboda, conductor.
Vienna: Universal Ed. <u>See</u>: B233-B256

W107. <u>Pièce brève</u>
Flute, oboe, and harp; 5 min.
Music derived from <u>Le Mystère de la Nativité</u>.
Premiere: May 10, 1957, Lausanne: soloists Edmond Defrancesco, Max Frankhauser, and Amedea Redditi.
Zürich: Hug.

<u>1958</u>

W108. <u>Ouverture en rondeau</u>
Orchestra; 11 min.
Commissioned for the Lucerne Festival.
Premiere: August 13, 1958, Lucerne: Ernest Ansermet, conductor.
First U.S. performance: July 9, 1967, Dartmouth College, Hanover, New Hampshire: Dartmouth Symphony Orchestra; Mario di Bonaventura, conductor.

W109. <u>Que Dieu se montre seulement</u>
Excerpt from <u>Pseaumes de Genève</u> for alto and tenor voice, flute, and piano.
Manuscript.

W110. <u>Pseaumes de Genève</u>
   Cantata for mixed chorus, boy's choir, organ, and orchestra; 22 min.
   Text: Psalms from the Old Testament translated into French by
      Clément Marot and Theodore Beze.
   Commissioned by Radio Genève to celebrate the 400th anniversary of
      the University of Geneva.
   Premiere: May, 1959, Geneva: Société de Chant Sacré; Ernest
      Ansermet, conductor.
   First U.S. performance: May 10, 1985, Minneapolis: chorus and
      orchestra of the Plymouth Music Series; Philippe Brunelle,
      conductor.
   Vienna: Universal Ed. <u>See</u>: B291

W111. <u>Sonata da chiesa</u>
   14 min.
   Version for flute and string orchestra, orchestrated by Victor
      Desarzens.
   Premiere: October 15, 1959, Lausanne: [radio broadcast] Marianne
      Clément, flute; Victor Desarzens, conductor.
   Vienna: Universal Ed. <u>See</u>: W51, W96

<u>1959</u>

W112. <u>In dulci jubilo</u>
   An arrangement of an old Dutch Carol prepared for the personal use
      of the Martin family.
   Manuscript.

<u>1960</u>

W113. <u>Drey Minnelieder</u>
   Song cycle for soprano and piano; 9 min.
   Text: 13 century anon., Dietmar von Eist, and Walter von der
      Vogelweide.
   Premiere: 1960, Berlin: R.I.A.S.
   Alternate edition: Soprano, flute, viola, and cello.
   Vienna: Universal Ed. <u>See</u>: B163; D67-D71

W114. <u>Monsieur de Pourceaugnac</u>
   Opera in 3 acts; 105 min.
   Text: Slightly abridged from the play by Molière.
   Premiere: April 23, 1963, Geneva: Ernest Ansermet, conductor.
   Vienna: Universal Ed. <u>See</u>: B226-B232; M9

1961

W115. Ode à la musique
       Mixed chorus, brass ensemble, double bass, and piano; 9 min.
       Written for the 30th congrés de la société pédagogique de la Suisse
           Romande.
       Text: Verses from Les Prologue by Guillaume de Machaut.
       Premiere: June 23, 1962, Bienne: directed by Frank Martin.
       Kassel: Bärenreiter. See: B261

W116. Verse à boire
       Mixed chorus a cappella; 3 min.
       Text: Folk verse from Anjou.
       Premiere: June 26, 1963, Amsterdam: Nederlands Kamerkoor; Felix de
           Nobel, conductor.
       Geneva: Editions Henn. See: D227-D228

1962

W117. Passacaille
       13 min.
       Version for grand orchestra. See: W66, W96
       Premiere: May 30, 1963, Berlin: Berlin Philharmonic; Frank Martin,
           conductor.
       Vienna: Universal Ed. See: B264-B265

1963

W118. Inter arma caritas
       Orchestra; 7 min.
       Written for the centennial celebration of the International Red Cross.
       Premiere: September 1, 1963, Geneva: Ernest Ansermet, conductor.
       Geneva: Radio Suisse Romande. See: B214-B215

W119. Nous sommes trois souverains princes
       Old French Christmas carol arranged for mixed voices a cappella; 3
           min.
       Composed for the private use of the Martin family.
       Manuscript. See: D136

1963-1964

W120. Les Quatre éléments
Symphonic etudes for large orchestra; 20 min.
Composed for the celebration of the 80th birthday of Ernest Ansermet.
Premiere: October 5, 1964, Lausanne: Orchestre de la Suisse
    Romande; Ernest Ansermet, conductor.
First U.S. performance: November 5, 1965: Pittsburgh Symphony
    Orchestra; William Steinberg, conductor.
Vienna: Universal Ed. See: B292-B298; M17

1964

W121. Pilate
Oratorio breve for baritone, mezzo-soprano, tenor, and bass soloists,
    mixed chorus and orchestra; 30 min.
Text: Arnoud Grèban from his Mystère de la passion.
Commissioned by the European Radio Union.
Premiere: November 14, 1964, R.A.I, Rome: soloists Jean-Christophe
    Benoit (Pilate), Jeanne Deroubaix, Louis Devos, and Derrik Olsen;
    directed by Armando la Rosa Parodi.
Vienna: Universal Ed.

1965

W122. Etude rythmique
Piano; 2:30 min.
Written to honor Jacques Dalcroze.
Premiere: February 22, 1965, Geneva: Arlette Stadelmann, pianist.
Wiesbaden: Breitkopf & Härtel. See: D80-D82

W123. Esquisse pour piano
Piano; 3:15 min.
Originally entitled Etude de lecture.
Composed for the sight reading piece at the Internationaler
    Musikwettbewerb held in Munich in September 1965.
Vienna: Universal Ed. See: D76-D78

1965-1966

W124. Concerto pour violoncelle et orchestre
28 min.
Premiere: January 26, 1967, Bâle: Pierre Fournier, cellist; Paul Sacher,
    conductor.
First U.S. performance: October 26, 1967: Pierre Fournier, cellist;
    Cleveland Symphony Orchestra; George Szell, conductor.
Vienna: Universal Ed. See: B150-B155; D62

1966

W125. Agnus Dei
        Organ; 5 min.
        Organ transcription of the Agnus Dei from Messe. See: W15
        Vienna: Universal Ed.

1966-1967

W126. Quatuor à cordes
        22 min.
        Commissioned by the Tonhalle Gesellschaft to celebrate the centennial
           of Zürich's concert hall.
        Premiere: June 20, 1968, Zürich: Tonhalle-Quartett.
        Vienna: Universal Ed. See: B303-B305; D186

1967

W127. Magnificat
        Soprano, violin solo, and orchestra; 11 min.
        Text: Luther's German translation from the New Testament.
        Commissioned by Irmgard Seefried and Wolfgang Schneiderhan.
        Premiere: August 14, 1968: Lucerne Music Festival: Irmgard Seefried,
           soprano, and Wolfgang Schneiderhan, violin; Bernard Haitink,
           conductor.
        Magnificat later became the second part of Maria-Triptychon. See:
           W130
        Vienna: Universal Ed. See: B217; D124

W128. O Dieu, c'est dans ta Sion Sainte
        Arrangement of Psalm 65 for alto voice and piano.
        Manuscript.

1968

W129. Concerto II pour piano et orchestre
        25 min.
        Commissioned by Paul Badura-Skoda.
        Premiere: June 24, 1970, Paris: [radio & television] Paul Badura-
           Skoda, pianist; Victor Desarzens, conductor.
        Public premiere: June 27, 1970, La Haye: Paul Badura-Skoda, pianist;
           Jerzy Semkow, conductor.
        First U.S. performance: April 7, 1972: Paul Badura-Skoda, pianist;
           Cincinnati Symphony Orchestra; Thomas Schippers, conductor.
        Vienna: Universal Ed. See: B127-B134; D52-D54

W130. Maria-Triptychon
Soprano and violin solo with orchestra; 22 min.
Text: Ave Maria (in German), Magnificat (in German) both from
Luther's translation of the New Testament. Stabat Mater (in Latin),
sequence from the Latin liturgy ascribed to Jacopone da Todi.
Premiere: November 13, 1969, Rotterdam: during the celebration of
the 500th birthday of Erasmus: Irmgard Seefried, soprano, and
Wolfgang Schneiderhan, violinist; Rotterdam Philharmonic; Jean
Fournet, conductor.
First U.S. performance: December 16, 1970, State University of New
York, Binghamton: Maria Dornya, soprano, and Eric Lewis, violin;
Harpur College Orchestra; David Buttolph, conductor.
Vienna: Universal Ed. See: B216-B219; D124; W127

1969

W131. Erasmi monumentum
Organ with large orchestra; 22 min.
Commissioned by the Kunststichting (Arts Foundation) of Rotterdam
as part of the celebration of the 500th birthday of Erasmus.
Premiere: October 27, 1969, Rotterdam: Arie Keijzer, organist;
Rotterdam Philharmonic; Jean Fournet, conductor.
Vienna: Universal Ed. See: B166-B168

W132. Ballade des pendus
Three male voices and three electric guitars; 9 min.
First version of a work that was to become the finale of Poèmes de la
mort.
Vienna: Universal Ed. See: D165; W133

1969 & 1971

W133. Poèmes de la mort
Three male voices and three electric guitars; 17 min.
Text: François Villon.
Commissioned by the Lincoln Center Fund for the Chamber Music
Society of Lincoln Center.
Premiere: December 12, 1971, Alice Tully Hall, New York: Grayson
Hirst, tenor, John Reardon, baritone, Herbert Beattie, bass, and
Martin Best, Edward Flower, and Stanley Silvermann, electric
guitars; directed by the composer.
Vienna: Universal Ed. See: B287-B288; D164-D165

1970

W134. Trois danses
Oboe, harp, solo string quintet, and string orchestra; 18 min.
Commissioned by Paul Sacher for Heinz and Ursula Holliger.
Premiere: October 9, 1970, Zürich: Heinz Holliger, oboist, and Ursula
Holliger, harpist; Collegium Musicum; Paul Sacher, conductor.
First U.K. performance: December 9, 1970: Heinz Holliger, oboist
Ursula Holliger, harpist; English Chamber Orchestra; Paul Sacher,
conductor.
Vienna: Universal Ed. See: B343-B348; D225-D226

1971-1972

W135. Requiem
4 soloists, mixed chorus, organ, and orchestra; 45 min.
Premiere: May 4, 1973, Cathedral of Lausanne, Lausanne: soloists
Elizabeth Speiser, Ria Bollen, Eric Tappy, Peter Lagger, and André
Luy, organist; Frank Martin, conductor.
First U.S. performance: March 9, 1978, North Texas State University,
Denton: University Symphony Orchestra and Grand Chorus; Anshel
Brusilow, conductor.
Vienna: Universal Ed. See: B306-B315; D188-D190; M7

1972

W136. Agnus Dei
Alto voice and organ; 5 min.
Separate publication of the Agnus Dei from Requiem.
Vienna: Universal Ed. See: D190; W135

W137. Ballade pour alto et orchestre à vent
Viola with orchestra of wind instruments; 13 min.
Commissioned by the Mozarteum of Salzburg.
Premiere: January 20, 1973, Saltzburg: Ron Golan, violist; Helmut
Eder, conductor.
Vienna: Universal Ed. See: D2-D3

1973

W138. Polyptyque Six images de la passion du Christ
Violin with double string orchestra; 25 min.
Written for Yehudi Menuhin for the celebration of the 25th anniversary
of the International Music Council.
Premiere: September 9, 1973, Lausanne: Yehudi Menuhin, violinist;
Chamber Orchestra of Zürich; Edmond de Stoutz, conductor.
Vienna: Universal Ed. See: B289-B290; D166

W139.   Fantaisie sur des rythmes flamenco
Piano with dancer (ad lib.); 14 min.
Commissioned by Paul Badura-Skoda.
Premiere: August 18, 1974: Lucerne Festival: Paul Badura-Skoda,
pianist, and Teresa Martin, dancer.
Vienna: Universal Ed. See: B174; D88-D89; M20

W140.   Notre Père
Unison choir and organ; 2 min.
Simplified version of the Our Father from In terra pax.
Fribourg: Editions de la Procure Romande. See: W68

1974

W141.   Et la vie l'emporta
Chamber cantata for alto and baritone soloists, small choir, and
instrumental ensemble; 26 min.
Completion of the end of l'Offrande by Bernard Reichel.
Text: Maurice Zundel, Martin Luther/Frank Martin, and 16th-century
anon.
Commissioned for the 75th anniversary of Zyma, Nyon
(Pharmaceutical firm).
Private premiere: June 12, 1975, Montreux: for the 75th Anniversary of
Zyma, Nyon.
Public premiere: August 24, 1975: Lucerne Festival: soloists Claudine
Perret and Philippe Huttenlocher; directed by Michel Corboz.
Vienna: Universal Ed. See: B164-B165; D79

Discography

"Il y a toujours, dans les fonctions
de notre esprit, une frange de
mystère."

"There always is, in the functions of
our spirit, an element of mystery."

This list includes all known commercial and non-commercial discs, whether or
not currently available.

Each entry contains as much bibliographic information as could be obtained
and is entered as follows: Entries are by title alphabetically; when there are
multiple entries, they appear chronologically whenever possible. Next follows
record label, serial number and format (stereo or otherwise). The first issue is
followed by subsequent reissues and/or issues licensed to other labels.
Additional content of the disc follows and the album title when appropriate.

L'AMOUR DE MOY

D1.   Opus One #83 stereo April 1982.
Johanna Arnold, soprano; Yolanda Liepa, piano.
With Trois chansons de Noël; Shields, Alice. Six Songs from Poems of
Pablo Neruda; Tsandoulas, Gerasimos. Elià.

BALLADE POUR ALTO ET ORCHESTRE À VENT

D2.   Pathé Marconi CO69-02688 stereo 1975; EMI ASD3185.
Yehudi Menuhin, viola; Menuhin Festival Orchestra; Michael Dobson,
conductor.
With: Ballade pour flûte; Polyptyque.

D3.   Pantheon D-0981X stereo 1987. FSM PD 0981X.
Ronald Golan, viola: M.I.T. Symphony Orchestra; David Epstein,
conductor.
With: Hindemith, Paul. Trauermusik; Holst, Gustav. Lyric Movement;
Martinu, Bohuslav. Rhapsodie.

BALLADE POUR FLÛTE ET PIANO

D4.   Lanier 5238 mono c. 1958.
Charles Delaney, flute; Edwin Thayer, piano.

D5.   Francis William Record Co. REV1107 mono.
William Watson, flute; Richard Kapp, piano.
With: Bach, J.S. Sonata in E Major, BWV1035; Falla, Manuel de. Five
Spanish Folk Songs; Marcello, Benedetto. Sonata no. 4 in g Minor.

D6.   Columbia (Switzerland) SEGZ 2073 mono c. 1961.
Peter-Lukas Graf, flute; Edith Fischer, piano.

D7.   Telefunken 641011 stereo May 12-17, 1966; Telefunken (Japan)
SH5270 January 1967.
Aurèle Nicolet, flute; Gerty Herzog, piano.
With: Bach, C.P.E. Sonata, Wq. 132; Bach, J.S. Sonata no. 3 BWV
1032; Messiaen, Olivier. Le Merle noir; Poulenc, Francis. Sonata.

D8.   Monitor MC2120 stereo 1967 reissued 1976.
William Watson, flute; Richard Kapp, piano.
With: Bach, J.S. Sonata in g Minor; Marcello, Alessandro. Sonata in g
Minor; Falla, Manuel de. 5 Popular Spanish Songs.

D9.   Da Camera Magna SM93118 stereo March 1970; Musical Heritage
Society MHS 3916A.
Susanne Lindtberg, flute; Monica Hoffman, piano.
With: Ballade pour violoncelle; Huit préludes pour piano.

D10.   Hungaroton SLPX11685 stereo 1973; Hungaroton (French) 11. 685.
        Istvàn Matuz, flute; Zoltan Benkö, piano.
        With: Sari, Joseph. Contemplazione; Boulez, Pierre. Sonatina;
        Prokofiev, Sergey. Sonata, op. 94; Messiaen, Olivier. Le Merle noir.

D11.   Jecklin 133 stereo 1973.
        Marianne Keller, flute; Hans Walter Stucki, piano.
        With: Reinecke, Carl. Sonata für Flöte und Piano e-Moll "Undine," Op.
        167; Hummel, Johann Nepomuk. Sonata für Flöte und Klavier
        D-Dur, Op. 50.

D12.   Musical Heritage Society MHS3450Y stereo October 14-15, 1975.
        Ingrid Dingfelder, flute; Anita Gordon, piano.
        With: Jolivet, André. Chant de linos; Martinu, Bohuslav. Sonata no. 1.
        In: 20th Century Flute Masterpieces.

D13.   Golden Crest RE/GC 7065 stereo April 14, 1976; reissued 1981.
        Virginia Nanzetta, flute; Milton Kaye, piano.
        With: Wilder, Alec. Sonata no. 2; Small Suite; Suite for
        Unaccompanied Flute.

D14.   Telefunken AP642364 stereo June 3, 1978.
        Wolfgang Schulz, flute; Helmut Deutsch, piano.
        With: Berio, Luciano. Sequenza I; Eder, Helmut. Sonatine; Jolivet,
        Andre. Suite en concert; Messiaen, Olivier. La Merle noir.

D15.   Opus One #76 stereo March 27, 1980.
        George Pope, flute; Mark Robson, piano.
        With: Froom, David. Ballade for Piano and Fender Rhodes; Pelosi,
        Louis. Seven In(ter)ventions.

D16.   Jecklin Disco 603 mono June 28, 1967. Issued 1985; Jecklin Disco
        JD563-2, 1989.
        Robert Willoughby, flute; Frank Martin, piano.
        With: Ballade pour violoncelle et piano; Huit préludes pour piano.
        In: Frank Martin interprète Frank Martin.

D17.   Bethmann 28290678 stereo 1984.
        Annegret Lucke, flute; Güher Pekinel, piano.
        With: Mozart, W. A. Sonate in B-dur, für vier Hände, K. 358; Bach, J.
        S. Tokkaten für Orgel, BWV 565 arr.; Lautensuite Nr. 1 e-Moll, BWV
        995; Mendelssohn-Bartholdy, Felix. Toccata und Fuge d-Moll;
        Schumann, Robert. Fantasiestücke, Op. 73; Weber, Carl Maria von.
        Adagio und Rondo; Scarlatti, Domenico. Sonaten C-Dur und D-Moll;
        Haydn, Joseph. Sonate B-Moll, Nr. 47; Debussy, Claude. Rhapsodie
        Klarinette und Klavier.
        In: Die Treppenhaus-Konzerte.

D18.   Opus One #123 stereo 1984.
Maxine Neuman, cello; Yolanda Liepa, piano.
With: Fine, Vivian. Fantasy for Cello and Piano; Levine, Jeffrey.
Variations Romanesca (1983).

BALLADE POUR FLÛTE (version for flute and string orchestra)

D19.   HMV (Switzerland) HEX 120 78 rpm mono.
Joseph Bopp, flute; Basle Chamber Orchestra; Paul Sacher,
conductor.

D20.   Pathé Marconi CO69-02688 stereo September 1974; EMI ASD3185
1976.
Aurèle Nicolet, flute; Zürich Chamber Orchestra; Edmond de Stoutz,
conductor.
With: Polyptyque; Ballade pour alto et orchestre à vent.

D21.   Crystal S503 stereo 1976.
Louise Di Tullio, flute; English Chamber Orchestra; Elgar Howarth,
conductor.
With: Ibert, Jacques. Concerto for Flute; Dubois, Pierre Max. Concerto
for Flute.

D22.   Eterna 827899 stereo 1984.
Johannes Walter, flute; Staatskapelle, Dresden; Sigfried Kurz,
conductor.
With: Ibert, Jacques. Konzerte für Flöte und Orchester; Jolivet, Andre.
Suite en concert.
In: Französische Flötenkonzerte.

D23.   Contemporary Record Society CD 8840 stereo 1988.
Samuel Baron, flute; Billings Symphony Orchestra; Uri Barnes,
conductor.
With: Donizetti, Gaetano. Studie für Klarinette; Ewazen, Eric. Ballade
for Clarinet, Harp and Strings; Jones, David Evan. Still Voices for
clarinet; Piston, Walter. Clarinet Concerto; Flute Concerto; Presser,
William. Partita for Clarinet; Rossini, Gioacchino. Variations for
Clarinet and Orchestra.
In: Flute and Clarinet Soloists.

BALLADE POUR FLÛTE (version for flute and orchestra)

D24.   Cook (Sounds of our times) 1037 mono 1952.
Camillo Wanansell, flute; Collegium Musicum; Kurt Rapf, conductor.
Orchestrated by Ernest Ansermet.
With: Hindemith, Paul. Sonata, Piano 4-hands.

BALLADE POUR PIANO ET ORCHESTRA

D25.   Jecklin 529 stereo 1972; Candide 31065; Vox (UK) STBGY669; FSM
31065; Jecklin Disco JD529-2 1989.
Sebastian Benda, piano; Chamber Orchestra of Lausanne; Frank
Martin, conductor.
With: Concert pour clavecin; Ballade pour trombone.

D26.   Claves D8509/CD8509 stereo August 1985.
Jean-François Antonioli, piano; I Filarmonici di Torino; Marcello Viotti,
conductor.
With: Concerto I pour piano; Concerto II pour piano.

BALLADE POUR SAXOPHONE ET ORCHESTRE

D27.   Colosseum STM 0525 stereo; Colosseum (US) 525 1983.
Marcel Perrin, saxophone; Nürnberger Symphoniker; Urs Schneider,
conductor.
With: Debussy, Claude. Rhapsody Nr. 2; Saint-Saëns, Camille.
Karneval der Tiere.

D28.   Zephyr 223 stereo.
Francois Daneels, saxophone; Orchestre Philharmonique de la BRT;
Fernand Terby, conductor.
With: Harvey, Paul. Concertino; Legley, Victor. Concert d'Automne;
Villa-Lobos. Heitor. Fantasia.
In: Saxophon in Konzert.

BALLADE POUR TROMBONE ET PIANO

D29.   Golden Crest RE7011 mono December 20, 1961.
Davis Schuman, trombone; Leonid Hambro, piano.
With: Goeb, Roger. Concertino; Hindemith, Paul. Sonata.

D30.   BIS LP258 stereo; Musical Heritage Society MHS7330Z 1986; BIS
CD258.
Christian Lindberg, trombone; Roland Pontinen, piano.
With: Rimsky-Korsakov, Nicolas. Flight of the bumble bee; Sulek,
Stjepan. Sonata, "Vox Gabrieli"; Monti, Vittorio. Czardas; Kreisler,
Fritz. Liebeslied; Pryor, Arthur. Blue bells of Scotland; Hindemith,
Paul. Sonata; Berio, Luciano. Sequenza V.

BALLADE POUR TROMBONE (version for trombone and orchestra)

D31.   Jecklin 529 stereo 1972; Vox (UK) STGBY669; Candide 31065;
FSM31065; Jecklin Disco JD529-2 1989.
Armin Rosen, trombone; Chamber Orchestra of Lausanne; Frank
Martin, conductor.
With: Concert pour clavecin; Ballade pour piano.

D32.   Claves D8407 stereo 1984.
   Branimir Slokar, trombone; Lausanne Chamber Orchestra; Jean-Marie
   Auberson, conductor.
   With: Wagenseil, George. Concerto for Alto Trombone; David,
   Ferdinand. Concertino; Tomasi, Henri. Concerto.

BALLADE POUR TROMBONE (version for tenor saxophone and orchestra)

D33.   Schwann VMS 2065 stereo October - December 1980.
   Detlef Bensmann, tenor saxophone; RIAS Sinfonietta; David Shallon,
   conductor.
   With: Glazunov, Alexander. Concerto; Rivier, Jean. Concerto;
   Villa-Lobos, Heitor. Fantasia.
   In: Virtuose Saxophonkonzerte.

BALLADE POUR TROMBONE (version for tenor saxophone and piano)

D34.   Opus One #92 stereo 1985.
   Tim Smith, tenor saxophone; Yolanda Liepa, piano.
   With: Theobald, Jim. Go in Green (times fifteen); Schubel, Max.
   Ylk-Dyrth; Wilson, Richard. Figuration.

BALLADE POUR VIOLONCELLE ET PIANO

D35.   Da Camera Magna 93118 stereo March 18, 1970; Musical Heritage
   Society MHS 3916A.
   Klaus Heitz, cello; Monica Hofmann, piano.
   With: Ballade pour flûte; Huit préludes.

D36.   Jecklin Disco 603 mono/stereo 1985; Jecklin Disco JD563-2 1989.
   Henri Honegger, cello; Frank Martin, piano.
   With: Huit préludes; Ballade pour flûte et piano.
   In: Frank Martin interprète Frank Martin.

D37.   Opus One #123 stereo 1987.
   Maxine Neuman, cello; Yolanda Liepa, piano.
   With: Fine, Vivian. Fantasy for Cello and Piano; Levine, Jeffrey.
   Variations Romanesca.

BALLADE POUR VIOLONCELLE (version for cello and orchestra)

D38.   Hungaroton 11749 stereo 1974.
   Miklós Perényi, cello; Budapest Symphony Orchestra; György
   Lehel,conductor.
   With: Lutoslawski, Witold. Concerto for Cello; Farkas, Ferenc.
   Concertino All'antica.

CANTATE POUR LE 1ER AOÛT

D39.   Opus One #84 stereo April 1982.
Choir of All Saints Church, New York; Dennis G. Michno, conductor.
With: Chanson 'le petite village'; Quant n'ont assez fait do-do; Quatre
pièces brèves; Loeb, David. Trois cansos; Wallach, Joelle. Three
Spanish Songs.

CHACONNE

D40.   Opus One #120 stereo 1984.
Maxine Neuman, cello; Yolanda Liepa, piano.
With: Read, Gardner. Sonata brevis; Miller, Dennis. Trio for Flute, Cello
and Piano; Hollister, David. String Quartet no. 2.

CHANSON DES MÉTAMORPHOSES

D41.   Opus One #86 stereo April 1982.
Johanna Arnold, soprano; Yolanda Liepa, piano.
With: Le Roy a fait battre tambour; Il Faut partir pour l'angleterre; Drey
Minnelieder; Gerber, Steven R. Songs from "The Wild Swans at
Colle"; Two Lyrics of Gerald Manley Hopkins.

CHANSON 'LE PETITE VILLAGE'

D42.   Opus One #84 stereo April 1982.
All Saints Church Choir, New York; Dennis G. Michno, conductor.
With: Cantate pour le 1er août; Quant n'ont assez fait do-do; Quatre
pièces brèves; Loeb, David. Trois cansos; Wallach, Joelle. Three
Spanish Songs.

CHANSON EN CANON

D43.   Gallo 30-329 stereo September 26-27, 1981.
Ars Laeta Groupe Vocal; Robert Mermoud, conductor.
With: Verse à boire; Vospoite Gospodi (Orthodox Liturgy); Duruflé,
Maurice. Ubi Caritas; Reichel, Bernard. Magnificat; Festa,
Constanzo. Quis Dabit Oculis (attributed to Senfl); Poulenc, Francis.
Vinea mea electa (Respons aux matines du vendredi-Saint); 1er
Nocturne; Lotti Antonio. Crucifixus; Fatise Kolo (air popular serbe);
Passereau, Pierre. Il est bel et bon; Sutermeister, Heinrich. Le vieux
jardin; Robin et Marion (melodie du XVe siècle); Mermoud, Robert.
La Tarasque de Tarascon; Binet, Jean. Chanson; Heiller, Anton.
Nörgeln; Kodaly, Zoltan, arr. Turot ëszik a Cigany.

D44.   Opus One 78 stereo April 1982.
        Choir of All Saints Church, New York; Dennis G. Michno, conductor.
        With: 5 Ariel Songs; Le Coucou; Dédicace; Es ist ein Schnitter, heisst
        der Tod; Nous sommes trois souverains princes; Ode et sonnet;
        Verse à boire; Gerber, Steven R. Dylan Thomas Settings.

LES CHANSONS DE "LA NIQUE À SATAN"

D45.   Ex Libris EL16506 stereo January 1969.
        Union Chorale de Lausanne; Robert Mermoud, conductor.

CLAIR DE LUNE

D46.   Opus One #68 stereo March 9, 1981.
        Rebecca La Brecque, piano.
        With: Esquisse; Etude rythmique; Fantaisie sur des rythmes flamenco;
        Guitare.
        In: The Piano Music of Frank Martin.

D47.   Accord 140059 stereo 1982.
        Nicole Wickihalder, piano.
        With: Huit préludes; Fantaisie sur des rythmes flamenco; Esquisse;
        Clair de lune; Guitare; Etude rythmique.
        In: Oeuvre intégrale pour piano.

LE COUCOU

D48.   Opus One #78 stereo April 1982.
        Choir of All Saints Church, New York; Dennis G. Michno, conductor.
        With: 5 Ariel Songs; Dédicace; Chanson en canon; Ode et sonnet; Es
        ist ein Schnitter, heisst der Tod; Verse à boire; Nous sommes trois
        souverains princes; Gerber, Steven R. Dylan Thomas Settings.

CONCERT POUR CLAVECIN

D49.   Oiseau-Lyre DL5300l mono 1954.
        Isabelle Nef, harpsichord; Ensemble de l'Oiseau-Lyre; Louis Froment,
        conductor.

D50.   Jecklin Disco 529 stereo 1972; Candide 31065; Vox (UK) STBGY 669;
        FSM 31065; Jecklin Disco JD529-2 1989.
        Christiane Jaccottet, harpsichord; Chamber Orchestra of Lausanne;
        Frank Martin, conductor.
        With: Ballade pour trombone et piano; Ballade pour piano et
        orchestra.

CONCERTO I POUR PIANO

D51.   Claves D8509 stereo August 1985; CD50-8509 1988.
Jean-François Antonioli, piano; I Filarmonici di Torino; Marcello Viotti, conductor.
With: Concerto II pour piano; Ballade pour piano et orchestre.

CONCERTO II POUR PIANO

D52.   Candide CE31055 stereo June 1971; Vox (UK) STBGY661; Vox (France) 36006; FSM 31055; Jecklin JD632-2 1989.
Paul Badura-Skoda, piano; Symphony Orchestra of Radio Luxembourg; Frank Martin, conductor.
With: Concerto pour violon.

D53.   Queen Elizabeth International Music Competition 1980030 stereo 1984.
Dominique Cornil, piano; Orchestre Symphonique National de la Radio Bulgare; Vassil Kazandjiev, conductor.
With: Huit préludes pour piano.

D54.   Claves D8509/CD8509 stereo August 1985; CD50-8509 1988.
Jean-François Antonioli, piano; I Filarmonici di Torino; Marcello Viotti, conductor.
With: Concerto I pour piano; Ballade pour piano et orchestra.

CONCERTO POUR SEPT INSTRUMENTS À VENT, TIMBALES, BATTERIE ET ORCHESTRE À CORDES

D55.   Nixa CLP1109 mono 1951; Concert Hall Society 1109.
Winterthur Symphony Orchestra; Victor Desarzens, conductor.
With: Ibert, Jacques. Concerto for Flute and Orchestra.

D56.   Decca (UK) LXT5676/SXL2311 mono/stereo November 1961; London CM/CS6241; Stereo Treasury STS15270; Eclipse 578; London (Japan) SLC1197/SLC; GT9250.
L'Orchestre de la Suisse Romande; Ernest Ansermet, conductor.
With: Etudes for String Orchestra.

D57.   RCA (US) LM/LSC2914 mono/stereo March 19, 1966; RCA (UK) RB/SB6710; RCA (Japan) RVC/SHP2453.
Chicago Symphony Orchestra; Jean Martinon, conductor.
With: Varese, Edgar. Arcana.

D58.   Harmonia Mundi 30. 736 stereo June 25, 1967.
Westflämisches Orchester; Dirk Varendonck, conductor.
With: Poot, Marcel. Ballade pour saxophone, alto et archets; Divertimenti pour petit orchestre.

CONCERTO POUR VIOLON ET ORCHESTRE

D59.   Decca (UK) LX3146 mono 1956; London LD9213.
Wolfgang Schneiderhan, violin; L'Orchestre de la Suisse Romande;
Ernest Ansermet, conductor.

D60.   Louisville LS-636 stereo 1963.
Paul Kling, violin; Louisville Orchestra; Robert Whitney, conductor.
With: Bloch, Ernest. Proclamation for Trumpet and Orchestra;
Mayuzumi, Toshiro. Pieces for Prepared Piano and Strings.

D61.   Candide 31055 stereo June 1971; Vox (UK) STGYB661; Vox (France)
36. 006; Jecklin JD632-2 1989.
Wolfgang Schneiderhan, violin; Symphony Orchestra of Radio
Luxembourg; Frank Martin, conductor.
With: Concerto II pour piano.

CONCERTO POUR VIOLONCELLE ET ORCHESTRE

D62.   Louisville LS731 stereo April 9, 1973.
Stephen Kates, cello; Louisville Orchestra; Jorge Mester, conductor.
With: Arnold, Malcolm. Concerto for two Violins and String Orchestra.

DER CORNET

D63.   Columbia (Switzerland) LZX15/7 LZX246/48 78 rpm mono.
Elsa Cavelti, mezzo-soprano; Collegium Musicum, Zürich; Paul Sacher,
conductor. No. 4,9,10,12,13,17-21,23 only.

D64.   Jecklin 539 mono May 1972; FSM 0539.
Ursula Mayer-Reinach, contralto; Orchestra della Radio Svizzera
Italiana; Frank Martin, conductor.

D65.   Orfeo A164881 C164881 stereo March 29-30,1988.
Marjana Lipovšek, mezzo-soprano; ORF-Symphonieorchester; Lothar
Zagrosek, conductor.

DÉDICACE DE PIERRE DE RONSARD

D66.   Opus One #78 stereo April 1982.
Thomas Bogdan, tenor; Dennis G. Michno, piano.
With: 5 Ariel Songs; Le Coucou; Chanson en canon; Ode et sonnet;
Es ist ein Schnitter, heisst der Tod; Verse à boire; Nous sommes
trois souverains princes; Gerber, Steven R. Dylan Thomas Settings.

DREY MINNELIEDER

D67.   Iramac 6520 stereo 1966; Jecklin 563 1981; BASF/Harmonia Mundi
         (Japan) UXL3160-V April 1975; Jecklin Disco JD563-2 1989.
         Elly Ameling, soprano; Frank Martin, piano.
         With: Huit préludes pour piano; Trois chants de Noël.

D68.   Opus One #86 stereo April 1982.
         Johanna Arnold, soprano; Yolanda Liepa, piano.
         With: Le Roy a fait battre tambour; Il Faut partir pour l'angleterre;
         Chanson des métamorphoses; Gerber, Steven R. Songs from "The
         Wild Swans at Coole"; Two Lyrics of Gerald Manley Hopkins.

DREY MINNELIEDER (version for soprano, flute, violin & cello)

D69.   Opus One #106 stereo.
         Elsa Charlston, soprano; Alex Ogle, flute; Tina Pelikan, viola; Ted
         Mook, cello.
         With: Quatre sonnets à Cassandre; Shapey, Ralph. Songs.

DREY MINNELIEDER - UNTER DER LINDEN

D70.   Carolina 712C-2538 stereo c. 1968.
         Ethel Casey, soprano; Janet Southwick, piano.
         With: Schoenberg, Arnold. Lied der Waltaube (from Gurre-lieder);
         Wenn Voglein Klagen (from Sechs Orchesterlieder, op. 8); Krenek,
         Ernst. Die Nachtigall, op. 68; Berg, Alban. Die Nachtigall (1907);
         Webern, Anton. Die Geheimnisvolle, op. 12, no. ?; Des Harzens
         Purpurvogel, op. 25, no. 2; Gerhard, Roberto. The Lark (1933).
         In: Contemporary Birds.

D71.   Columbia M35119 stereo November 1977; CBS (UK) 76738; CBS
         (Japan) 25AC680.
         Elly Ameling, soprano; Dalton Baldwin, piano.
         With: Rossini, Gioacchino. La Danza; Canteloube, Joseph. Brezairola;
         Rodrigo, Joaquin. De los alamos; Vuillermoz, Jean. Jardin d'amour;
         Rachmaninoff, Sergei. Spring Waters; Hahn, Reynaldo. La Dernière
         Valse; Ives, Charles. Memories; Schoenberg, Arnold. Gingerlette;
         Nakada, Yoshinao. Oyasumi Na Sai; Purcell, Henry. Music for
         Awhile; Weldon, John. The Wakeful Nightingale; Britten, Benjamin. O
         Waly Waly; Liszt, Franz. O Lieb; Sibelius, Jean. Varen Flyktar
         Hastigt; Dutch folksong. Moeke; Hullebroeck, Emiel. Afrikaans
         Wiegeliedjie.
         In: Souvenirs.

DU RHÔNE AU RHIN

D72.   HMV HE1939 mono 78rpm. 1939.
       Exhibition Band; G. C. Mantegazzi, conductor.

D73.   Disques Serp 796/99 mono 78 rpm. 1939.
       Musique des Gardiens de la Paix de Paris; Désiré Doneyne,
          conductor.

D74.   Serp MC7036 stereo
       Musique des Gardiens de la Paix de Paris; Désiré Doneyne,
          conductor.
       With: Saint-Saëns, Camille. Marche du couronnement d'Edouard VII,
          Op. 117; Smetana, Bedrich. Marche pour la garde nationale de
          Prague (1848); Strauss, Johann, Père; Marche de Radetzky, Op.
          228 (1849); Kodaly, Zoltan. Marche de parade pour les héros
          (1948); Rowley-Bishop, Henry, Sir. Marche pour la Société Royale
          des Musciens de Londres.

ES IST EIN SCHNITTER, HEISST DER TOD

D75.   Opus One #78 stereo April 1982.
       Choir of All Saints Church, New York; Dennis G. Michno, conductor.
       With: 5 Ariel Songs; Dédicace; Chanson en canon; Ode et sonnet;
          Verse à boire; Nous sommes trois souverains princes; Gerber,
          Steven R. Dylan Thomas Settings.

ESQUISSE POUR PIANO

D76.   BIS LP71 stereo 9-10 October 1976.
       Lucia Negro, piano.
       With: Brahms, Johannes. Variationen über ein eigenes Thema, Op. 21,
          no. 1; Mendelssohn-Bartholdy, Felix. Variations Sérieuses.

D77.   Opus One #68 November 18, 1980.
       Rebecca La Brecque, piano.
       With: Clair de lune; Etude rythmique; Fantaisie sur des rythmes
          flamenco; Guitare.
       In: The Piano Music of Frank Martin.

D78.   Accord 140059 stereo June 1982.
       Nicole Wickihalder, piano.
       With: Huit préludes; Clair de lune; Fantaisie sur des rythmes flamenco;
          Guitare; Etude rythmique.
       In: Oeuvre intégrale pour piano.

ET LA VIE L'EMPORTA

D79. Erato ERA9137 stereo February 1975.
Claudine Perret, contralto; Philippe Huttenlocher, baritone; Les Solistes de L'ensemble Vocal et L'ensemble Instrumental de Lausanne; Michel Corboz, conductor.
With: Debussy, Claude. Préludes: Le Vent dans la plaine; Des Pas sur la neige; La Cathedrale engloutie; La Danse de Puck; Children's Corner Suite.

ETUDE DE LECTURE

See Esquisse

ETUDE RYTHMIQUE

D80. FSM Aulos 53537 stereo March 1979.
Monica Hofmann, piano.
With: Sechs Monologe aus Jedermann; 4ème Etude-Pour le jeu fugue; Guitare; Overture and Foxtrot.

D81. Opus One #68 stereo March 9, 1979.
Rebecca La Brecque, piano.
With: Clair de lune; Esquisse; Fantaisie sur des rythmes flamenco; Guitare.
In: The Piano Works of Frank Martin.

D82. Accord 140059 stereo June 1982.
Nicole Wickihalder, piano.
With: Huit préludes; Esquisse; Clair de lune; Fantaisie sur des rythmes flamenco; Guitare.
In: Oeuvre intégrale pour piano.

ETUDES POUR ORCHESTRE À CORDES

D83. Decca (UK) LXT5676/SLX2311 mono/stereo November 1961; London CM9310/CS6241; Stereo Treasury STS15270.
L'Orchestre de la Suisse Romande; Ernest Ansermet, conductor.
With: Concerto for Seven Wind Instruments, Timpani, Percussion, and String Orchestra.

D84. Philips PHS900198, 802865; Philips (UK) SAL3678; Philips (Japan) SLF8551.
I Musici.
With: Hindemith, Paul. Mourning Music for viola & string orchestra; Roussel, Albert. Sinfonietta, op. 52; Nielsen, Carl. Little Suite, op. 1.

D85.   Balkanton BCA1056.
       Sofia Chamber Orchestra; Vasil Kazandjiev, conductor.
       With: Handel, George Frideric. Overture and Dances from "Alcina";
           Vivaldi. Antonio. Sinfonia no. 3 in g Minor.

ETUDES POUR ORCHESTRE A CORDES (version for 2 pianos)

D86.   FSM Aulos 53537 stereo March 1979.
       Monica Hofmann and Machiko Hari, pianists. 4ème Etude-Pour le jeu
           fugué only.
       With: Sechs Monologe aus Jedermann; Guitare; Overture and Foxtrot;
           Etude rythmique.

D87.   Opus One #102 stereo January 1983.
       Eliza Garth and Yolanda Liepa, pianists.
       With: Johnson, Roger. Layers; Echo II; Improvisation IV.

FANTAISIE SUR DES RYTHMES FLAMENCO

D88.   Opus One #68 stereo April 1980.
       Rebecca La Brecque, piano.
       With: Etude rythmique; Clair de lune; Esquisse; Guitare.
       In: The Piano Music of Frank Martin.

D89.   Accord 140059 stereo June 1982.
       Nicole Wickihalder, piano.
       With: Huit préludes; Esquisse; Clair de lune; Guitare; Etude rythmique.
       In: Oeuvre intégrale pour piano.

IL FAUT PARTIR POUR L'ANGLETERRE

D90.   Opus One 86 stereo April 1982.
       Johanna Arnold, soprano; Yolanda Liepa, piano.
       With: Le Roy a fait battre tambour; Chanson des métamorphoses;
           Drey Minnelieder; Gerber, Steven R. Songs from "The Wild Swans
           at Coole"; Two Lyrics of Gerald Manley Hopkins.

5 ARIEL SONGS

D91.   Philips N00679 mono 1955.
       Netherlands Chamber Choir; Felix de Nobel, conductor.
       With: Poulenc, Francis. Quatre pour les temps de Noël; Salve Regina.

D92. BASF 29-25476-3 stereo 1974.
Nederlands Kamerkoor; Felix de Nobel, conductor.
With: Sweelinck, Jan Pieterszoon. Canticum in honorem nuptiarum Johannis Stoboei; Josquin des Pres. Ave Maria-Virgo serena; Lassus, Orlando d'. Responde mihi wit; (Sacrae lectiones novem ex propheta Hiob, 1575); Monteverdi, Claudio. Ecco mormorar l'onde; Cor mio, mentre vi miro; Lamento d'Arianna I; Bach, J. S. Komm, Jesu, komm, BWV 229; Brahms, Johannes. Warum ist das licht gegeben dem Mühseligen?, Op. 74, no. 1; Vaughan Williams, Ralph. 3 Shakespeare Songs; Schoenberg, Arnold. De Profundis, Op. 50B.
In: Zes Eeuwin Koorklanken.

D93. Electrola IC165-30796/99 stereo 1975.
Stockholm Kammerchor; Eric Erickson, conductor.
With: Messe pour double choeur a cappella; Jolivet, André. Epithalame; Poulenc, Francis. 7 Chansons; Strauss, Richard. Die Göttin im Putzzimmer; Die Abend; Messiaen, Olivier. 5 Réchants. Monteverdi, Claudio. Sestina "Lagrime d'Amante al Sepolcro dell'Amata"; Dallapiccola, Luigi. Il Coro Dei Malmaritate; Il Coro Dei Malammogliati; Pizzetti, Ildebrando. Tre Composizione Corali; Tallis, Thomas. Spem in Alium; Edlund, Lars. Elegi.
In: Virtuose Chormusik.

D94. Opus One #78 stereo April 1982.
Choir of All Saints Church, New York; Dennis G. Michno, conductor.
With: Chanson en canon; Le Coucou; Dédicace; Es ist ein Schnitter, heisst der Tod; Nous sommes trois souverains princes; Ode et sonnet; Verse à boire; Gerber, Steven R. Dylan Thomas Settings.

GOLGOTHA

D95. Erato STU70497/98 stereo November 1968; Musical Heritage Society MHS1337/38.
Walli Staempfli, soprano; Marie-Lise Montmollin, contralto; Eric Tappy, tenor; Pierre Mollet, baritone; Philippe Huttenlocher, bass-baritone; André Luy, organ; Symphony Orchestra and Chorus of the University of Lausanne; Robert Faller, conductor.

D96. Vengo 3544002/3 stereo April 1, 1988.
Martina von Bargen, soprano; Margit Hungerbühler, alto; Friedhelm Decker, tenor; Joachim Gebhardt, baritone; Martin Blasius, bass; Chor der Erlöserkirche, Bad Homburg; Offenbacher Kammerorchester; Frankfurter Bläservereinigung; Hayko Siemens, conductor.

LES GRENOUILLES, LE ROSSIGNOL ET LA PLUIE

D97.   Opus One #104 stereo January 1983.
        Eliza Garth and Yolanda Liepa, pianists.
        With: Petite marche blanche et trio; Pavane couleur du temps;
            Rosenblum, Mathew. Harp Quintet; Alrich, Alexis. Prelude and Jig.

GUITARE - QUATRE PIÈCES BRÈVES POUR PIANO

D98.   FSM Aulos 53537 stereo March 1979.
        Monica Hofmann, piano.
        With: 4ème etude-Pour le jeu fugué; Sechs Monologe aus Jedermann;
            Overture and Foxtrot; Etude rythmique.

D99.   Opus One #68 stereo November 18, 1980.
        Rebecca La Brecque, piano.
        With: Clair de lune; Etude rythmique; Fantaisie sur des rythmes
        flamenco; Esquisse.
        In: The Piano Music of Frank Martin.

D100.   Accord 140059 stereo June 1982.
        Nicole Wickihalder, piano.
        With: Huit préludes; Esquisse; Clair de lune; Fantaisie sur des rythmes
            flamenco; Etude rythmique.
        In: Oeuvre intégrale pour piano.

HUIT PRÉLUDES POUR PIANO

D101.   Elite 7078/80 mono 78rpm.
        Peter Speiser, piano.

D102.   Columbia (Switzerland) ZCX5053 mono.
        Jürg Vintschger, piano.
        With: Honegger, Arthur. Sept pièces brèves; Préludes, arioso et
            fughetta sur le nom Bach; Schieck, Othmar. Consolations; Toccata.

D103.   Columbia (US) ML5639/MS6239 mono/stereo November 1960.
        André Previn, piano (no. 7 only).
        With: Hindemith, Paul. Piano Sonata no. 3; Barber, Samuel. Four
            Excursions.

D104.   Qualiton LPX1181 stereo 1963.
        Janos Sebestyén, piano (no. 2, 4, 5 only).
        With: Bach, J. S. Concerto in D Major, BWV 972; Italian Concerto;
            Prokofiev, Sergey. Four Pieces from Visions Fugitives, Op. 22, no.
            1, 10, 11, & 15; Prelude, Op. 12, no. 3; Rigaudon, Op. 12, no. 3;
            Petrovics, Emil. Four Masked Self-Portraits.

D105.   Decca (US) DL710133/DL10133 mono/stereo 1966.
        Marjorie Mitchell, piano (no. 2, 3, 5, 7, 8 only).
        With: Britten, Benjamin. Piano Concerto.

D106.   Iramac 6520 mono January 1966; Jecklin Disco 603 1985. Jecklin
        Disco JD563-2 1989.
        Frank Martin, piano.
        With: (Iramac) Trois chants de Noël; Drey Minnelieder. (Jecklin)
        Ballade pour violoncelle; Ballade pour flûte.

D107.   Swiss Broadcasting Corp. MH3+4 stereo January 1966
        (non-commercial).
        Frank Martin, piano (no. 4 only).
        With: Trois danses pour hautbois, harpe et orchestre à cordes-
        Rumba; Poèmes de la mort-Ballade des pendus; Requiem-In
        Paridisum; Le Vin herbé-Epilogue.
        In: Musica Helvetica-Programme no. 4.

D108.   Da Camera Magna 93118 stereo March 18, 1970; Musical Heritage
        Society MHS3916.
        Monica Hofmann, piano.
        With: Ballade pour flûte; Ballade pour violoncelle.

D109.   Armida KE119 stereo August 1971; FSM A119KE.
        Karl Engel, piano.
        With: Schoeck, Othmar. 2 Klavierstücke, op. 29; Consolation; Toccata;
        Honegger, Arthur. Sept pièces brèves; Alessandro, Rafaele d'. 4
        etudes, op. 66, no. 2, 7, 8, 11.
        In: Schweizer Interpreten (V).

D110.   BASF 25-21638-1 stereo May 7-12, 1971; Acanta EA21638.
        Werner Genuit, piano.
        With: Trio für Violine, Viola und Violoncello; Trio sur des mélodies
        populaires irlandaises.

D111.   Martina 30-329 stereo May 11-12, 1972.
        Christina Meyer, piano.
        With: Haydn, Joseph. Sonata, Hob: XVI:52; Brahms, Johannes.
        Capricci, op. 76.

D112.   Educo 8027 stereo c. 1975.
        Nelita True, piano (no. 3 only).

D113.   BIS LP71 stereo October 9-10, 1976.
        Lucia Negro, piano.
        With: Esquisse; Mendelssohn-Bartholdy, Felix. Variations Sérieuses;
        Brahms, Johannes. Variationen über ein eigenes Thema, Op. 21,
        no. 1.

D114.   Gallo 30-229 stereo 1978; MXT VG30229.
Denise Bidal, piano.
With: Ravel, Maurice. Le Tombeau de Couperin.

D115.   Orion 79328 stereo December 1978.
Robert Silverman, piano.
With: Prokofiev, Sergey. Sonata no. 6.

D116.   Accord 140059 stereo June 1982.
Nicole Wickihalder, piano.
With: Esquisse; Clair de lune; Fantaisie sur des rythmes flamenco;
Guitare; Etude rythmique.
In: Oeuvre intégrale pour piano.

D117.   Queen Elizabeth International Music Competition 1980030 stereo 1984.
Dominique Cornil, piano.
With: Concerto no. 2.

D118.   Opus One #94 stereo January 1983.
Yolanda Liepa, piano.
With: Schubel, Max. Klish Klash; Gulda, Friedrich. Prelude and Fugue;
Shields, Alice. Rhapsody for piano and tape.

D119.   Laurel LR135 stereo 1986.
Veronica Jochum, piano.
With: Busoni, Ferruccio. Seven Short Pieces for the Cultivation of
Polyphonic Playing; Prelude; Etude; Perpetuum Mobile.

IN TERRA PAX

D120.   Communauté de Travail CT64-12 stereo October 20-23, 1963; Decca
(UK) SXL6098/LXT6098; London OS25847/OL5847; Decca (UK)
DPA593-4.
Ursula Buckel, soprano; Marga Höffgen, contralto; Ernst Haefliger,
tenor; Pierre Mollet, baritone; Jakob Stämpfli, bass; L'Orchestre de
la Suisse Romande; Ernest Ansermet, conductor.

D121.   Saint-Céré (unnumbered) stereo 1964 (non-commercial).
Lise Arseguet, soprano; Marie-Louise Gilles, contralto; Georg Jelden,
tenor; Jacques Villisech, bass; Choeurs et Orchestre de la Session
de Saint-Céré; Paul Nitsche, conductor.
In: 1964 cinquième Session Internationale.

D122.   Johannes-Kantorei Düsseldorf 3E 168-3607 stereo November 28, 1982
(non-commercial).
Jeannette Zarou, soprano; Christa Wellner, alto; Takeshi Wakamoto,
tenor; Werner Maxin, bass; Chor und Orchester Johannes-Kantorei,
Düsseldorf; Almut Rössler, conductor.

IN TERRA PAX - PATER NOSTER

D123. Abbey LPB707 stereo 1973.
Canterbury Cathedral Choir; Alan Wicks, conductor.
With: Mozart, Wolfgang Amadeus. Agnus Dei (last mov. from K. 195);
Agnus Dei (from Mass in C Maj.); Fauré, Gabriel. Pie Jesu; Vierne,
Louis. Prelude; Bach, J. S. Psalm 4 - Sighing, Weeping; Ridout,
Alan. Resurrection Dances.
In: Andrew Lyle, treble with Canterbury Cathedral Choir.

MARIA-TRIPTYCHON

D124. Schwann AMS3555 stereo August 22, 1984.
Edith Mathis, soprano; Wolfgang Schneiderhan, violin; Schweizerisches
Festspielorchester; Jean Fournet, conductor.
With: Fauré, Gabriel. Messe de Requiem.

MESSE POUR DOUBLE CHOEUR A CAPPELLA

D125. Musical Heritage Society 3167 stereo March 1974.
Wartburg College Choir; James Fritschel, conductor.
With: Copland, Aaron. In the Beginning; Fritschel, James. Be Still.

D126. Wartburg College Choir S80-639-3391S-A stereo.
With: Pachelbel, Johann. Gott is unser Zuversicht; Brahms, Johannes.
Regina Coeli; Sweelinck, Jan Pieterszoon. Venite; Exultamus
Domino; Nystedt, Knut. Thou, O Lord; Beck, John Ness. Ye Shall
Go Out with Joy; Fissinger, Edwin, arr. Witness; Shaw, Robert -
Parker, Alice, arr. I Got a Key; Decormier, Robert, arr. Rainbow
Round My Shoulder.
In: Wartburg College Choir. Fritschel, James, conductor.

D127. Electrola 1C165-30796/99 stereo 1975.
Stockholm Radio Choir; Eric Erikson, conductor.
With: 5 Ariel Songs; Jolivet, André. Epithalame; Poulenc, Francis. 7
Chansons; Strauss, Richard. Die Göttin im Putzzimmer; Der Abend;
Messiaen, Olivier. 5 Réchants; Monteverdi, Claudio. Sestina
"Lagrime d'Amante al Sepolcro dell'Amata"; Dallapiccola, Luigi. Il
Coro Delle Malmaritate; IL Coro Dei Malammogliati; Pizzetti,
Ildebrando. Tre Composizioni Corali; Tallis, Thomas. Spem in Alium;
Edlund, Lars. Elegi.
In: Virtuose Chormusik.

D128. Gallo 30-157; stereo September 1976; MXT VG30157.
La Psallette de Genève; Pierre Pernaud, conductor.
With: Poulenc, Francis. Quatre motets pour le temps de Noël.

D129.   Proprius PROP7782 stereo May 9-10, 1977.
Storkyrkans Kör; Gustaf Sjökvist, conductor.
With: Britten, Benjamin. Rejoice in the Lamb; Larsson, Lars-Erik. Missa
Brevis.

D130.   Cantate JSV657617 stereo February 1978; Bard 657617.
Kölner Kantorei; Volker Hempfling, conductor.

D131.   FSM Aulos 53528 stereo September 1978.
Bach Chor, Gütersloh; Hermann Kreutz, conductor.
With: Kodaly, Zoltan. Missa Brevis.

D132.   Crest ACDA79-7/8 LAU-51279-B stereo March 9, 1979.
Lawrence University Concert Choir; Karle Erickson, conductor.
With: Homilius, Gottfried August. Deo dicamus gratius; Casals, Pablo.
O vos omnes; Brahms, Johannes. O Heiland reiss die Himmel auf;
Gretchaninoff, Alexandre. Our Father; Nunc dimittis; Poulenc,
Francis. Tenebrae factae sunt; Duruflé, Maurice. Ubi caritas; Tu es
Petrus.

D133.   Mirasound KS7038 stereo 1981 (non-commercial). (Kyrie and Gloria
only)
Eindhovens Kamerkoor; Andries Clement, conductor.
With: Gabrieli, Andrea. Non vedi o sacr' Apollo; Frescobaldi, Girolamo.
Canzona in a klein; Canzona in G groot; Castello, Dario. Sonata
prima in a klein; Lasso, Orlando di. O faible espirit; Petite folle;
Reger, Max. O Tod, wie bitter bist du.

D134.   Waterloo WR8028/29 stereo June 1984.
Elmer Iseler Singers and Netherlands Chamber Choir; Elmer Iseler,
conductor.
With: Zbinden, Julien. Te Deum; Willan, Healey. An Apostrophe to the
Heavenly Hosts; Brahms, Johannes. Three Motets; op. 110, no. 1,
op. 29, no. 1 & 2; Strauss, Richard. Deutsche Motette.
In: Serenade in Harmony.

D135.   Proprius PRCD 9965 stereo October 11-13, 1985.
Mikaeli Kammarkör; Anders Eby, conductor.
With: Pizzetti, Ildebrando. Messa di Requiem.

NOUS SOMMES TROIS SOUVERAINS PRINCES

D136.   Opus One #78 stereo April 1982.
Choir of All Saints Church, New York; Dennis G. Michno, conductor.
With: 5 Ariel Songs; Chanson en canon; Le Coucou; Dédicace; Es ist
ein Schnitter, heisst der Tod; Ode et sonnet; Verse à boire; Gerber,
Steven R. Dylan Thomas Settings.

ODE ET SONNET

D137. Communauté de Travail CTS47 stereo February 18, 1967.
La Psallette de Genève; Pierre Pernoud, conductor; Francois
Courvoisier, cello.
With: Apothelos, Jean. Concertino, flute, piano, & string orchestra;
Schibler, Armin. Concerto, viola, cello and string orchestra;
Marescotti, André Francois. Mere, mariez-moi cet an; Jeanneton du
Vieux Testament; Binet, Jean. Qui veut avoir liesse; Qui veut entrer
en grâce; Les Comptines de l'oiselier; Hemmerling, Carlo. Don
Quichotte et Sancho Panca.

D138. Opus One #78 stereo April 1982.
Choir of All Saints Church, New York; Dennis G. Michno, conductor;
Holly Singer, cello.
With: 5 Ariel Songs; Chanson en canon; Le Coucou; Dédicace; Es ist
ein Schnitter, heisst der Tod; Nous sommes trois souverains
princes; Verse à boire; Gerber, Steven R. Dylan Thomas Settings.

OUVERTURE ET FOXTROT

D139. FSM Aulos stereo March 1979.
Monica Hofmann and Machiko Hari, pianists.
With: Sechs Monologe aus Jedermann; 4ème Etude-Pour le jeu fugué;
Guitare; Etude rythmique.

D140. Opus One #103 stereo 1983.
Eliza Garth, and Yolanda Liepa, pianists.
With: Boyadjian, Hayg. Sonata for 2 Pianos; Maves, David. Sonatine
par deux pianistes pitoyables; Schoenberg, Arnold. Sechs Stücke
für Klavier zu vier Handen.

PASSACAILLE POUR ORGUE

D141. AGK 30203 stereo.
Tragott Timme, organ.
With: Alain, Jehan. Le Jardin suspendu; Variationen über ein Thema
von Clement Jannequin; Reger, Max. Fantasie und Fuge über den
Namen Bach, op. 46.
In: Orgelmusik 1900-1950.

D142. Cathedral CRM/CRMS848 mono/stereo May 15-17, 1967; Mixtur
Schallplatten CRMS 848.
Brian Runnett, organ.
With: Alain, Jehun. Trois danses; Messiaen, Olivier. Le Banquet
celèste.
In: Brian Runnett plays Alain, Messiaen, and Martin at Norwich
Cathedral.

D143.   EMI CSD3659 stereo 1970; Music Guild S-876.
Lionel Rogg, organ.
With: Buxtehude, Dietrich. Prelude and Fugue in g Minor; Reger, Max.
Fantasia and Fugue in d Minor, Op. 135b; Alain, Jehun. Variations
sur un thème da Clément Jannequin; Litanies.
In: Lionel Rogg at the Royal Festival Hall.

D144.   Pelca PSR41008 stereo July 1974; Musical Heritage Society
MHS3582K.
Bernhard Billeter, organ.
With: Frescobaldi, Girolamo. Toccata Prima-Terza-Quinta; Muffat,
Georg. Toccata Septima; Burkhard, Willy. Fantasie und Choral: Ein
Feste Burg.
In: Orgel-Landschaften der Schweiz.

D145.   Da Camera Magna 93276 stereo March 1975; Turnabout TVS 34627;
FSM34627.
Edgar Krapp, organ.
With: (DaCamera Magna) Genzmer, Harald. Sinfonisches Konzert;
Hindemith Paul. Kammermusiken Nr. 7; Peeters, Flor. Konzertstuck,
Op. 52a.
In: Konzertante Orgelmusik d. 20. Jh.

D146.   Abbey LPB719 stereo 1977.
Josef Bucher, organ.
With: Franck, César. Pièce héroïque; Ibert, Jacques. Pièce solonelle;
Honegger, Arthur. Fugue; Mottu, Alexandre. Prelude et chorale.
In: Josef Bucher plays the organ of New College, Oxford.

D147.   Wealden WS195 stereo April 12, 1980.
Ivor Bolton, organ.
With: Nielsen, Carl. Commotio; Schoenberg, Arnold. Variations on a
Recitative.
In: Organ Music from Clare College.

D148.   Priory PRCD228 stereo September 8-9, 1987.
James Lancelot, organ.
With: Reger, Max. Introduction and Passacaglia in d Minor;
Rheinberger, Josef. Sonata no. 11 - Cantilene; Howells, Herbert.
Psalm Prelude, Op. 32, no. 3. Mathias, William. Berceuse, Op. 96;
Mendelssohn, Felix. Organ Sonata, Op. 65, no. 2 in C Major; Alain,
Jehan. Postlude pour office de compline; Langlais, Jean. Hymne
d'action de grace "Te Deum".
In: Great European Organs no. 5.

PASSACAILLE (version for string orchestra)

D149. Decca (UK) LXT5153 mono October 1955; London LLP1395; Eclipse
ECS668 September 1973; Decca (German) 6.48136DT.
Stuttgart Chamber Orchestra; Karl Munchinger, conductor.
With: Hindemith, Paul. Five Pieces for String Orchestra, Op. 44, no. 4;
Berkeley, Lennox. Serenade for Strings; Barber, Samuel. Adagio for
Strings.

PAVANE COULEUR DU TEMPS (version for full orchestra)

D150. Jecklin 203 stereo 1981.
Jungend-sinfonie-Orchester; Klaus Cornell, conductor.
With: Weber, Carl M. von. Concertino für Klarinette und Orchester,
Op.26; Moscheles, Ignaz. Concertante für Flöte, Oboe und
Orchester; Gade, Niels W. Mariotta: Lustspielouverture; Pleyel,
Ignaz. Sinfonia Concertante Nr. 5, F-Dur.

PAVANE COULEUR DU TEMPS (version for string orchestra)

D151. Classic Pick PR70-118 stereo May 10, 1976; Everest 3420.
Solisti di Zagreb.
With: Vivaldi, Antonio. Concerto pour guitare et cordes en do majeur;
Kohaut, Carl. Concerto pour guitare et cordes en fa majeur;
Brouwer, Leo. Trois danses concertantes pour guitar et cordes.

PAVANE COULEUR DU TEMPS (version for 2 pianos)

D152. Opus One #104 stereo January 1983.
Eliza Garth and Yolanda Liepa, pianists.
With: Les Grenouilles, le rossignol et la pluie; Petite marche; Blanche
et trio noir; Rosenblum, Mathew. Harp Quartet; Alrich, Alexis.
Prelude and Jig.

PETITE MARCHE BLANCHE ET TRIO NOIR

D153. Opus One #104 stereo 1987.
Eliza Garth and Yolanda Liepa, pianists.
With: Les Grenouilles, le rossignol et la pluie; Pavane couleur du
temps; Rosenblum, Mathew. Harp Quartet; Alrich, Alexis. Prelude
and Jig.

PETITE SYMPHONIE CONCERTANTE

D154. Oiseau-Lyre LD17 mono 1951.
M.G. De Francesco, piano; Isabelle Nef, harpsichord; E. Cariven, harp;
Lausanne Chamber Orchestra; Victor Desarzens, conductor.

D155. Decca (UK) LXT2631 mono March 1951; London LLP390.
Doris Rossiaud, piano; Germaine Vaucher-Clerc, harpsichord; Pierre
Jamet, harp; L'Orchestre de la Suisse Romande; Ernest Ansermet,
conductor.

D156. Polydor 72064/5 78 rpm mono; Deutsche Grammophon MG3961
18494; Decca (US) DL9774 1955.
Gerty Herzog, piano; Silvia Kind, harpsichord; Irmgard Helmis, harp;
RIAS Symphony; Ferenc Fricsay, conductor.
With: Blacher, Boris. Variations on a Theme of Paganini, Op. 26;
Einem, Gottfried von. Capriccio for Orchestra, Op. 2.

D157. Capitol P/PS8507 mono/stereo 1960; Recorded Music Circle CM69.
Mitchell Andrews, piano; Albert Fuller, harpsichord; Gloria Agostini,
harp; Leopold Stokowski conducting his Symphony Orchestra.
With: Bartók, Béla. Music for Stringed Instruments, Percussion and
Celesta.

D158. Communauté de Travail CTS42 stereo November 12-13, 1967.
Rudolf Am Bach, piano; Hans Andreae, harpsichord; Emmy
Hürlimann, harp; Collegium Musicum Zürich; Paul Sacher,
conductor.
With: Burkhard, Willy. Concerto pour violon.

D159. Unicorn UNS233 stereo January 5-6, 1971.
Michael Reeves, piano; Leslie Pearson, harpsichord; John Mason,
harp; London Chamber Orchestra; Paul Tortelier, conductor.
With: Tortelier, Paul. Offrande; Roussel, Albert. Sinfonietta.

D160. RCA (Australia) VRL1-0122 stereo June 6, 1975; Chandos
ABR1060/ABT1060 (cass.) 1982; Disco Center CHA1060.
Joyce Hutchinson, piano; Colin Forbes, harpsichord; Louise Johnson,
harp; Sydney Symphony Orchestra; Willem van Otterloo, conductor.
With: Debussy, Claude. Danses sacrée et profane; Ravel, Maurice.
Introduction and Allegro.

D161. EMI ASD3723 stereo May 21-22, 1978; Angel S37577; Electrola
06503519; Pathé Marconi 2C06903519; EMI-Odeon (Spain) 10C067-
003. 519; EMI (Japan) EAC80550.
Philip Ledger, piano; Simon Preston, harpsichord; Osian Ellis, harp;
Academy of St. Martin in-the-Fields; Neville Marriner, conductor.
With: Bloch, Ernest. Concerto Grosso No. 1.

D162. Supraphon 11103187 stereo January 20-23, 1981; Supraphon (US)
SO3187.
Josef Páleníček, piano; Zuzana Růžičková, harpsichord; Renata
Kodadová, harp; Czech Philharmonic; František Vajnar, conductor.
With: Debussy, Claude. Premiere rapsodie.

D163. NDR 66. 23816 stereo November, 26, 1984 (non-commercial).
Jürgen Lamke, piano; Wilhelm Neuhaus, harpsichord; Ludmila Muster, harp; Sinfonie Orchester des Norddeutscher Rundfunks; Günter Wand, conductor.
With: Haydn, Joseph. Symphonie E-flat, Nr. 76.

POÈMES DE LA MORT

D164. Opus One #122 stereo November 1984.
Ed Cohn, bass; Baker Peoples, tenor; John Rouse, baritone; Paul Binkley, Douglas Hensley, Larry Polonsky, electric guitars; Kent Nagano, conductor.
With: Wallach, Jaelle. Orison of Ste. Theresa; Plaint for a Prince and King; Three Short Sacred Anthems; Five American Echoes.

POÈMES DE LA MORT - BALLADE DES PENDUS

D165. Swiss Broadcasting Corp. MH 3+4 stereo (non-commercial).
Pierre-André Blaser, tenor; Etienne Bettens, baritone; Francois Loup, bass-baritone; Tony d'Adario, Bobbio Gino, Mario Gabbi, electric guitars; Frank Martin, conductor.
With: Huit préludes-no. 4; Trois danses pour hautbois, harpe et orchestre à cordes-Rumba; Requiem-In Paridisum; Le Vin herbé-Epilogue.
In: Musica Helvetica - Programme no. 4

POLYPTYQUE

D166. Pathé Marconi 2C069-02588 stereo September 1974; EMI ASD3185.
Yehudi Menuhin, violin; Menuhin Festival Orchestra and Zürich Chamber Orchestra; Edmond de Stoutz, conductor.
With: Ballade for Flute and String Orchestra; Ballade for Viola, Wind Orchestra and Percussion.

QUANT N'ONT ASSEZ FAIT DO-DO

D167. Opus One #84 stereo April 1982.
Thomas Bogdan, tenor; J. William Meyer, guitar; Francis Brancaleone and Dennis G. Michno, pianists.
With: Cantate pour le 1er août; Quatre pièces brèves; Cantate pour 'Le Petite village'; Loeb, David. Trois Cansos; Wallach, Joelle. Three Spanish Songs.

QUATRE PIÈCES BRÈVES POUR GUITARE

D168. RCA (US) LM/LSC2964 mono/stereo September 1966; RCA (UK)
       RL/RK43373/RK43373; RCA (France) SB6723; RCA (German) 26.
       41070S.
       Julien Bream, guitar.
       With: Brindle, Reginald Smith. Polifemo de Oro; Britten, Benjamin.
       Nocturnal; Henze, Hans Werner. Drei Tentos; Villa-Lobos, Heitor.
       Etudes no. 5 & 7.
       In: 20th Century Guitar.

D169. Gallo 30-152 stereo; MXT VG30152.
       Raùl Sanchez, guitar.
       With: Pièces de la renaissance: Danses et lieder; Fritz, Gaspar. Sonata
       en mi-mineur; Zbinden, Julien-Francois. Quatre miniatures, op. 14;
       Burkhard, Willy. Serenade, Op. 71, no. 3.
       In: Musique Suisse des XVIe, XVIIIe, XXe Siècle.

D170. Arion 30S150 stereo January 1972; Quintessence ARN31953 May
       1981; Musical Heritage Society MHS36032 1977.
       Alberto Ponce, guitar.
       With: Dodgson, Stephen. Partita; Ohana, Maurice. Si le jour parait;
       Brouwer, Leo. Eloge a le danse; Sojo, Vincente. 4 Pieces
       Venezueliennes; Turina, Joaquin. Sonatine.
       In: Prestige de la Guitare au XXe siècle (Quintessence); In: Florilège
       de la guitare (Arion).

D171. Disco-Center DIC78308 stereo May 1974.
       Masayuki Hirayama, guitar.
       With: Bach, J.S. Tänze und Stücke a.d.2. Notenbüchlein (BWV Anh.
       115); Brouwer, Leo. Elogio de la danza; Ohana, Maurice. Tiento;
       Villa-Lobos, Heitor. Prelude Nr. 4.
       In: Gitarrenmusik I.

D172. Love LRLP140 stereo June 11-13, 1975.
       Seppo Siirala, guitar.
       With: Castelnuovo-Tedesco, Mario. Sonatina; Ibert, Jacques. Piece
       pour le flûte seul; Entr'acte; Duarte, John. Danse joyeuse, op. 42;
       Fukushima, Katsuo. Shun-San.

D173. CRCI 180630 stereo July 15-16, 1975.
       Jan Wolf, guitar.
       With: Sauguet, Henri. Musiques pour Claudel; Berkeley, Lennox.
       Theme & Variations (1970); Eastwood, Tom. Ballade-Phantasy
       (1968); Petrassi Goffredo. Nunc (1971).
       In: Contemporary Music for Guitar.

D174.   Guitar G105 stereo 1977.
John Mills, guitar (no. 2 only).
With: Absil, Jean. Scherzo; Havg, Hans. Alba; Brouwer, Leo. Simple
Studies 1-10; Pratesi, Mira. Air, Muzurka; Tansman, Alexandre.
Entree, Gaillarde, Kolysanke no. 2; Walton, William. Bagatelle no. 2;
Ponce, Manuel. Mexican Song, Six Preludes; Dodgson, Stephen.
Study; Serenade; Rutter, John. Rondeau Caprice.
In: 20th Century Guitar Music.

D175.   MDG J1037/38 stereo 1982. MD+G 3292 1988.
Reinbert Evers, guitar.
With: Falla, Manuel de. Homenaje "Le tombeau de Claude Debussy";
Brindle, Reginald Smith. El Polifemo de Oro; Henze, Hans Werner.
Drei Tentos; Britten, Benjamin. Nocturnal; Medek, Tilo. Erdrach;
Trojahn, Manfred. Fantasia per chittara; Brandmüller, Theo.
Canzona liriche e danza di morte.
In: Gitarrenmusik des 20. Jahrhunderts.

D176.   Jecklin 209 stereo 1982.
Christoph Jäggin, guitar.
With: Kelterborn, Rudolf. Music für Violine und Gitarre; Gasser, Ulrich.
Herbstzeichen; Herbstkälte im Nebel; Diethelm, Caspar. Ukiyoye;
Peyrot, Fernande. Suiten.
In: Herbstzeichen Gitarrenmusik von Schweizer.

D177.   Gitarre & Laute G&L8201 stereo September 1982.
Eliot Fisk, guitar.
With: Scarlatti, Domenico. Sonatas, K. 27, K. 164, K. 96; Ponce,
Manuel. Valse; Theme varie et final; Raffman, Relly. For Eliot;
Paganini, Nicolo. Caprices, no. 7, 9, 13, 21.

D178.   Opus One #84 stereo 1982.
Douglas Hensley, guitar.
With: Cantate pour 1er août; Quant n'ont assez fait dodo; Chanson 'le
petite village'; Loeb, David. Trois Cansos; Wallach, Joelle. Three
Spanish Songs.

D179.   Da Camera Magna 93610.
Tilman Hoppstock, guitar.
With: Brouwer, Leo. Elogio de la Danza; La Espiral eterna; Tarantos;
Falla, Manuel de. Tanz des Müllers; Farruca; Lucia; Tarantos;
Ponce, Manuel. Cabezon-Variations; Paco de Lucia. Tarantos.

D180.   Eterna 827466 stereo 1983.
Monika Rost, guitar.
With: Narvaez, Luis de. Libros del delphin de Musica; Sor, Fernando.
Soli, op. 14; Carulli, Ferdinando. Duos, op. 34, no. 2; Rodrigo,
Joaquin. Invocation et danse; Brouwer, Leo. Micropiezas.
In: Music für Gitarre.

D181.   Preludio PH/PHC2116 stereo October/November 1987.
Nicholas Petrou, guitar.
With: Barrios, Agustin. La Catedral; Villa-Lobos, Heitor. Five preludes;
Mersson, Boris. Sonata per chitarra.

D182.   Harmonia Mundi DMR2028 stereo 1987
Jürgen Ruck, guitar.
With: Bach, J.S. Lautensuite, BWV 996; Milhaud, Darius. Segoviana;
Dowland, John. Variet of Lute Lessons; Fürtig, Peter. Intermezzi;
Heusinger, Detlef. Spurem-Elemente.
In: Preisträger Deutscher Musikrat 1987.

QUATRE SONNETS À CASSANDRE

D183.   ASCAP CB173 mono November 23, 1952 (non-commercial).
Nell Rankin, mezzo-soprano; Bernard Z. Goldberg, flute; Kras Malno,
viola; Theo Salzman, cello.
With: Walton, William. String Quartet; Prokofiev, Sergey. Sonata for
Flute and Piano, Op. 94.
In: Pittsburgh International Contemporary Festival.

D184.   Orion ORS82422 stereo January 15, 1982.
Carol Kimball, mezzo-soprano; Richard Soule, flute; Lewis Rosove,
viola; Barbara Gurley, cello.
With: Satie, Erik. Ludions; Berger, Jean. Cinq chansons; Poulenc,
Francis. La Frâicheur et le feu; Quatre poèmes d'Apollinaire; Deux
melodies; Milhaud, Darius. Six chansons de théâtre.
In: Mélodies.

D185.   Opus One #106 stereo.
Elsa Charlston, soprano, Alex Ogle, flute; Tina Pelikan, viola; Ted
Mook, cello.
With: Shapey, Ralph. Songs for Soprano and Piano.

QUATUOR À CORDES

D186.   Ex Libris EL 16951 stereo September 24, 1984.
Amati Quartett, Zürich.
With: Honegger, Arthur. Quatuor à cordes no. 1.

QUINTETTE EN RE MINEUR

D187.   Jecklin 159 stereo 1976; Spectrum SR-171 1983.
Zürich Piano Quintet.
With: Martinu, Bohuslav. Klavierquintett no. 1.

REQUIEM

D188.   Jecklin 190 stereo May 4, 1973; Jecklin DISCO 631-2 1989.
Elisabeth Speiser, soprano; Ria Bollen, contralto; Eric Tappy, tenor;
Peter Lagger, bass; André Luy, organist; Robert Mermoud,
choirmaster; Union chorale et Choeur de dames de Lausanne;
L'Orchestre de la Suisse Romande; Frank Martin, conductor.

REQUIEM - IN PARADISUM

D189.   Swiss Broadcasting Corp. MH3+4 (non-commercial).
Soloists, Union chorale et Choeur de dames de Lausanne;
L'Orchestre de la Suisse Romande; Frank Martin, conductor.
With: Huit préludes-no. 4; Trois danses pour hautbois, harpe et
orchestre è cordes-Rumba; Poèmes de la mort-Ballade des
pendus; Le Vin herbé-Epilogue.
In: Musica Helvetica - Programme no. 4.

REQUIEM - AGNUS DEI

D190.   RBM 3070 stereo.
Roswitha Sperber, contralto; Peter Schumann, organ.
With: Bonnet, Joseph. Caprice heroique; Dubois, Theodore. Cantilene
nuptiale; Herbold, Joachim. O Orients; Johner, Hans Rudolf.
Jubilate Deo; Kameke, Ernst-Ulrich. Wenn ich mitten in der Angst
wandle; Lefébure-Wély, Louis. Sortie Es Dur; Liszt, Franz.
Cantantibus Organis.
In: Jubilate Deo.

LE ROY A FAIT BATTRE TAMBOUR

D191.   Opus One #86 stereo April 1982.
Johanna Arnold, soprano; Yolanda Liepa, piano.
With: Il Faut partir pour l'angleterre; Chanson des métamorphoses;
Drey Minnelieder; Gerber, Steven R. Songs from "The Wild Swans
at Coole"; Two Lyrics of Gerald Manley Hopkins.

SECHS MONOLOGE AUS JEDERMANN

D192.   Decca (UK) LW5236 mono October 1955; London LL1405; Jecklin 563
1981; Jecklin Disco JD563-2 1989.
Heinz Rehfuss, baritone; Frank Martin, piano.
With: Schubert, Franz. Der Storm; Der Wanderer, Op. 65, no. 2;
Totengrabers Heimweh; Auf der Donau, Op. 21, no. 1;
Fischerweise, Op. 96, no. 4; Der zürnende Barde; Gruppe aus dem
Tartarus, Op. 24.

D193. CBC International Service 248 stereo January 1969.
John Boyden, baritone; John Newmark, piano.
With: Fleming, Robert. Four Songs on Poems by John Coulter;
Poulenc, Francis. Le Travail du peintre.

D194. FSM Aulos 53537 stereo March 1979.
Günther Massenkeil, baritone; Monica Hofmann, piano.
With: 4ème Etude-Pour les jeu fugué; Guitare; Etude rythmique;
Overture and Foxtrot.

D195. Eterna 827924 stereo.
Theo Adam, bass-baritone; Rudolf Dunckel, piano.
With: Schütz, Heinrich. Symphoniae sacrae, Teil 1; Jubilate Deo Omnis
terra; Geistliche Konzerte, Teil 2; Ich liege und schlafe und
erwache; Bach, Johann Sebastian. Beschränkt, ihr Weisen dieser
Welt, BWV 443; Ich halte treulich still, BWV 466; Der Tag is hin,
BWV 447; Der Tag mit seinem Lichte, BWV 448; Bist du bei mir,
BWV 508; Franz, Robert. Jagdlied, op. 1, no. 9; Gewitternach, op. 8
no. 6; Auf dem Merre, op. 5, no. 3; Es hat die Rose sich beklaght,
op. 42, no. 5; Widmung, op. 14, no. 1; Strauss, Richard. Heimliche
Aufforderung, op. 27, no. 3; Ach weh mir unglückhaftem Mann, op.
21, no. 4; Die Georgine, op. 10, no. 4; Allerseelen, op. 10, no. 8;
Ich liebe dich, op. 37, no. 2.
In: Liedmatinee mit Theo Adam.

SECHS MONOLOGE AUS JEDERMANN (version with orchestra)

D196. Deutsche Grammaphon LPM18871/SLPM138871 mono/stereo May 24-
28, 1963; DG2530630IMS October 1975; DG (French) 2530. 630;
DGCollector 2543819 1983.
Dietrich Fischer-Dieskau, baritone; Berlin Philharmonic; Frank Martin,
conductor.
With: Der Sturm - 3 Fragmente aus der Oper; (2530630) Lieder eines
Fahrenden Gesellen.

D197. FSM stereo RSM 68213EB/ FCD97213.
Martin Egel, baritone; Nürnberg Symphonie Orchester; Pierre-
Dominique Ponnelle, conductor.
With: Bach, J. S. Ich habe Genug, BWV 82.

SONATA DA CHIESA (version for flute and organ)

D198. Erato STU70649 stereo January 1971; Electrola IC06328289; RCA
(German) ZL30573DX; Musical Heritage Society MHS1277.
Jean-Pierre Rampal, flute; Marie-Claire Alain, organ.
With: Blavet, Michel. Sonata, B Minor, Op. 3, no. 2; Marcello,
Benedetto. Sonata, G Major; Krebs, Johan Ludwig. Fantasia for
Transverse Flute, 2 Keyboards & Pedal; Pugnani, Gaetano. Sonata
no. 3, F Major; Alain, Jehan. Trois mouvements.

D199. FSM 33501 stereo July 1974.
       Andreas Bossler, flute; Helmut Schroder, organ.
       With: Bach, J. S. Partita e-Moll für Flöte solo, BWV 1013; Pralüdium
       und Fuge C-Dur, BWV 547; Bossler, Kurt. Dialog I; Dialog II, für
       Flöte und Orgel.
       In: Musik in der Abtei Brauweiler.

D200. BIS LP-160 stereo February 27-29, 1980.
       Gunilla von Bahr, flute; Hans Fagius, organ.
       With: Hartmann, J. P. E. Preludium g-Moll; Olsson, Otto. Romance, op.
       24; Badings, Henk. Dialogues; De Frumerie, Gunnar. Aria, op. 77b.
       In: Meditation for flute and organ.

D201. Vista VPS1098 stereo May 7-8, 1980.
       Edward Beckett, flute; Nicolas Jackson, organ.
       With: Bach, J. S. Fantasia and Fugue in g Minor, BWV 542; Siciliano
       (from Sonata in E-flat); Alain, Jehan. Trois mouvements; Litanies;
       Fauré, Gabriel. Après un Rêve; Villette, Pierre.
       In: Music for Flute and Organ from St. Davids.

D202. Opus One #72 stereo November 28, 1980.
       Katherine Hoover, flute; Dennis G. Michno, organ.
       With: Chance, Nancy Laird. Daysongs; Mamlok, Ursula. Variations for
       Solo Flute.

D203. MZ 30 869 stereo 1987.
       Doris Geller, flute; Hans-Jürgen Kaiser, organ.
       With: Alain, Jehun. Mouvements 1-3; Bach, Johann Sebastian. Sonate
       für Flöte und cembalo, BWV1030; Krebs, Johann Ludwig. Fantasie
       C-Dur, Fantasie g-Moll; Lachner, Franz. Elegie C-Dur; Marais, Marin.
       Folies d'Espagne: Variationen 1-15.
       In: Musik für Flöte und Orgel.

SONATA DA CHIESA (version for viola d'amore and string orchestra)

D204. Turnabout 34687 stereo January 1976.
       Marcus Thompson, viola d'amore; M.I.T. Symphony Orchestra; David
       Epstein, conductor.
       With: Bloch, Ernest. Suite hébraïque; Hindemith, Paul. Der
       Schwanendreher.

SONATE I POUR PIANO ET VIOLON

D205. Opus One #89 stereo April 1983.
       Carol Sadowski, violin; Yolanda Liepa, piano.
       With: Fromm, Herbert. Sonata for Piano.

SONATE II POUR PIANO ET VIOLON

D206.   Opus One #98 stereo April 1982.
Carol Sadowski, violin; Yolanda Liepa, piano.
With: Iannaccone, Anthony. Aria Concertante.

DER STURM - 3 FRAGMENTE AUS DER OPER

D207.   Deutsche Grammaphon LPM18871/SLPM138871 mono/stereo May 24-
28, 1963; DG Collector 2543819 1983.
Dietrich Fischer-Dieskau, baritone; Berlin Philharmonic; Frank Martin,
conductor.
With: Sechs Monologe aus Jedermann.

SYMPHONIE POUR ORCHESTRE BURLESQUE SUR DES MÉLODIES
POPULAIRES SAVOYARDES

D208.   Jecklin 172 stereo October 28-30 1977.
Orchester der Kantonschule Stadelhofen, Zürich; Walter Ochsenbein,
conductor.
With: Telemann,Georg Ph. Orchestersuite G-Dur-Ouverture-Air-
Gavotte; Reichardt, B. J. F. Sinfonie G-Dur-Andantino-Presto;
Dittersdorf, Ditters von. Le Carnaval ou la redoute-Le Carnival;
Gluck, Christopf W. Sinfonie G-Dur-Allegro-Presto; Genzmer, Harald.
Miniaturen-Ausschnitte; Fecker, Adolf. Das kleine
Orchester-Festmusik; Martin, Orlando de. Rondo.
In: Schweizerisches Jungendorchester Treffen 1977.

TRIO À CORDES

D209.   BASF 2521638 stereo May 7-12, 1971; Acanta EA21. 638.
New String Trio: Charles Castleman, violin; Paul Doktor, viola; Jennifer
Langham, cello.
With: Trio sur des mélodies populaires irlandaises; Huit préludes pour
piano.

TRIO SUR DES MÉLODIES POPULAIRES IRLANDAISES

D210.   Columbia (Switzerland) DZX 17-18 78 rpm mono.
Walter Lang Trio: Walter Kägi, violin; Franz Hindermann, cello; Walter
Lang, piano.

D211.   Rimaphon RILP30-021 mono.
Sattler Trio: Klaus Sattler, violin; Samuel Langmeir, cello; Gerty Sattler,
piano.
With: Ravel, Maurice. Trio pour piano, violon et violoncelle.

D212. BASF 2521638-1 stereo 7-12 May 1971; Acanta 2521638-1; Bellaphon
EA21638.
New String Trio: Charles Castleman, violin; Jennifer Langham, cello;
Werner Genuit, piano.
With: Trio für Violine, Viola und Violoncello; Huit préludes pour piano.

D213. Jecklin 156 stereo 1976.
Trio Montavo: Marlis Mose, violin; Klära Tanner-Egyedi, cello; Rita
Wolfensberger, piano.
With: Turina, Joaquin. Trio (1926); Gal, Hans. Variationen über eine
Weiner Heurigenmelodie, Op. 9.
In: Folklore im Klaviertrio.

D214. Verceau M10093 stereo December 1980.
Le Clavier Trio Francais: Bernard Mauppin, violin; Yves Potrei, cello;
Susan Campbell, piano.
With: Ravel, Maurice. Trio en la mineur.

D215. Gallo 30-424 stereo 1984.
Trio Musiviva: Patrick Genet, violin; Marc Jaermann, cello; Philippe
Dinkel, piano.
With: Dvorak, Antonin. Trio in f Minor, Op. 65.

D216. Harmonia Mundi HM669D stereo 1983.
Trio Fontenay: Michael Mücke, violin; Niklas Schmidt, cello; Wolf
Harden, piano.
With: Henze, Hans Werner. Kammersonaten; Mendelssohn-Bartholdy,
Felix. Trio, op. 66.

TROIS CHANTS DE NOËL

D217. Carolina 712C2143 stereo October 1963.
Ethel Casey, soprano; Bill Sidell, piano; Don Adcock, flute.
With: Debussy, Claude. Fetes galantes, Bk. I; Proses lyriques; Trois
chansons de Bilitis; Fetes galantes Set II; Ballade des femmes de
Paris; Mandoline;
In: Debussy Recital.

D218. Iramac 6520 mono/stereo January 1966; Jecklin 563 1981; Jecklin
Disco JD563-2 1989.
Elly Ameling, soprano; Frank Martin, piano; Pieter Odé, flute.
With: Huit préludes; Drey Minnelieder.

D219.   CBC SM96 stereo March 28-29, 1969.
Lyric Arts Trio: Mary Morrison, soprano; Marion Ross, piano; Robert
Aitkin, flute.
With: Roussel, Albert. Deux poèmes de Ronsard; Lasala, Angel E.
Poemas Nortenos; Gaubert, Philippe. Soir Païen; Riegger,
Wallingford. Music for Voice and Flute; Freeman, Harry. Toccata for
Soprano and Flute; Three old Dutch Christmas Carols.

D220.   Jecklin 137 mono/stereo 1974.
Kammertrio Bern: Brigitte Kuhn-Indermühle, mezzo-soprano; Hansjörg
Kuhn, piano; Heidi Indermühle, flute.
With: Handel, George Frideric. Nell dolce dell' oblio; Burkhard, Willy. 4
Lieder aus Op. 25: Wandern; Des Morgens Schale; Szervansky,
Endre. Szent vagy Uram; Jolivet, André. Chant de linos; Roussel,
Albert. Deux poèmes de Ronsard.

D221.   BIS LP37 stereo 23, August 31, 1975.
Jacqueline Delman, soprano; Lucia Negro, piano; Gunilla von Bahr,
flute.
With: Shostakovich, Dmitrii. Seven Poems by Alexander Blok;
Messiaen, Olivier. Poèmes pour mi, Livre I; Pergament, Moses. Vem
Spelar Natten; Head, Michael. A Piper.

D222   Claves 604 stereo February 1-3, 1976.
Kathrin Graf, soprano; Michio Kobayashi, piano; Peter-Lukas Graf,
flute.
With: Bach, J. S. Cantata Nr. 204: Meine Seele sei Vergnugt; Handel,
George Frideric. Deutsche Arien Nr. 6: Meine Seele hort im Sehen;
Rameau, Jean-Philippe. Rossignols amoureux; Ravel, Maurice.
Chansons medécasses; Roussel, Albert. Lieder, op. 26; Scarlatti,
Alessandro. Solitudini Amene.
In: Musik für Gesang und Flöte.

D223.   Wealden WS156 stereo 1978.
Petronella Dittmer, soprano; Andrew Ball, piano; Lyn McLarin, flute.
With: Darke, Harold. In the Bleak Midwinter; Ord, Boris. Adam lay y
bounden; Terry, Richard. Myn Lyking; Holst, Gustav. Christmas Day
in the Morning, Op. 46, no. 1; Jesu Sweet; I Sing of a Maiden;
Bach, J. S. Fantasia on In Dulci Jubilo, BWV 729; Howells, Herbert.
Here in the Little Door; Leighton, Kenneth. Lully, Lulla, Thou Little
Tiny Child; Poston, Elizabeth. Jesus Christ the Apple Tree; Davies,
H. Walford, arr. The Holly and the Ivy; A Sacred Cradle Song; O
Little town of Bethlehem; Haas, Joseph. Kirchensonata on "In Dulci
Jubilo," Op. 62, no. 1; Wilcocks, David, arr. Infant Holy, Infant
Lowly; Wood, Charles, arr. Ding! Dong! Merrily on High; Jacques,
Reginald, arr. Away in a Manger.
In: Christmas music from St. Martin-within-Lidgate.

D224. Opus One #83 stereo April 1982.
Johanna Arnold, soprano; Steven Gerber, piano; Theresa Aiello, flute.
With: L'Amour de Moy; Shields, Alice. Six Songs from Poems of Pablo
Neruda; Tsandoulas, Gerasimos. Elià.

TROIS DANSES POUR HAUTBOIS, HARPE ET ORCHESTRE À CORDES

D225. Opus One #125 stereo 1985.
Philip Teachey, oboe; Lynne Abbey, harp; Richmond Sinfonia;
Jacques Houtmann, conductor.
With: Allen, Judith. Aura.

TROIS DANSES POUR HAUTBOIS, HARPE ET ORCHESTRE À CORDES -
NO. 3 RUMBA

D226. Swiss Broadcasting Corp. MH3+4 stereo (non-commercial).
Heinz Holliger, oboe; Ursula Holliger, harp; Basel Chamber Orchestra;
Paul Sacher, conductor.
With: Huit préludes-No. 4; Poèmes de la mort-Ballade des pendus;
Requiem-In Paridisum; Le Vin herbé-Epilogue.
In: Musica Helvetica - Programme no. 4.

VERSE À BOIRE

D227. Gallo 30-32g stereo September 1981.
Ars Laeta Groupe Vocale; Robert Mermoud, conductor.
With: Chanson et cannon; Vospoite Gospodi (Orthodox Liturgy);
Duruflé, Maurice. Ubi Caritas; Reichel, Bernard. Magnificat; Festa,
Constanzo. Quis Dabit Oculis (attributed to Senfl); Poulenc, Francis.
Vinea mea electa (Respons aux matines du vendredi-Saint); 1er
Nocturne; Lotti Antonio. Crucifixus; Fatise Kolo (air popular serbe);
Passereau, Pierre. Il est bel et bon; Sutermeister, Heinrich. Le Vieux
jardin; Robin et Marion (melodie du XVe siècle); Mermoud, Robert.
La Tarasque de Tarascon; Binet, Jean. Chanson; Heiller, Anton.
Nörgeln; Kodaly, Zoltan, arr. Turot ëszik a Cigany.

D228. Opus One #78 stereo April 1982.
Choir of All Saints Church, New York; Dennis G. Michno, conductor.
With: 5 Ariel Songs; Chanson en canon; Ode et sonnet; Es ist ein
Schnitter, heisst der Tod; Nous sommes trois souverains princes;
Gerber, Steven R. Dylan Thomas Settings.

LE VIN HERBÉ

D229. Westminster XWN2232/WST232 mono/stereo September 1961; Music
Guild MS6210 1969; Jecklin 581/82 1983; FSM 0581/82; Jecklin
DISCO 581/2-2 1989.
Soloists, Chamber Ensemble; Frank Martin, piano; Victor Desarzens,
conductor.

LE VIN HERBÉ - EPILOGUE

D230. Swiss Broadcasting Corp. MH3+4 (non-commercial).
Soloists, Chamber Ensemble; Frank Martin, piano; Winterthur
Symphony Orchestra; Victor Desarzens, conductor.
With: Trois danses pour hautbois, harpe et orchestre à cordes-no. 3
Rumba; Huit préludes-no. 4; Poèmes de la mort-Ballade des
pendus; Requiem-In Paridisum.
In: Musica Helvetica - Programme no. 4.

ZWISCHEN RHÔNE UND RHEIN

See Du Rhône au Rhin

DIRECTORY OF PUBLISHERS

Bärenreiter Verlag
Heinrich Schütz Allee 31-37
D3500 Kassel-Wilhelmshöhe, West
   Germany
U.S. Agent: Foreign Music Dist.
305 Bloomfield Ave.
Nutley, NJ 07110

Gérard Billaudot
14 rue de l'Echiquier
F-75010 Paris, France
U.S. Agent: Theodore Presser
Bryn Mawr, PA 19010

Breitkopf & Härtel
Walkmühlstrasse 52
D-6200 Wiesbaden, West Germany
U.S. Agent: Associated Music
   Publishers
8112 W. Bluemound Rd.
Milwaukee, WI 53213

Edition de la Procure Romande
Fribourg, West Germany

Editions Henn
8 Rue de Hesse
1211 Geneva, Switzerland

Hug & Co.
Flughofstrasse 61
CH-8152 Glattbrugg, Switzerland

Müller & Schade
Kramgasse 50
CH-3011 Berne, Switzerland

Pierre Noël, Editeur
see Billaudot

G. Schirmer Inc.
8112 W. Bluemound Rd.
Milwaukee, WI 53213

Société des Chanteurs Bernois
Berne, Switzerland

Universal Edition
Bösendorferstrasse 12
A-1015 Wien, Austria
U.S. Agent: European American
   Music Dist. Corp.
P.O. Box 850
Valley Forge, PA 19482

Writings by Martin

"Si ce n'est pas nécessairement la
paixet la consolation que l'artiste
doit donner aux autres hommes, ce
devait être en tout cas cette
libération que produit en nous la
beauté."

"If it is not necessarily peace and
consolation which the artist should
give to others, it should in any case
be that liberation which produces
beauty in us."

Over a span of many years Frank Martin wrote program notes for his new
works, gave lectures and interviews, made speeches and wrote letters and
essays on topics that were of particular interest to him. Many of these are
collected in two monographs, Un Compositeur médite sur son art (see M11)
and A propos de...commentaires de Frank Martin (see M2). Some of these
topics were repeated, and as the situation required they were expanded or
summarized. The entries which follow represent an attempt to present to
English-speaking readers the most important writing of Frank Martin which
also reflects the greatest variety.

M1.   "A la mémoire de Dinu Lipatti." In Hommage à Dinu Lipatti, 71.
       Genève: Labor et Fides, 1951.
       Trans. as: "Dinu Lipatti zum Gedächtnis." Schweizerische
       Musikzeitung. Revue musicale suisse 91 (1952): 38.
       Frank Martin wrote this brief eulogy almost immediately after
hearing of the great pianist's death. The composer describes Lipatti
as an artist whose deep humility coexisted with his self confidence,
and whose nature combined irony with a deep seriousness. In brief
reminiscences that follow, Martin recalls how he met the pianist as a
guest of the Romanian legation in Geneva, where he was invited to
listen to a young pianist play. After hearing the unknown pianist play
Bach, Martin was convinced of a very unique talent. Subsequently a
lasting friendship arose that remained throughout the brief seven
years that remained for Lipatti.

M2.   A propos de...commentaires de Frank Martin sur ses oeuvres.
       Neuchâtel: A la Baconnière, 1984.
       This monograph collects in one volume the many program note
essays which Frank Martin prepared for premieres, subsequent
performances and recordings of his works. They span a period of
years from his Symphonie pour orchestre burlesque (1915) to the
Fantaisie sur des rythmes flamenco (1973). Some of the articles such
as the final work E la vie l'emporta were done by Maria Martin.
Together their work constitutes a valuable source of program
information reflecting the composer's own view of his compositions,
and they are brought together from diverse sources many of which
would now be difficult to obtain in their original format.

M3.   "A propos de mon de concerto de violon." Revue musicale No. 212
       (April 1952): 111-115.
       Reprinted in: A propos de ...commentaires de Frank Martin sur ses
       oeuvres, (1984): 169-173.
       Here is an essay by the composer written in response to a
request for an article on "The development of my musical language."
It is only secondarily "about" the Violin Concerto. Using a quotation
from the poet Baudelaire in which the poet in mock seriousness
proposes to explain his method, and to teach everyone how to do it,
as a point of departure, Frank Martin attempts to explain his lifelong
search for his own musical voice and his philosophy and the means
to achieve it. The composer identifies one element which has
remained constant in his life work of composing but admits that it's
not easy to define. He sees a work of art not as a self-propelled
organism but the product of a composer's "inner capacity" or total
personality combined with his intellect or skill in fashioning a musical
entity from the technical resources at his disposal. Martin asserts that
it is his preoccupation with this "centrality of sensibility" that is the one
constant in his conceptual goals and requires that the two elements
remain in balance with one another. From this concept, the composer
reviews the various means through which his music has evolved in

order to achieve his true and unique musical voice. This has been achieved by reconciling a need to expand and enrich his musical language through serial procedures, while at the same time retaining a fundamental tonal link with traditional harmonic practice. Finally, the Violin Concerto is seen as a natural consequence of this search. The work is cast in the traditional mold of the romantic concerto only because the musical elements fit naturally into this form. This imaginative use of material from his previous work of choruses from Ariel's songs in the Tempest adds a fantasy element to the Violin Concerto. See: W92

M4.   "A propos des 'Six Monologues de Jedermann.'" Kunst-Zeitung Nr. 12 (December 1944): 3.

   Frank Martin uses an article about his Jedermann Songs, as a forum to share his thoughts about the difficulties that modern audiences have in comprehending the new technical and musical devices that composers have employed in searching for new means of expression. The composer finds that it is especially difficult in the area of instrumental music for the listener to grasp the new and often complex musical syntax. There is, however, for the listener an enormous advantage in being able to relate to a literary text set to music, even if the text is not fully comprehended on a single hearing. Because of the need to be able to grasp the written words at a single hearing, poetic works from the past are generally more appropriate than contemporary poems which often have irregular poetic meter and difficult intellectual concepts. Martin then explains his good fortune in finding just the right text for a song cycle for baritone in von Hofmannsthal's Jedermann setting. The needed element is there-- pure and simple poetic expression to convey an eternal message of confrontation with death and its acceptance through redemption.

M5.   "A propos du 'Cornet.'" In Alte und neue Musik - Das Baseler Kammerorchester unter Leitung von Paul Sacher 1926-1951. Zürich: Atlantis, 1952.

   In writing program notes for Paul Sacher's Baseler Kammerorchester (February 2, 1945), Frank Martin describes in detail how, in searching for a suitable text for a projected song cycle, he was introduced to Der Cornet by his wife. Despite the fact that the prose poem was too long, that it was in German which he did not feel comfortable with, and that it was a narrative poem rather than one describing feelings which was what he was searching for, the attraction of Rilke's poem was so insistent that he abandoned the original search in order to devote himself to composing music for Der Cornet. Enlisting aid from Maria Martin whose command of German was excellent, the music was conceived for alto voice and chamber orchestra. For each tableau the composer sought a musical form that most nearly fit the literary form of Rilke's rambling and episodic poem.

M6.   "A propos du language musical contemporain." <u>Schweizerische</u>
       <u>Musikzeitung. Revue musicale suisse</u> 77 (October 1937): 501-505.
       Reprinted in: <u>Un Compositeur médite sur son art</u>. Neuchâtel: A la
       Baconnière 72-77.

       In this essay, the composer shares his thoughts on the present
       state of contemporary music as he perceives it, but focuses his
       attention primarily on the twelve-tone system of Schoenberg and its
       impact on younger composers. Martin argues that, faced with the
       demand of absolute originality from both the public and the critical
       establishment, the twentieth-century composer has experienced an
       extended period of experimental and anarchistic composition. Having
       lost the guidelines of the carefully codified rules that have been the
       basis for western European music in past centuries, composers of
       today have had to rely mainly on their individual sensitivity. Martin
       sees ahead a new era of academism where conventionality and
       banality will reassert themselves. He believes that the only direction
       which will permit music to produce new masterpieces in an original
       way will be to maintain the tension induced by the search for new
       expressive means. The composer acknowledges that Schoenberg
       has produced the only new set of rules, that is, he has created a
       school from which composers working now can benefit. While
       rejecting the concept of absolute atonality, Martin sees the importance
       of the Schoenberg system as one which creates demands on future
       composers by creating a set of new rules from which composers
       must deviate as they have from past formulations of rules in order to
       produce new masterworks. The composer concludes that: "Si notre
       musique actuelle ne doit pas périr sous une vague en retour de
       simplisme, j'ai la conviction qu'elle peut trover son point d'èquilibre
       dans la conciliation du principe harmonique et du système
       chromatique inauguré par Schoenberg." "If our present music is not
       to perish under the wave of a return to simplism, I am convinced that
       it will find its equilibrium point in the conciliation between the harmonic
       principle and the chromatic system instituted by Schoenberg."

M7.   "A propos du 'Requiem.'" [Program Notes] for the premiere
       performance of <u>Requiem</u> May 4, 1973.
       Reprinted in: <u>Un Compositeur médite sur son art</u>. Neuchâtel: A la
       Baconnière, 1977. 141-143.

       The composer discusses the background of composing his
       <u>Requiem</u> which he resolved to write in mid-life, but found it difficult to
       undertake even when he realized that the time to commence was at
       hand. Martin found the impetus to write from a trip to Italy where he
       visited churches and Greek temples that expressed perfectly the
       feeling of adoration that he wanted to incorporate into his <u>Requiem</u>.
       After due consideration of alternatives, the composer found the
       medieval imagery of the Latin mass of the dead and the traditional
       resources of oratorio: large chorus, solo vocal quartet, organ and
       orchestra to best fulfill his expressive needs. Writing about the
       technical means, Martin states that he tried to reflect the beauty and

value of the text by using contrapuntal writing very sparingly, and also in introducing melodic lines accompanied only by a chord.

Expressively, Martin tried to put into his music the thought or consideration of death when he wrote "Ce que j'ai tenté d'exprimer ici c'est la claire volonté d'accepter la mort, de faire la paix avec elle, de la voir pleinement dans tout ce qu'elle comporte d'angoisse, physique et morale, en nous mettant face à face avec ce qu'a été notre vie..." "What I attempted to express in my work is the will to accept death, to make peace with it, to be aware of its physical and moral anguish by making us face our lives..."

M8. "A propos du 'Vin Herbé.'" <u>Schweizerische Musikzeitung. Revue musicale suisse</u> 82 (March 1942): 73-75.

This early article has proved to be one of Martin's most important statements concerning his own working philosophy toward composing and contains elements that are reflected in many of his subsequent writings and speeches. Before addressing the subject of <u>Le Vin herbé</u>, Martin discusses the difficulty he experiences in writing about his own work from either a technical viewpoint or in terms of thoughts and feelings. He further states that, despite what the public may believe, works of art are derived from both inspiration and the application of hard work. Unlike mathematics which produces indisputable truths, works of art which are artistic truths must succeed by convincing an audience. The composer pursues further the elements that he perceives to be required, including intimate feeling, sensitivity to tonal, literary, and psychological elements, and, above all, judgment in the selection or rejection of ideas and technical devices to achieve the desired goals. Returning to the subject of <u>Le Vin herbé</u>, Martin again affirms his belief that intimate feeling, not obedience to technical rules, is the only proof of the success of an artistic work. He then states that he has followed certain arbitrary rules up to a point in <u>Le Vin herbé</u>, but only for their expressive value in this work. Then follows the composer's often quoted lines: "Toute règle, du reste, n'a en vue que l'enrichissement du style, ... L'obéissance à des règle de style n'est qu'une élégance, un plaisir de l'espirit qui ne fait preuve d'aucune valeur, qui n'emporte aucune conviction." "Rules exist only to enrich style... to obey stylistic rules is an elegance only, a pleasure of the spirit; it is no proof of value and does not indicate conviction." Martin concludes with a brief history of how <u>Le Vin herbé</u> came to be written and the process of adoption from the novel by Bédier.

M9. "Anmerkungen zu 'Monsieur de Pourceaugnac.'" <u>Musik und Szene</u> 8 (1962); 1-4.

In an article that begins by reproducing the composer's own handwriting (in French), Frank Martin extends his best wishes to the Deutsche Opera am Rhein prior to a performance of his Molière opera in a German language production. Then follows (in German) the composer's essay on <u>Monsieur de Pourceaugnac</u> in which he explains some of the problems and solutions involved in setting Molière's play to music. Frank Martin identifies a fundamental problem--modern music per se is not funny. The reason is that what makes us laugh are well-known things placed in an unusual context. The composer's solution to this problem was to just write what pleased him. Some of the devices he uses are simple repetitive twelve-tone series alternating between voices and the orchestra, which are embellished by the addition of unaccompanied speech, rhythmic speech accompanied, recitative, dance and even yodeling. The orchestra is of Mozartean dimensions but augmented by the use of piano, saxophone, harp, vibraphone, and harpsichord. The composer concurs with Molière that: "Es ist ein schwieriges Unternehmen, die ehrbaren Leute zum Lachen zu bringen." "It's a difficult task to make honest people laugh."

M10. "Ballade pour piano et orchestre." Orchestre de la Suisse Romande. Neuvième concert de l'abonnement (February 19, 1945).

Writing in program notes for a concert in which the soloist was Dinu Lipatti in a performance of the Piano Ballade, Martin places the work in its historical perspective as being written in 1939 along with other Ballades and in the midst of completing his Le Vin herbé. The composer asserts that the common bond of the pieces written at that time was that they were intended to be more epic than lyric. There follows a brief but analytical description of the piece section by section to the end.

M11. Un Compositeur médite sur son art. Neuchâtel: A la Baconnière, 1977.

A collection of writings gathers together in a single volume Martin's most important essays, lectures, and letters, which reflect his thought on various aspects of music including his own music during a period that spans nearly forty years. Despite its title, the various articles say more about trends in the twentieth century than about the composer's own works. Many of Martin's favorite topics are represented here, such as his relationship to Schoenberg's twelve-tone system, the difficulties that audiences experience in assimilating new music, the dominance of harmony over other elements in European music, and the composer's responsibility in the creation of new works. Finally, there are articles on some of his own works. For a composer whose works reflected ever increasing refinement and a deliberate search for a stylistic synthesis consistent with European art music of the past, much of what was taking place among the avant-garde was distasteful to him. This, too, is expressed in his writings. Taken as a whole, the articles present a clear summary of the thought and position of an important composer whose life and works span a considerable portion of the twentieth century.

M12.   "Le Compositeur moderne et les textes sacrés." Schweizerische
        Musikzeitung. Revue musicale suisse 86 (1946): 261-266.
        Reprinted in: Un Compositeur médite sur son art. 123-132.
        Neuchâtel: A la Baconnière, 1977.

        In an extended article originally presented as a talk on the
        occasion of a performance of his In terra pax, Frank Martin shares his
        views on writing music to a sacred text. In the view of the composer,
        the situation of writing music for the church which in the past
        produced so many masterpieces has been changed unalterably. In
        our modern society, the church no longer exerts its former dominance
        in the area of the arts. Works written now to a sacred text are judged
        on the same basis as secular works which today are dominated by
        the cult of the individual creator, not by the quality of the text or by
        the success of the work in awaking a religious feeling or re-animating
        the faith of a listener. Martin believes that a truly spiritual work should
        not direct attention to the creator, but to the work's message, while
        the composer remains anonymous, however impractical this may be.
        Faced with this dilemma, Martin retained his Mass and an incomplete
        Christmas Cantata in a drawer, unheard and unpublished for many
        years. He then describes how the ending of World War II created the
        necessary conditions to resolve his personal impasse. Because of the
        universality of the theme of war and peace, Martin felt that only a
        passage drawn from the Bible and expressing the theme of
        forgiveness could satisfy the need for a text to fulfill a commission for
        a new work to be heard on the day that peace was declared. Linking
        this with his nearly completed passion music Golgotha, the composer
        describes in detail the selection of texts and the structure of each
        work, emphasizing that they are works to be presented in church, but
        are not by his definition church music.

M13.   "Concerto for Seven Wind Instruments, Timpani, Percussion and String
        Orchestra" (1949) and 'Etudes' for string orchestra (1955-56)."
        Jacket notes.
        Reprinted in: A propos de...commentaires de Frank Martin sur ses
        oeuvres, 211-212. Neuchâtel: A la Baconnière, 1984.

        Here are succinct program notes in English that were prepared
        for the 1961 recording of these works (see D56). Martin describes
        how the two pieces are so completely different, yet have in common
        the challenge (for the composer) of technical problems to be solved,
        which become the agent that sets his creative energy in motion. He
        then briefly describes the structure of each piece.

M14.   "Défense de l'Harmonie. "Schweizerische Musikzeitung. Revue
        musicale suisse 83 (1943): 8-10.

        This article reveals Frank Martin as educator and pedagogue, as
        well as in his usual role of composer. The argument concerns the
        definition given in a published article by Pierre Wissmer, of harmony
        as a "vertical effect," a definition to which Martin takes exception. For
        the reader the argument is relatively unimportant, but Martin's

explication of the function and importance of harmony is masterful in its presentation and reveals the importance that the composer attaches to harmony when he says "c'est, en effet, à l'harmonique nous devons la marque distinctive de notre musique européenne; je veux dire le sens tonal. C'est ce sens tonal seul qui a permis la composition de morceaux étendus de musique pure. Cest le sens tonal qui a permis l'eclosion de la musique symphonique avec toute l'infinie richesse de ses ramifications." "We owe the distinctive mark of European music to harmony--I am speaking of the tonal sense. This tonal awareness is the only thing which made the composition of extensive pieces of pure music possible." Returning to the issue of vertical versus horizontal writing or whether great composers thought of melody or harmony first, Martin states that "L'harmonie se passe dans la durée, comme la mélodie; comme elle, est modifiée par le facteur durée, par le rythme." "Harmony takes place over a duration of time, as does melody. Like melody, it is modified by duration and by rhythm." Thus these elements interact with one another to form a unity that cannot be meaningfully separated.

M15.   Entretiens avec Frank Martin. Zodiaque no. 103 (January 1975): 7-28.
         This is an interview conducted in the Martin home using a tape recorder. The series of questions or statements, designed to elicit an opinion, center first on the composer's background and then on his compositions, with specific emphasis on those of a religious nature. Additional questions probe Martin's approach to composing, and conclude with a question of the role of the artist in today's society. The questions and responses reflect, at times, the direction a conversation might take, rather than a carefully organized interview. The questions also sometimes overlap similar interviews or subjects on which the composer has already expressed his opinion in published essays, etc. The interview may be considered a valuable document on the thoughts (not always musical) of a contemporary composer who expressed himself well in prose as well as in his music.

M16.   Entretiens sur la musique: with J. Claude Piquet. Neuchâtel: A la
         Baconnière, 1977.
         Trans. as: Conversations About Music. Trans. by Leonard Lythgoe.
         unpubl.
         Of the several published interviews with Frank Martin by reviewers, journalists, critics and others, this monograph is by far the most comprehensive in depth probing of the composer's life, work and thoughts about matters musical. Jean-Claude Piquet, philosopher and long time friend and confidant of Frank Martin, demonstrates in these thoughtful conversations with the composer his own very thorough knowledge of the craft of musical composition, and of Martin's works in particular. The ten conversations are divided into three series under the headings of "Frank Martin, musician" (three sessions), "The music" (five sessions), and "The musician opposite

music" (two sessions). The first series explores the composer's background and his vocation as a composer. The second series develops the topics of harmony, melody, and rhythm, while the third series addresses general musical problems, including the composer's responsibility. These discussions reflect the concerns which the composer has written and spoken about during his long career. The analytical nature of these questions and answers presupposes some musical knowledge on the part of the reader.

M17.   "Etudes pour orchestre à cordes." Schweizerische Musikzeitung. Revue musicale suisse 97 (June 1957): 250-251.
      In program notes for a concert of all Swiss composers performed on June 5, 1957, Frank Martin describes the background of his Etudes for String Orchestra. Responding belatedly to a commission by Paul Sacher for his Basel Chamber Orchestra, the composer was obliged to write for string orchestra, with only occasional divisi into additional parts, and to include no soloists. As the composer has confided in other writings, without a literary text for support, he often needed a technical problem whose solution became the pathway to the creation of a new work. Thus it followed in the four Etudes: the composer chose what he called "links," the movement of a melodic passage quickly from one section of the orchestra to another with absolute smoothness, free from any disjointedness. Similarly, the second etude explores as many varieties of pizzicato as he could devise. The third is a study in legato playing by divided viola and cello sections, while the final movement is a fugal study.

M18.   "L'expérience créatrice." Schweizerische Musikzeitung. Revue musicale suisse 90 (1950): 350-353.
      Reprinted in: Un Compositeur médite sur son art, 43-48. Neuchâtel: A la Baconnière, 1977.
      Trans. as: "Erfahrung des Schöpferischen." Musica 4 (September 1950): 321-324.
      Reprinted in: Musik der Zeit: Schweizer Komponisten Heft 1. 59-62 Bonn: Boosey & Hawkes, 1955.
      With his usual modesty and a certain reticence to talk about himself, the composer at once recognizes that truly creative genius is an extremely rare quality reserved to only a chosen few throughout all of history. Nevertheless, there is within all humans a desire to invent, in the sense of discovering and defining something of one's own individuality, even at the most mundane level. Focusing on the creative experience of the composer, Martin identifies false pride and false modesty as both originating in the fact that the creator identifies himself with his creation and considers it to be himself. He then cites the poet Paul Valery as one who has most successfully tried to define the creative process, and who has identified two aspects of this process. "Observez bien cette dualité possible d'entrée enjeu: parfois qulque close veut quelque close à servir." "We should note that there

are two possibilities of engagement in the creative process: sometimes an idea has a need to be expressed, other times the means of expression is searching for an idea to be served." For the composer, Martin sees a vocal work with a set text to be set to music as an expression of the former, while an instrumental work of pure music is an example of the latter. Borrowing from Valery again, the composer asserts that in every artist there are two fundamental values: the musical materials he has to work with, and the talent and skill he has to fashion something of value from them. Finally Martin sees the creative process as acting in two different ways upon the artist. For some, creativity is an inner thrust seeking release, while for others the creative experience is derived from an anxiety over the still unknown and shapeless entity that is to come. In fact, both of these aspects are present in the creative process, as the artist expresses both the joy and the anguish of his labors. Martin believes that the public should not have to participate in the creative process, but only experience the result: "...son oeuvre devrait toujours porter le signe de cette sérénité qu'évoque en nous une forme accomplie et qui est, je pense, ce qu'on appelle la beauté." "...his work should always bear the sign of that serenity which an accomplished form evokes in us, and which is, I believe, what we call beauty."

M19.   "Expression ou incarnation." Lettres IV (1944, no. 3).
        Reprinted in: Un Compositeur médite sur son art, 160-163.
            Neuchâtel: A la Baconnière, 1977.

            In this essay, Martin defines and explains his use of the term incarnation. "Il symbolise pour moi ce fait que l'oeuvre d'art n'exprime pas les mouvements les plus intérieurs de l'artiste mais peut, si elle atteint à la beauté, incarner en quelque sorte, ces mouvements de son esprit, et parfais les recréer chez d'autres." "This term signifies for me the fact that a work of art does not express the innermost movements of the artist, but rather, if it has attained beauty, it can in a way incarnate these movements of his mind, and sometimes recreate these movements in others." While Martin disagrees with Stravinsky who wrote in his Chronicles of My Life that "I consider music by its very essence, powerless to express anything...," Martin believes that the expression of feelings by a composer is not the primary purpose of music. The composer asserts that the great musical masterpieces of all time, such as works by Bach and Beethoven, are loved for the works themselves, not for the feelings which may be expressed by the composer, or experienced by the listener. These masterpieces then, have succeeded in incarnating the movements of the composer's mind, and recreating them for the listener. A composer carries within himself an ideal image of art that goes beyond feelings. It follows that a true artist does not need to experience a feeling at the moment he expresses it. Paradoxically, feelings and the (spiritual) quality of feelings do play an independent part in the process that cannot be directly controlled by the will of the artist. The artist then must concentrate his will on the two elements of technique and expression, especially the latter, these being the elements from which he is free to choose, and for which he is ultimately responsible. Beyond this, there is nothing more the artist can, by his own effort, accomplish.

M20. "Fantaisie sur des rythmes flamenco." Concert en hommage à Frank Martin à l'occasion du 3e anniversaire de sa mort (November 21, 1977).

In program notes reused on this anniversary concert, the composer describes the circumstances that led to the composition of this work for solo piano and dancer. In composing his Fantaisie, three needs were fulfilled: the composition of a dance piece which his daughter Teresa could use, the fulfillment of a long promised fantasy piece for pianist Paul Badura-Skoda, and the completion of a new work requested for the 1974 Lucerne International Music Festival. Martin then describes his fascination with the rhythmic aspects of flamenco music and comments briefly on the structure of each of the four sections of the piece.

M21. "Frank Martin" In Pour ou contre la musique moderne?, 203-210. Paris: Flammarion, 1957.
Trans. as: "Moderne Musik und Publikum." Österreichische Musikzeitschrift 15 (September 1960): 412-417.
Trans. as: "Novaya Muzyka i Publika." [abridged] Soviet Music 25 (January 1961): 181-184.

Writing on the subject of new music and the public, Frank Martin lists and discusses the elements that he perceives to be the obstacles to public acceptance of new music. These include a new piece which is performed on a program with popular classical favorites, thus automatically eliciting a negative response from veteran listeners. Also he cites the differences in quality of audiences from one country to another and even from city to city. The degree of excellence experienced in the performance should not be taken for granted, as many new musical works are poorly comprehended by the musicians, and are often under rehearsed. Even the nationality of the composer, and the juxtaposition of lightweight and serious pieces on the program, can affect the reception of a new piece. The composer then turns his attention to the composers of new music, and the obstacles they have erected to public acceptance of their music. Predictably, Martin reaffirms his total allegiance to the traditional tonal function of music, while admitting that he and other composers are concerned with enlarging the scope of this concept but not with destroying it. The composer then must avoid musical avenues that lead to self-impoverishment, whether it be atonality, concrete music, or even totally diatonic music that limits its expressive possibilities severely. The young composer must guard against permitting his technical skill to supplant his humanity by creating complex abstractions which the public will never be equipped to comprehend, much less to love. Finally the author offers some practical suggestions to the listener: adopt a position of neutrality at the start, do not dismiss a piece after a single hearing as incomprehensible-- because music is not written to try to elude the listener, look for elements that are pleasing even in a piece that contains much that is not, and try to hear it again. Do not pursue a piece that offends, move on to something else. Sometimes we later return to such a piece and like it better. Facetiously, the composer concludes by advising listeners not to believe in artists who have been writing for fifty years or more.

M22.   "Golgotha." Schweizerische Muzikzeitung. Revue musicale suisse 90
        (1950): 205-209.
        Reprinted in: A propos de... commentaire de Frank Martin, 70-73.
        Neuchâtel: A la Baconnière, 1984.
            The composer describes, in considerable detail, the background and motivation for having undertaken a modern setting of the passion, and then describes step-by-step his approach and methodology to achieve the desired result. The initial impetus or inspiration came from an exhibition in the spring of 1945 of etchings by Rembrandt, and the composer's response to one in particular, which is called "The Three Crosses." After rejecting a desire to express the music of the passion in a brief and concentrated manner, much as the artist had achieved on a small rectangle of paper, the composer finally elected the medium of the sacred oratorio, just as J.S. Bach and others had in the baroque period. Martin asserts that each epoch has the right to re-express great themes which had preceded it, and that a new setting of the passion could provide a more meaningful and relevant vision of Christ's sufferings and victory over death to at least some of modern society. In this context, the composer argues that in the classical passions we are exposed to an account of Christ's death presented to a group of the faithful, who respond with hymns and choruses. He then determined to have his setting of the sacred drama evoke the divine person of Christ, and to present him as a man of action to a modern audience that may not be believers. In so doing, all other characters remain in the background and some secondary events and characters are omitted, including the traditional role of the evangelist. Just as in Bach's settings of the passion, meditative passages drawn from St. Augustine's writings are used to emphasize Christ's various attitudes, and to draw the gospel narratives together into a musical unity. Organized in two parts with seven scenes, the action begins on Palm Sunday and concludes with the scene at Calvary.

M23.   "In terra pax." In Alte und neue Musik - Das Baseler
        Kammerorchester unter Leitung von Paul Sacher 1926-1951.
        Zürich: Atlantis, 1952.
            In program notes of the Baseler Kammerorchester for April 29, 1946 Frank Martin describes the circumstances of his composing In terra pax. In the summer of 1944, he was commissioned by Radio

Geneva to compose a work to be performed and broadcast on the actual armistice day of World War II. Martin was thus faced with his own thoughts about war and peace as he anticipated the monumental event of great joy mixed with sadness. The composer then describes how he divided the forty-five-minute work into four parts and searched the Bible for passages to reflect these feelings of war and peace, and joy and sorrow. Using passages from Revelation, Isaiah, Psalms and the gospels, Martin wrote a work in which his own feelings are expressed in a musical idiom intended to reach the largest possible number of listeners. The four sections, beginning with passages from the Apocalypse expressing war and God's anger, ultimately conclude with the vision of a new heaven and a new earth from the same Biblical source.

M24.   "Littérature et Musique." Schweizerische Musikzeitung. Revue musicale suisse 98 (1958): 246-249.
Trans. as: "Literatur und Musik." Österreichische Musikzeitschrift 14 (October 1959): 403-407.

In a lecture presented on May 4, 1958 to the Swiss Author's and Musician's Festival in Lucerne, the composer speaks to the subject of how music and literature differ, and what they have in common. The composer asserts that while the poet and musician do not speak the same language, their respective languages have elements in common. Just as everyday speech is not a poetic art form, music can also satisfy obvious needs that are not art forms. Bugle calls, jungle drumming, and military marches are examples. Thus, music, like basic speech, is an articulate language, not of itself an art form. The fundamental difference between the two art forms is that the poet must deal with ideas and concepts, as well as emotions through the spoken language, while music must strive to be fully human without the help of thoughts. "...qui ne fait appel à aucun concept et ne connaît pas les prises de position philosophiques ou métaphysiques." "...it must be able to penetrate into places which require no concept, no philosophical or metaphysical position." Finally, that which music and literature have most in common is that they exist in a framework of time, but not the same time. Thus a combining of a poetic text with music raises the immediate problem that speech moves at a faster pace than song. This fundamental problem remains a verity which poets and musicians must find new solutions to with each new work created.

M25.   "Maurice Ravel." Schweizerische Musikzeitung. Revue musicale suisse 78 (March 1938): 137-138.

In this article Martin relates his one experience in talking with Ravel, who he describes as a modest man, especially when speaking about himself. Martin's article responds to Ravel's paradoxical statement "Le plus grand danger pour un artiste, c'est sincérité. Si nous avions été sincères une seue instant, nous n'aurions écrit que de la musique de Wagner." "The artist's greatest danger is that of sincerity. If we had been sincere for only an instant, we would have written only Wagner's music." Martin poses the question; what did Ravel mean by sincerity, and then attempts to answer it. Martin believes that Ravel used the term honestly--that it means to write the most beautiful music that one is capable of at the moment. At the same time, there is within a truly creative artist an expression of beauty which exists only in the creator's imagination and that has never been heard. This is an inner conflict that repeats itself in each new generation. Ravel speaks of a first-degree sincerity; that is a sincerity that moves one to compose based on youthful or momentary taste, to repeat the means of expression already time-tested, and to offer easy and comfortable solutions. The danger of sincerity then lies in the failure to resist following in the path that preceded, and instead to search for one's own voice wherever that may lead. Martin concludes that Ravel's paradoxical comment on the dangers of sincerity was really a profound lesson in courage and faith.

M26.   "La Musique moderne est-elle <<cérébrale>>?" Echo, La Revue des suisses à l'étranger No. 24 (February 1944): 9-10.
Reprinted in: Un Compositeur médite sur son art, 156-159. Neuchâtel: A la Baconnière, 1977.

The composer introduces his use of the term incarnation in another article (see M19) that also appeared in 1944. "Elle symbolise simplement pour moi ce fait que l'oeuvre d'art dans sa conception la plus haute, n'exprime jamais directement les mouvements les plus intérieurs de l'artiste." "For me, it symbolizes the fact that the work of art in its highest conception never directly expresses what is going on deep inside the artist." Martin believes that feelings expressed in a work of art are of secondary importance. What is really important is that a work be beautiful. Secondly, for a work of art to live it must have a public audience to respond to and be moved by it. Human feelings expressed in works of art become a powerful way of penetrating the listener's mind, thus it is important but not the primary goal of the artist. The great masterpieces from the past are loved and re-experienced for their beauty, not for feelings invoked in the listener or expressed by the artist. The answer to the title question seems to be sometimes yes, but for truly great new works the answer will ultimately be no. Only when the modern artist achieves a balanced and perfect work will his work move from the realm of the cerebral and technical to that of the masterwork and the heartfelt.

M27.   "Nécessité d'une musique contemporaine." In Lettres 3 (1943, no. 1): 55-62.
Trans. as: "Das Absolute und das Werdende." Österreichische Musikzeitschrift 11 (May 1956): 176-180.

Frank Martin in his letters, essays, and speeches several times addressed the topic of the difficulties which the public, that is musical audiences, encounters in listening to and comprehending new music. In this essay the author asserts that contemporary society living in a fast changing and often chaotic world seeks in music and the other arts a stability which represents an absolute, and that the listener finds this quality in art works of a past age. This concentration on artists and works of art from the past creates a cult status that leads to a form of idolatry. The argument then is against the misuse of masterpieces from the past which the composer sees as the practice of adoration, in which the entire interest and emphasis center on the interpretation of overly well-known musical works. The modern listener does not require art to contain that stimulating element which puts one in touch with the creative past. The listener then assigns to works of the past the quality of perfection, and at the same time from each new work demands the same perfection. Today's composer faces the impossible dilemma of trying to create a work of art that is both new and classical (perfect) at the same time.

M28.   "The Petite symphonie concertante and Les Quatre éléments" In The Orchestral Composer's point of View, edited by R.S. Hines, 152-165. Norman: University of Oklahoma Press, 1970.
    Reprinted in: A Propos de ---commentaries de Frank Martin sur ses oeuvres. 217-227 [in English], 130-137 [in French]. Neuchâtel: A la Baconnière, 1984.
        Written for an American publication of essays of composers writing about their own music, Frank Martin discusses the background and circumstances of writing each piece and briefly analyzes each work with musical examples. The composer, as elsewhere in his writings, makes a distinction between compositions in which a poetic text or other limiting factors are used and a purely abstract work that has only the limitations of its internal logic.

M29.   "Que peut-on atendre d'une oeuvre musicale nouvelle?" Journal de Genève (Supplément - October 30, 1943); In Dissonances 16 (no. 7/8 1943): 102-106.
    Reprinted in: Un Compositeur médite sur son art, 152-155.
    Neuchâtel: A la Baconnière, 1977.
    Trans. as: "Was kann Man von einem neuen Musikwerk erwarten?" Österreichische Musikzeitschrift 35 (November 1980): 594-596.
        Frank Martin responds to this essay question with another question, "What is one able to hear?" In speech, to hear is to understand or comprehend. In music, there is an intermediate level of partial understanding not shared by speech. Thus a third question is posed: what does understanding mean in this context? The composer asserts that understanding music does not mean an ability to analyze it technically, rather "...c'est donner un nom à des sensations proprement musicales..." "...it means to give a name to the feeling that the music provokes." Thus understanding music becomes a mysterious spiritual act that requires being able to follow its basic components--rhythm and melody. Finally, it means to be able to relate these elements in a new work to those of an older work that is already a part of the listener's musical comprehension. In addition,

idea-association, especially as it relates to a literary text, gives the listener a tool by which he can approximate the same feelings and responses that the creator may have had at the outset of writing the piece. Only later, with the experience of repeated listening, does a new work take its place in the listener's repertoire of assimilated musical experiences.

M30.   "Quelques réflexions sur la rythmique Jacques-Dalcroze." Feuilles musicales 14 (March - April 1961): 38-39.
        Frank Martin poses the question: What is the Jacques-Dalcroze rhythm method and what is its value? He responds that the Dalcroze method is not an art, not exactly a discipline, but a pedagogical method that complements intellectual, artistic, and athletic disciplines. Based on solfège, the Dalcroze method teaches the study of music through the development of the musical ear in which solfège is linked to bodily movement. The unique aspect of the method is that it creates an interaction of the principle activities of our being: attention and listening, intelligence or comprehension of what one has heard, sensitivity, in which the listener becomes embodied with the musical sentiment, and finally bodily movement that provides an access to and an outlet for one's response. The Dalcroze system is especially effective with children who do not separate the various elements of the method and who respond to it very naturally.

M31.   "Responsabilité du compositeur." Polyphonie 2 (1948): 85-88.
        Reprinted in: Un Compositeur médite sur son art, 15-29. Neuchâtel: A la Baconnière, 1977.
        Trans. as: "Die Verantwortung des Komponisten" Stimmen 1 (1948): 339-341.
        In an article first written in 1948 and later adapted for a lecture given in 1966, the composer addresses the question: to what degree is a composer responsible for his work, and also the question pressed still further, what is his responsibility toward others or mankind? This frequently cited article has become to some extent the composer's artistic credo, for in it he reveals a great deal about his own approach to the creative process and attempts to analyze it step by step for the reader. Martin explains that neither in the initial stages of conception and exploratory first draft, nor during the taxing actual labor of composing can the artist examine his work objectively. Only afterwards can he meditate on what has been achieved, although even then only its technical realization can be evaluated. "On peut admirer l'ouvrage de ses mains, non pas l'ouvrage de son esprit." "One can admire the work of one's hand but not the work of one's mind." From this, Martin describes what he calls the technique of inspiration in which future works benefit from an examination of those already completed. Looking at the question of ethical responsibility, Martin quotes from Joseph Haydn writing after he had already achieved worldwide fame, and observes the profound humility of Haydn and his acute awareness of a responsibility towards his public.

Martin believes that works of art contain within themselves an ethic which can be either positive or negative. It follows that beauty bears in itself a virtue that liberates our minds and it is the ultimate responsibility of the composer to create beauty which, "Et si ce n'est pas nécessairement la paix et la consolation que l'artiste doit donner aux autres hommes, ce devrait être en tous cas cette libération que produit en nous la beauté." "If it cannot give peace and consolation in a troubled world, it can give us that liberation of the spirit that is produced in us by beauty."

M32.   "Le rôle de l'art dans la société d'aujourd'hui." Schweizerische
        Musikzeitung. Revue musicale suisse 116 (September - October
        1976): 329-343.
            In this extended and thoughtful essay, first presented as a
speech, Frank Martin defines two distinct ways of looking at the world.
These he defines as exteriority (extériorité), that is examining things
from the outside, thus by analysis, and interiority (intériorité), that is by
looking at things from an inner prospective, an un-scientific way that
he calls global. The composer recognizes that these two attitudes
may be contradictory but that they are also complementary.
Recognizing a need for both, Martin sees that systematic analysis can
destroy a global concept, thus removing from society that which
permits us to live and grow. The composer asserts that musical
thought is necessarily interior and is therefore inexpressible any other
way. He believes that art exists to speak to mankind "through the
heart." For the creative artist, this seeking to create beauty is in itself
an act of love. Directing his attention more directly to the topic,
Martin sees a need in modern society for works of art from the past
as well as new expressions reflecting our own age. Works of art
involve both the aesthetic and the ethic, thus one can admire a work's
beauty (aesthetic) or listen to the spiritual message (ethic) present in
the work. For complete fulfillment one must experience both. Martin
identifies two tendencies that in modern art works can lead to
imitation and sterility; one is an attempt to express our unconscious,
the other is to assume an aggressive attitude. From the former is
derived obscurity, that is esoteric expression that creates difficulty in
comprehension, while the latter concerns efforts to shock at all costs.
In music the avant-garde has moved steadily toward greater
incomprehension and risks destroying itself. The composer concludes
that it is his opinion that, in music, the artist's essential role is to
search for an aestheticism that fits his deepest thoughts. Interiority,
by its very global character, is the most important element in art. We
must rediscover global thought and contemplate all things through
interiority. In doing this, we are free of eternal solitude and art is that
which frees us. This, he believes, is the role that art should play in
our contemporary society.

M33.   "Schönberg et les conséquences de son activité." Schweizerische
       Musikzeitung. Revue musicale suisse 116 (September - October):
       359-364.
           Speaking to a Conference on August 18, 1974 during the
       International Music Festival at Lucerne, Frank Martin defines his
       attitude toward atonal music and Schoenberg's twelve-tone system, as
       well as his own response to these developments, in a paper that
       together with his article "Schönberg et nous" (see M34) gives the
       clearest picture of the composer's thoughts on a subject that he
       frequently alluded to in other writings and speeches. The composer
       first attempts to arrive at a comprehensive definition of tonal-atonal
       and quotes from both Messiaen and Boulez to make his point. Martin
       asserts that it is the rapport or relationship of musical tones among
       themselves that is important and is the foundation of all tonal music.
       Schoenberg wanted to "free" musical tones from this order or
       relationship, and systematically and gradually devised a system in
       which the twelve tones within a chosen series must appear
       sequentially in a predetermined order before any tone may be
       repeated, and that octaves and unisons must be avoided. Ironically,
       the hierarchy of tones is so strongly imbedded that a determined
       effort must be made to create truly atonal music. This usually
       requires extremely wide spacings to avoid the return of at least partial
       key relationships. Martin acknowledges his debt to Schoenberg while
       at the same time rejecting atonality. From Schoenberg he learned to
       construct chromatic melody lines, to keep separate melody lines from
       accompanying music and to avoid traditional repetitions and cadences
       while at the same time developing and maintaining a function of
       tonality regardless of how temporary or unsettled and transitory it
       might be. The author concludes that truly atonal music can be
       powerfully expressive and dynamic and is therefore not without merit.
       For him, however, true music is that which can be followed, identified
       with, and which one could sing internally.

M34.   "Schönberg et nous." Polyphonie 4 (1950): 68-71.
       Reprinted in: Un Compositeur médite sur son art, 1977, 108-112.
       Trans. as: "Schönberg and ourselves." The Score no. 6 (May 1952):
       15-17.
           Frank Martin presents his position with regard to the twelve-tone
       system as one of assimilation and synthesis. Martin rejects
       Schoenberg's system as a total replacement of traditional western
       harmonic practice, but rather sees it as a means of enrichment
       through incorporating twelve-tone elements into the harmonic
       language developed over the centuries. In so doing, new expressive
       resources are opened to the composer working today. Martin says
       "working with tone-rows then, will teach us to think and work in a new
       language, which everyone must develop for himself. And the first
       thing we shall learn will be to invent rich melodies, since they must
       use all twelve notes of the chromatic scale before going back to the
       first again."

M35.   "Les sources du rythme musical." Revue musicale de suisse romande
            28 (1975): 1, 3-6.
            Frank Martin addresses the question of the sources of musical
    rhythm in terms of the movements and responses of the human body
    and of language. He asserts that three elements are the basis of
    rhythm: heavy (or large movement), light (or small movement) and yet
    a third element which he calls the awareness of number. It is from
    heavy movement such as walking that we derive the concept of
    tempo, that is rhythmic continuity and repetition. The light movements
    which can be represented by the movements of the tongue or a
    finger are those which we use to produce music and its rhythms.
    Especially is this true in the ability to speak and to sing. To this end
    speech itself becomes a rhythmic source. The relationship of
    language and music is only truly manifest, however, in the use of a
    poetic rhyme. This brings into focus the third element which the
    composer calls awareness of number. This is first defined as similar
    to an ability to hear a clock bell tower chime and be aware of being
    on the third or fourth chime without having consciously counted. This
    limited skill goes only up to perhaps a count of five. In summary, one
    can say that continuity, regularity, and its beat are derived from a
    body (heavy movement), that its structure in musical phrases or
    sentences derives from language (light movement), and is thus our
    thought. Tying it together is the awareness of number, actually of
    twos and threes. From this we derive a sense of measure which can
    be extended to the awareness of groups of measures and thus the
    feeling of form.

M36.   "Een zwitsers componist over het nederlandse Muziekleven." Mens en
            melodie 26 (August - September 1971): 267-269.
            In an article "ghost written" by Jaap Geraedts, the composer
    responds to a question and answer session called "a Swiss composer
    talks about musical life in the Netherlands." Martin responds to such
    questions as why he happened to settle in Holland, and is there such
    a thing as a Swiss style of composing? As usual, the composer uses
    these interview questions to share his opinion about whatever he feels
    strongly about. In this instance he sees a common problem in the
    difficulty of a creative artist from a small country whether it be
    Switzerland or the Netherlands, rather than France, Germany, or Italy,
    for example. Frank Martin also believes that the artist must make his
    own way and not automatically enjoy a privileged status as a ward of
    the government. He also rejoices in the number of choirs and
    orchestras that are active in a country as small as Holland, and sees
    this as an asset to be proud of, rather than as in some countries, to
    have only a few highly professional elitist performing organizations that
    have little impact on the ongoing musical life of provincial cities and
    towns.

Bibliography

"Cherchez à créer de la beauté est
un acte d'amour, encore même que
cet amour ne se dirigerait vers
personne, non pas même vers
l'humanité comme telle; c'est un
acte d'amour en sol. Le fait
d'exclure la recherche de la beauté,
de la nier ou simplement d ela
négliger, c'est refuser cet acte
d'amour."

"To seek to create beauty is an act
of love, even though this love were
not directed toward anyone or even
toward humanity as such; it is an
act of love in itself. The act of
refusing the quest for beauty, of
denying or simply ignoring it, is to
refuse this act of love."

General

B1.   Abendroth, Walter. "Martins unzeitgemässer Modernismus."
       Bayerische Rundfunk Symphonie Konzerte [program notes]
       (October 14-15, 1965).
       In program notes for a performance of the Petite symphonie
       concertante by the Bavarian Radio Symphony conducted by Karl
       Böhm, the annotator asserts that "Wenn es wahr ist, dass
       musikalische Modernismus unserer Tage im Zeichen einer
       wachsenden Beziehungslosigkeit zum Gedanken-und
       Empfindungleben des Menschen, dann kann man den Schweizer
       Frank Martin, ... gewiss keinen modernen Musiker nennen." "If it is
       true, that the musical modernism of our time is a sign of a
       progressing dehumanization, a growing lack of relationship to the
       thoughts and feelings of people, then one certainly cannot call the
       Swiss Frank Martin, ... a modern musician." The reputation of this
       composer's art rests on its solid humanistic values and speaks to the
       times in a language that is independent and in no way typical of the
       times. Martin has evolved through stimulation from Debussy and
       Ravel to Schoenberg, but has avoided both a faded eclecticism or a
       rigid adherence to the principles of Schoenberg. Instead he has
       drawn from various sources to find his own way. "Ohne Frage ist
       Frank Martin der heute ziemlich vereinzelt dastehende Vertreter eines
       romantischen Spiritualismus, betroffen werden kann, sondern in gültig
       bleibenden Neigungen des denkenden und fühlenden Menschen
       wurzelt." "Without question Frank Martin is the singular representative
       of a romantic spiritualism which is not swayed by epochal changes of
       opinion, but which is rooted in the mainstream of thinking and feeling
       people. The common characteristic of all of his works is noble
       invention with a very selective treatment."

B2.   Alte und neue Musik. Das Baseler Kammerorchester unter Leitung
          von Paul Sacher 1926-1951. Zürich: Atlantis, 1952.
       Alte und neue Musik II. Das Basler Kammerorchester (Kammerchor
          und Kammerorchester) unter Leitung von Paul Sacher 1926-1976.
       Zürich: Atlantis, 1977.
          Here are two commemorative volumes that document the fifty-
       year span of the Basel Chamber Orchestra and its founder-director
       Paul Sacher. The volumes contain individual essays that pay tribute
       to Paul Sacher and his orchestra, a chronological calendar of the
       concert seasons, and biographical sketches of some of the
       composers and program notes for many works. A comprehensive list
       by composer reveals fourteen different works by Frank Martin
       spanning the years from 1941-1975.

B3.   Ansermet, Ernest and Frank Martin. Correspondance 1934-1968.
          Neuchâtel: A la Baconnière, 1976.
          A unique record of nearly thirty-five years of a personal and
       professional working relationship is documented in letters between the

composer and his advisor, confidant, friend and most influential advocate. From these letters, the reader gains insights into the problems, uncertainties, trials, and failures as well as the successes of the creative process. One learns how the composer felt about certain aspects of his work and how other individuals and events impacted on the composer's life and work. There are also references to specific works by other composers. From letters, the reader shares a perspective of the composer's life and work that is not possible from reading more formal articles and essays by the composer or by other writers.

B4.   Ansermet, Ernest. "Frank Martin." In <u>Larousse Encyclopedia of Music</u>, 1971 ed. 486-487. New York: World, 1971.
　　　　A brief survey of Frank Martin's achievement up through the mid-sixties was written by his greatest advocate Ernest Ansermet. <u>Le Vin herbé</u> is the pivotal work in which Martin discovered his unique musical voice which can be identified in all subsequent works. "Martin excels in nuances of orchestral colour, and his musical palette is perfectly suited to giving life to impalpable concepts and fantasy. But he is equally capable of expressing a tragic vehemence, and of showing an epic quality necessary to the construction of immense choral and religious works."

B5.   Ansermet, Ernest. "Frank Martins historische Stellung." <u>Österreichische Musikzeitschrift</u> 24 (March 1969): 137-141.
　　　　In his last article, Ernest Ansermet pays tribute to Frank Martin, and also defines his position with respect to Schoenberg's twelve-tone system. Ansermet asserts that Frank Martin's study and experimentation with a new system, which eliminates a harmonic tonal center, created the necessity to "reestablish a sense of tonality, but one which exists in a state of permanent instability, a sense which then creates still more unrest than the dissonances in the tonal style. Frank Martin's historic position, then, is "...in der Evolution der tonalen Organisation, die mit der Chromatik begann, die historische Kontinuität wiederhergestellt zu haben." "...to have restored historic continuity to the evolution of tonal organization, which had begun with chromaticism."

B6.   Ansermet, Ernest. "Situation de Frank Martin." <u>Grand Théâtre de Genève</u> (July 25, 1982): 13.
　　　　Writing in program Notes for a double bill of Puccini's <u>Gianni Schicchi</u> and Martin's <u>Le Vin herbé</u>, Ernest Ansermet's 1969 essay (see B5) is paraphrased in which he describes Frank Martin's development as a Genevan and thus of French ancestry and persuasion, while at the same time, his musical training was mainstream turn-of-the-century Germanic, in which the traditional harmonic practice was dominated by tonal cadences. Martin's compositions thus evolved from the influence of César Franck and the Germanic tradition of his time to the twelve-tone system of Arnold

Schoenberg. However, in so doing, Martin re-introduced a tonal feeling and direction to his music through an independent tonal bass combined with serial procedures, thus creating a tonal instability which keeps the musical feeling in a state of suspense and which became the basis of his harmonic style from the composition of Le Vin herbé and thereafter.

B7.   Ansermet, Ernest. "Der Weg Frank Martins." Österreichische Musikzeitschrift 11 (May 1956): 172-175.

Writing at the time just prior to the premiere of Der Sturm, the Swiss conductor traces the path followed, and the important influences that shaped the personal and musical development of Frank Martin. Throughout this essay, the author points out his own influence in shaping the thought and development of the young composer. Ansermet describes the turn-of-the-century musical environment of Geneva and all of French-speaking Switzerland as being totally dominated by German musical culture. The author indicates that Martin's first important breakthrough toward his own stylistic development resulted from exposure to Debussy's music and through performances on the piano and harpsichord of both Bach and Debussy. From both of these composers, Martin learned the concept of how the bass line can free itself from the single function to support the harmony above, and can function independently and create its own melody. In time, Martin was able to combine this technique with twelve-tone devices and achieve his own harmonic synthesis from which he derived his own stylistic identity. Ansermet speaks of the inner law and the outer law (in creating music) in which he defines Schoenberg, Webern, and Stravinsky as practitioners of the outer law in which intellectuality, lust for experimentation, and abstractionism prevail. At the same time, Debussy and Martin are said to practice the inner law, in which the personal and spiritual elements of inward listening are operative, and technical means and options that avoid formulas and severe abstractions are employed.

B8.   Appia, Edmond. "Frank Martin et la conquête de la personnalité." In De Palestrina à Bartók etudes musicologiques, 367-378. Paris: Flammarion, 1965.

This essay examines the environment and prospective in which a composer of our time must develop and work, reflecting the accumulated knowledge and various styles which have slowly evolved from the past and the need to assimilate the fast-moving constantly changing new ideas that are a part of the current scene. This process of acquiring knowledge carries with it the danger of being dominated and subjugated by the great masters of the past. To achieve success, the effort must lead to liberation of the artist at some point. The author asserts that to attain this "consciousness of self," one must first willingly accept certain influences from others in order to subsequently break away from them. The process of assimilation and liberation is then applied to the development of Frank Martin's creative life. He then demonstrates the process through which Martin's compositions reflect the learning process of borrowing from the style of others and his eventual liberation after twenty-five years of diligent application to achieve a style uniquely his own. When the creative artist has reached this level of mastery he may be said to have achieved the "conquest of personality." "Frank Martin appartient à cette catégorie d'artistes. Son oeuvre nous touche et nous convaine parce qu'elle est l'expression d'un engagement total; c'est aussi parcequ'elle a le sens d'une "communication" qu'il nous est possible de participer à sa création et de la vivre plus intensément qu'une autre." "Frank Martin is one of these artists. His work touches us because it is the expression of total evolvement...we participate in its creation and live it more intensely than we would another work."

B9.   Austin, William W. "Frank Martin." In Dictionary of Contemporary Music, 453-454. New York: Dutton, 1974.
        A biographical sketch of the main periods and activities of the Swiss composer is followed by an assessment of his compositional style and technique with particular reference to his distinctive treatment of triads which permit serialistic writing with harmonic underpinnings. "His music is not only idiomatic as Hindemith's or effective as Shostakovich's, but fresh and grateful as Ravel's (whom Martin acknowledges as an early model)." A works list and brief bibliography conclude the article.

B10.   Austin, William. In Music in the 20th Century from Debussy through Stravinsky, 496-497. New York: Norton, 1966.
        Prophetically, the author sees how "The predominance of chromaticism in his melodies, the occasional appearance of twelve-tone themes and ostinato patterns together with the distinctive free forms, the fresh sonorities, the splendidly idiomatic writing for voices and all sorts of instruments, and the consistent mellow expressiveness of his music won for a moment the attention of many adventurous younger composers, including Roman Vlad and Karlheinz Stockhausen. ...The adventures of the young carried them past Martin before his work had time to reach an audience as wide as Berg's or Bartók's. And without the help of fashion his later works, continually more refined and powerful... would need many years to win the popularity they deserve."

B11.   Bach, Hans-Elmar. "Martin, Frank." Beträge zur Rheinische Musikgeschichte reinische Musiker. Folge 6 (1969): 124-130.
        This is an encyclopedic entry in which a detailed year by year account of Martin's family background, musical training, principal interests, and his stylistic development are documented succinctly but in detail. The article concludes with a works list and writings by and about the composer in chronological order.

B12.   Badura-Skoda, Paul. "Frank Martin, le maître angélique." <u>Journal de Genève</u> 10 (November 1984).

In an article written on the occasion of the Exposition commemorating the tenth anniversary of the death of Frank Martin, Viennese pianist Paul Badura-Skoda reminisces about his feelings, experiences and reactions to meeting and working with Frank Martin during the writing and preparation for performance of the <u>Second Piano Concerto</u>. The author then alternates between expressions of awe and admiration for the composer's vast knowledge of music and anecdotes on his experiences as a house guest of Frank and Maria Martin. The pianist also shares some insights into Martin's composing philosophy and methodology, a topic developed in more detail in an earlier article on the "genesis" of the <u>Second Piano Concerto</u> (see B127). Badura-Skoda concludes by referring to the composer as the "angelic master," so great is his admiration for Frank Martin as friend, mentor, and confidant.

B13.   Billeter, Bernhard and Maria Martin. "Dokumente Werkverzeichnis. Bibliographie der Schriften von Frank Martin." <u>Schweizerische Musikzeitung. Revue musicale suisse</u> 116 (September-October): 1976.

A comprehensive bibliography of writing by and about Frank Martin is a particularly valuable resource for English-speaking readers in that it contains many sources not brought out elsewhere, even though some of these may be difficult to obtain. Secondly, the bibliography provides strong support for the assertion that substantive scholarly writing about Frank Martin in English is woefully inadequate.

B14.   Billeter, Bernhard. <u>Frank Martin ein Aussenseiter der neuen Musik</u>. Frauenfeld: Huber 1970.

A biographical-analytical monograph, written in "popular style" in that it integrates biographical data with analytical insights in a work that updates the work of Rudolf Klein (see B64) which was published twelve years prior to the composer's death. The subtitle, "an outsider of new music," seems to indicate that Martin does not fit into any of the various schools or new directions taken by his peers. To some extent his music is accepted into the mainstream of public performance, while his penchant for synthesis and consolidation has caused him to remain only briefly on the cutting edge of modernism. Billeter, who has explored Martin's uses of harmony in his previously published dissertation (see B15), asserts that harmony is the decisive factor that gives Martin's music its unique and distinct sound. This, he states, is achieved by a "gliding tonality" in which there is not a single defined key, and yet the rules of close and distant relationships between tones continue to apply, giving the music a quasi-tonal feeling while not precisely defining a particular key. The author traces the influences on the composer's development beginning with the Germanic cultural environment of his youth in French-speaking Geneva. The influence of Bach and Franck and the subsequent attempt to follow the path of Ravel all led ultimately to Schoenberg's twelve-tone system which the composer modified for his own expressive purposes. Billeter writes about Martin's important works and the particular influences as he systematically proceeds through early, middle and late musical works.

B15. Billeter, Bernhard. "Die Harmonik bei Frank Martin. Untersuchungen zur Analyse neuerer Musik." [Frank Martin's harmony. Studies on the analysis of 20th century music.] Ph.D. diss., University of Zürich, 1970.

In his important dissertation, now published as a monograph, the Swiss scholar Bernhard Billeter provides his own best annotation which we quote from RILM 1972, no. 1882, p. 143. "Frank Martin's early works employ the functional harmony of the late romantic tradition. With the assistance of modal melody Martin freed himself from that idiom. His marked inclination toward chromaticism and modulation led him to a style using non-functional harmony with dodecaphonic elements ('gliding tonality'). Since there is no satisfactory analytic method for non-functional harmony, the author offers a definition of harmony and discusses the uses of interval and functional theory, major-minor dualism, the method of Heinrich Schenker and its extension by Felix Salzer, and above all of the Unterweisung in Tonsatz [The craft of musical composition] of Paul Hindemith. Fundamental aspects of the theory of the latter are rejected. Hindemith's method of analysis may with several modifications, however, furnish the basis for an analysis of Frank Martin's harmony."

B16. Billeter, Bernhard. "Die letzten Vocalwerke von Frank Martin." Schweizerische Musikzeitung. Revue musicale suisse 116 (September-October 1976).

Writing in a special issue that focuses on the achievement of Frank Martin, Professor Billeter's essay discusses in depth the composer's last three vocal compositions: Poèmes de la mort, Requiem, and E la vie l'emporta. All of these pieces are on the subject of death. Frank Martin repeatedly concerned himself with the subject of death in his music, and by so doing also raised final questions of humanity, of the reason for life, acceptance of one's limitations, the admission of guilt, and the whole religious dimension of this theme. Poèmes de la mort are settings of poems by François Villon about death, including the "Ballade des pendus" (Ballad of the hanged ones) in which the composer employs three male voices and three electric guitars to evoke this grotesque image. Both the poem and the electric medium were suggested by Martin's son, Jan Frank, but the outcome reflects the composer's still active and searching mind to bring new expressive means into his music. Requiem, according to Martin, was a long time in coming. Yet it was the composer's expressed intent to write a requiem for many years, but it was only getting to it that proved to be very difficult. Before any composing could be done, Martin had first to select the format in which it would be written. Gradually eliminated was a novel approach that would borrow from the pop culture and further extend his use of electric instruments. Likewise an alternate modern text was searched for and finally abandoned. The result was that, moved by the powerful imagery of the Latin requiem mass, Martin created a work of enormous expressive power utilizing the composing skills acquired over a lifetime, and employing the traditional resources of oratorio: a quartet of soloists, mixed chorus, organ and orchestra. Although already in failing health, Frank Martin was attracted by a commission to write yet another vocal-choral work on the universal theme of human triumph over suffering and adversity. Again a search for a suitable text was undertaken that resulted in three texts from as many sources, but all of which underlined the concept of the triumph of the human spirit over suffering and death. The final scoring of E la vie l'emporta was entrusted to the composer's friend and fellow composer Bernard Reichel following Martin's death in November of 1974.

B17.   Billeter, Bernhard. "Martin, Frank." In Musik in Geschichte und
        Gegenwart 16 (Supplement E-Z 1979): 1210-1212.
            In a supplement volume issued nineteen years after the original article by Ernst Mohr (see B75), there appears a complete works list using the same format as in the original volume, along with a bibliography of works about Martin written after 1960.

B18.   Boepple, Paul. "Music of Frank Martin belongs to no School." New
        York Times 13 January 1952.
            In a preview article which preceded the New York and American premiere of Martin's Golgotha, Paul Boepple, conductor of the Dessoff Choirs, reminisces about his relationship with the composer as a student in Geneva during the twenties. From this he addresses the question of how to classify Martin and his music with respect to his composer peers and with what movement or school he can be linked. The author then describes Martin as an eclectic, and briefly describes his stylistic evolution in terms of his modified use of the twelve-tone techniques within a framework of traditional tonality. See: W80

B19.   Bonte, Hans Georg. "Frank Martin: Alte und neue Chorwerke."
        Zeitschrift für Musik 114 (June 1953): 347-348.
            Writing about the choral music of Frank Martin, the author confines his comments to the two works Le Vin herbé and Golgotha. In the first work is outlined the broad structural lines of the Tristan legend based on the literary work by Joseph Bédier in which the contrast between Martin's work and that of Wagner's opera is delineated. In particular there is the employment of the small chorus in both the role of soloist and as chorus, much in the manner of ancient Greek tragedy. So also the small instrumental ensemble supports both the mood and the action of the drama. In Golgotha, Martin's setting of the passion eliminates the role of the narrator, and

it is the person of Jesus (baritone solo) and the chorus that carry forward the narrative of the passion with contrasting "meditations" from the writing of St. Augustine assigned to solo voices and the chorus. Using means that range from a simple declarative style to the use of a serialistic tone row, the composer develops and sustains interest in this new setting of the passion.

B20.   Brandt, Maarten. "Frank Martin 'Elke regel heeft slechts tot doel de tijl te verrijken.'" HG Opmaat [Programmas concerten] (April 1985): 3-6.

Writing in the program notes of the Symphonie Concertante voor Groot Orkest, Maarten Brandt translates into Dutch in his title the frequently quoted "every rule has as its objective the enrichment of style" from the composer's 1942 article A propos du Vin herbé see (M8). The formation and structure of the Frank Martin Society in Lausanne and the Frank Martin Foundation in Naarden are described along with their principle activities in producing the traveling exhibition commemorating the tenth anniversary of the composer's death, the issue or reissue of important recordings and publications and the performance competition for young musicians in Utrecht. There follows a summary of Frank Martin's musical life, emphasizing the influences both Germanic and French on his development, and his ultimate success in merging these diverse elements into a unique style of his own. Finally, there is the recognition of Martin's unshakable belief in the ultimate triumph of good in which optimism is always expressed even in works whose subject is death.

B21.   Brashovanova-Stancheva, Lada. "Frank Martin." [in Bulgarian] Bulgarska Muzika 32 (1971): 91-92.

It is difficult to assess the impact of Frank Martin's music on eastern European nations on the basis of the sparse number of publications. This brief article contains a biographical sketch of the composer and mentions some of his best known works.

B22.   Cadieu, Martine. "Duo avec Frank Martin." Les Nouvelles litteraires (April 3 1963): 11.

In another interview with Frank Martin conducted at his home in Naarden (near Amsterdam), the interviewer takes great pains to share with her readers the atmosphere of joy and the quiet working environment enjoyed by the composer. The series of questions tends to evolve as casual conversation that touches on a variety of subjects and ideas, from the specific composing project of the moment, to teaching activities in the past, to his influences and working habits, to speculations about the avant-garde. As always, the composer speaks candidly, and each of these interviews reveals some aspect of his personality not otherwise available to us in his writings or in the more formal writing of others.

B23.   Carner, Mosco. "Music in the mainland of Europe: 1918-1939,
         (Switzerland)." New Oxford History of Music Vol. X: 320-321. New
         York: Oxford UP, 1974.
              In a survey article of the main stream of development during the
         period between the world wars, the author summarizes the work of
         the most important composers either individually or as a
         representative of their respective country or area of Europe. Frank
         Martin is singled out to represent French-speaking Switzerland, where
         the author describes his early development in rhythmic
         experimentation, and his development of a synthesis of serial
         technique with tonal writing in the three important works: Le Vin
         herbé, Der Cornet, and the Sechs Monologe aus Jedermann.

B24.   Chapallaz, Gilbert. "Autour de Frank Martin pour le Xe anniversaire de
         sa mort." Revue musicale de suisse romande 37 (1984): 135-136.
              In an article commemorating the tenth anniversary of Frank
         Martin's death, three topics are discussed: bibliographic notes,
         discographic notes, and the Frank Martin Exposition. In bibliographic
         notes are cited the four published volumes (in French) of writings,
         letters, interviews and some commentary about the composer. Writing
         under the title of "A propos...," Frank Martin sometimes used the
         occasion of writing program notes and articles to express his view on
         whatever was on his mind at the time, but always encompassing a far
         broader scope than a summary analysis of the particular work at
         hand. The composer's essay on his Violin Concerto (see M3) is a
         particularly good example. The discographic notes concern
         themselves with recordings in which the composer takes part as
         conductor or pianist, and the brief description of the tenth anniversary
         exposition describes its itinerary and recognizes those individuals and
         agencies responsible for its success.

B25.   Dovaz, René. "Quelques propos d'introduction à un concert
         exceptionnel dédié à la mémoire du plus illustre des compositeurs
         suisses." [Introductory remarks on an exceptional concert
         dedicated to the memory of the most renowned of Swiss
         composers.] Concert extraordinaire Orchestre de Chambre de
         Zürich (September 1, 1984): 1.
              Writing in the program booklet for a concert by the Zürich
         Chamber Orchestra with soloists Yehudi Menuhin, Heinz and Ursula
         Holliger, the author responds to a statement by the conductor
         Edmond de Stoutz, made on a previous occasion, that it is difficult to
         say which is more important, the thinking of Frank Martin as
         expressed in his writing or the music itself. Dovaz believes that the
         music alone expresses the entire message of the composer and
         therefore transcends his ideas expressed in prose, important though
         they may be. Next, he addresses the question of the appropriateness
         of having two works of Martin, the Trois danses and the Polyptyque,
         on a program with music by Bach. To this point the author quotes
         from an essay by Ernest Ansermet (see B7) that describes how Martin

discovered for himself the manner in which Bach in his recitatives used the bass line for any melodic enharmonic structure above.

B26.   Duck, Leonard. "Aims and development of Frank Martin." Musical Opinion 78 (October 1954): 19-20.
       The author suggests that, for the young composer seeking to find his own way through the variety of styles and techniques that the twentieth century has produced, two directions seem to be open to him. One is to devise new forms and techniques for each new work as, notably, Stravinsky has done. The other is to progress work by work to achieve a synthesis of all available musical materials to achieve the means of expressing one's unique voice. A most remarkable example of this eclectic approach is Frank Martin's long search for his unique style and sound. Martin's development is summarized from early influences of Franck and Fauré, through rhythmic experimentation with Dalcroze and finally Schoenberg's twelve-tone system. Martin's unique voice is identified as his rapprochement between traditional triadic harmony and the demands of the twelve-tone system. By using the tone row as a melodic device, he is able to combine the two seemingly irreconcilable systems to achieve a unique individual voice. In so doing, the question is raised--but not answered--has the element of communicability with the public been sacrificed?

B27.   Dull, Ben. "Teresa Martin." [in Dutch] Preludium (February 1976): 13-14.
       Writing in the Concertgebouw publication prior to a performance of the Trois danses, the author introduces the composer's daughter by letting her speak about herself, her family, and her career as a flamenco dancer, and how, in time, this became the basis for Frank Martin's increasing interest in the rhythmic aspects of flamenco music. Martin was attracted to flamenco music through his daughter practicing at home in Naarden and from seeing her perform in Spain. At the end of his life, he composed two important works: the Trois danses and the piano work, Fantaisie sur des rythmes flamenco, both based on flamenco rhythms, and both performed with original choreography by Teresa Martin. Thus was brought into being two works in which father and daughter succeeded in creating something uniquely special as a gift of love for each other, and, at the same time, enriching the musical world with a legacy of two pieces that might never have been produced except for this unique relationship.

B28.   Ehinger, Hans. "Frank Martin." Canon 10 (September 1956): 52-53.
       For the benefit of Australian readers, this is one of a series of brief summary articles on Swiss composers, written by Swiss authors whose work normally appears in German and French language music journals. Frank Martin's background and composing style are briefly summarized, with specific works identified up to the opera Der Sturm (The Tempest).

B29.   "Einführung zum Program." Berliner Philharmonisches Orchester (May 30, 1963).

    In a unique program, Frank Martin conducted the Berlin Philharmonic in an entire program of his music which included the premiere of his Passacaille, originally a work for solo organ, and subsequently rescored for string orchestra in a new version for full orchestra. In addition, there were two vocal works performed by the celebrated German baritone Dietrich Fischer-Dieskau. These are the Overture and two arias of Prospero from his opera Der Sturm, followed by the Sechs Monologe aus Jedermann, a song cycle on texts by Hugo von Hofmannsthal. The concert concluded with the popular Concerto pour sept instruments à vent, timbales, batterie et orchestre à cordes. In the brief descriptions that follow, the annotator discusses the background and formal structure of each of the four works.

B30.   Epstein, Rhea S. "The String Music of Frank Martin." Master's thesis, Boston University, 1978.

    In this thesis thirteen works of Frank Martin are divided into early, middle and late periods and then subjected to detailed analysis. This spans a creative period from the First Violin Sonata of 1913 to the Polyptyque of 1973, completed only the year before the composer's death.

B31.   Evans, Peter. "Music of the European mainstream: 1940-1960." New Oxford History of Music, Vol.X, 419-420. New York, Oxford UP, 1974.

    Frank Martin's place in the European mainstream is defined in terms of his approach to the serial method of composition. Martin used twelve-tone devices particularly to expand, enrich and liberate his melodic line, but, at the same time, retained harmonic underpinnings which could be entirely diatonic, with an independent bass line which assumed a guiding role. The author finds that, in this compromise, Martin's music never "seethes with the inner tensions that are the source of Schoenbergian angst."

B32.   "Exposition Frank Martin 1890-1974 Palais Wilson - 16 November-13 December." Journal de la Haut-ville 6 December 1984).

    In a brief announcement of the Frank Martin Exposition in Geneva for the newspaper at Caroege, the author stresses how the displays give the viewer an idea of how an old Geneva family lived at the turn of the century, as well as the documentation (letters, scores, photos, etc.) that chronicles both the personal and professional life of the composer through many decades.

B33.   Fiechtner, Helmut. "Frank Martin." [in German] Musica 6 (July-August, 1952): 271-275.

    Writing in 1952, a period when many of Frank Martin's most important works were being written, the author offers what he calls a short study about the personality and development of the Swiss composer. "Der Erfolg von Martins Musik scheint uns um so bemerkenswerter in einer Zeit, welche von Schlagzeile, Lärm un Plakat beherrscht wird. Martin aber ist der Meister der diskreten Aussage under der massvollen Gebärde." "The success of Martin's music seems even more remarkable to us in a time ruled by headlines, noise and posters. But Martin is the master of discreet statement and moderate expression." Then follows a succinct but thorough summary of the composer's early training in Geneva with Joseph Lauber, his subsequent travels to Zürich, Rome and Paris, followed by his return to Geneva, with further study, teaching and performing, all leading to his eventual assimilation of the twelve-tone system of Schoenberg. The author asserts that confrontation with the Schoenberg teachings "...Lehre führte bei Martin weder zur Ablehnung noch zur bedingungslosen Unterwerfung, sondern zu einer völlig eigenständigen Assimilation." "...led to neither a rejection nor to a total submission, but rather to a total independent assimilation." Following a period when the composer learned the discipline of dodecaphony by employing it in a series of his own works, the result was a new and simplified style, beginning with Le Vin herbé, and, with some further refinement, continuing with the works that were to follow. The article concludes with brief commentaries on Le Vin herbé and Golgotha with a word of admiration for the purely instrumental pieces that were produced during this period.

B34.   Fiechtner, Helmut. "Frank Martin zum 60. Geburtstag." Österreichische Musikzeitschrift 10/11 (October-November 1950); 211-214.

In a tribute to the composer on the occasion of his sixtieth birthday, this essay traces the development of a musical life beginning with childhood pieces from as early as 1899 to his passion oratorio Golgotha (1948). Frank Martin's late musical maturity is inextricably tied to his conservative background and the turn of the century musical outlook of French Switzerland. Private study with Joseph Lauber led to annual performances of his works by the League of Swiss Musicians, and the early formative period of the composer's musical life was launched. A second phase followed from about the mid-twenties to the mid-thirties during which the young composer was finally exposed to the music of Debussy, Ravel, Stravinsky, and, most importantly, to a serious study of Schoenberg's twelve-tone system. Works written in this period reflect a serious effort to incorporate this new language into his music, the final formative work being the seldom played Symphony of 1938-39. At this point, the composer at last discovered his true language, one which created a synthesis between traditional harmonic practice and the twelve-tone system, and which resulted in his first great success Le Vin herbé, which in turn led to international recognition through his Petite symphonie concertante. The author concludes that "...dass neue Musik nicht mehr im guten glauben an die alten Mittel, sondern nur aus einem neuen Glauben mit neuen Mitteln zu machen ist." "...new music no longer needs to be created by old means, but a new belief can be established by virtue of new means."

B35.   Fischer, Kurt von. "Expressionistische und impressionistische Ausdruckswerte in der Musik des 19. und 20. Jahrhunderts." Schweizerische Musikzeitung. Revue musicale suisse 86 (1946): 1-4.

This essay examines the expressive values of musical impressionism and expressionism, terms borrowed from the world of painting. The author sees elements of each developing in the nineteenth and extending into the twentieth century, sometimes from the same composer in the same piece. In the early twentieth century, as in the art world, the two expressive forms congealed into styles as we define them today. This is seen as an evolutionary characteristic of romanticism and reflects the enormous upheavals wrought by the devastation of two world wars. The author sees impressionism as derived from the romantic or Latin culture, while expressionism is fundamentally Germanic. Carrying the idea a step further, he sees the combination of the two stylistic elements as a Swiss characteristic, particularly western (French-speaking) Switzerland and finds the music of Honegger, and especially that of Frank Martin, as primary evidence of this conclusion. Finally, impressionism and expressionism values of expression are mixed down to the individual tone in the works by Frank Martin such as Le Vin herbé and Der Cornet. It is the mixture of tension and the atmospheric absence of tension that makes Martin's compositions so unique.

B36.   Fischer, Kurt von. "Frank Martin." Grove's Dictionary of Music and Musicians, 5th ed. Vol. V, pp. 592-593. New York: St. Martin's, 1954.

In an analytical summary of Frank Martin's creative life from his early studies with Joseph Lauber to the creation of the passion oratorio Golgotha, the author quotes and cites from Martin's own writings and explains with incipits Frank Martin's handling of the twelve-tone system. An expanded analysis of Martin's music can be seen in the author's German language articles. See: B37, B38

B37.   Fischer, Kurt von. "Frank Martin." [in German] Schweizerische Musikzeitung. Revue musical suisse 111 (January-February 1971): 3-6.

In a birthday tribute to Frank Martin on the occasion of his eightieth birthday(1970), the author summarizes the composer's aesthetic, ethical and musical position as both man and musician. He first relates Martin to his role models, the three composers--Bach, Haydn, and Debussy--to whom the composer frequently made reference and paid tribute. Each of these three have made their mark on Martin's musical technique, but especially on his aesthetic and ethical disposition which, in turn, profoundly interact with one another. The author follows the path of Martin's musical development through

three distinct phases of his career, finally arriving at the conclusion
that through his music Frank Martin, the world humanist, becomes a
link with all of European musical art from the past; and in his highly
developed sense of a composer's responsibility toward his fellow men,
Frank Martin will leave a permanent link from which future artists and
indeed the whole European musical tradition can add another role
model.

B38.   Fischer, Kurt von. "Frank Martin Überblick über Werk und Stil."
        Schweizerische Musikalische Zeitung. Revue musicale suisse 91
        (1951): 91-96.
            This chronological and analytical survey of the works and the
        evolution and development of Frank Martin's style traces the
        development of the composer from his early student works through
        the composition of the passion oratorio Golgotha, which the author
        asserts is in certain respects a synthesis of the style of his later
        compositions. Beginning with the Trois poèmes païens in 1911, we
        follow the influences and stylistic changes that the composer
        experienced in first assimilating the music of Bach, and then of Franck
        and Fauré. His study and association with Jacques Dalcroze,
        resulting in a lifelong interest in rhythmic experimentation, was followed
        by intensive study of the Schoenbergian twelve-tone system. During
        this period came works such as the String Trio, the string quintet
        Rhapsodie, the 1st Piano Concerto, and the Symphony which
        represent Martin's effort to master this new technique by applying it
        rigorously to his own compositions. At this point, the composer
        achieved his stylistic breakthrough in the composition Le Vin herbé
        (1939) in which he successfully found a right balance between the
        expressive freedom which the twelve-tone system provides and his
        own need to remain in the tradition of western art music by retaining
        a tonal feeling. A further development was Martin's response to and
        his solution to writing sacred music. After completing an eight-part
        Mass and working on a Christmas Cantata, the composer put these
        works aside without either a performance or publication, so strong
        was his feeling concerning the separate worlds occupied by art and
        church music. "Der Diskrepanz von subjektivem Kunstausdruck und
        objectiver, nur der Sache dienenden Kirchenmusik..." "The
        discrepancy between subjective artistic expression and objective
        church music, serving only the religious purpose..." led him to
        abandon writing sacred music for many years. The impasse was
        finally overcome by a commission from Radio Geneva to write a work
        to be performed on the armistice day of World War II. Using texts
        from the Old and New Testaments, the oratorio In terra pax fulfilled
        the commission and was soon followed by his Golgotha, which in turn
        led to several major sacred choral works. The author concludes with
        an analysis, with musical examples from Golgotha in which he
        demonstrates how Frank Martin was able to utilize twelve-tone
        technique and functional harmony and, at the same time employ

impressionistic coloration and expressionistic harmony of tension. The result produces a synthesis which has led to a new harmonic style.

B39.   Frank, Alan. "New Music Works by Frank Martin." Musical Times 94 (October 1953): 461-462.

In this review of four Martin scores published by Universal Ed. the reviewer concludes that "Frank Martin is one of the most distinguished and distinctive composers now working in Europe." The four works--Flute Ballade, Sonata da chiesa, Six Monologues from Jedermann, and In terra pax--are each given a summary evaluation with the honors going to In terra pax as the best of the four, with a larger proportion of the commentary allotted to this work.

In summation, the question is raised, "Is Frank Martin a composer of the very highest rank?" The author responds to his own question by saying, "I have only one small doubt: his style of writing, particularly his harmonic style, is highly idiosyncratic but slightly limited, and one is aware of a certain sameness from work to work."

B40.   "Frank Martin." [in Swedish and English] Nutida Musik 19 (1976-77): 19-20.

A brief thumbnail biographical sketch of Frank Martin which asserts that Martin is a single answer to the question as to whether Switzerland has any significance in the field of contemporary music.

B41.   "Frank Martin et la Vie Musicale." Journal de Genève 10 November 1984).

This brief summary statement of the composer's many achievements was prepared from a special newspaper section on Frank Martin presented on the occasion of the traveling Exposition commemorating the tenth anniversary of the composer's death. A brief bibliography of the published writing of Frank Martin concludes the article.

B42.   Frank Martin L'univers d'un compositeur: Catalogue de l'exposition commémorant le dixième anniversaire de la mort de Frank Martin. Lausanne: Société Frank Martin, 1984.

As the title suggests, an exhibition of the life and work of Frank Martin was organized to commemorate the tenth anniversary of the composer's death. This traveling exhibit of photographs, letters, manuscripts, and memorabilia, organized into eleven general headings, was conceived and brought to fruition by Eugénia Catala and Maria Martin. The exhibit was presented in several Swiss and Austrian cities, and was concluded some two years later at the Hague. The Catalogue follows the organization of the exhibition and contains eleven sections that review the family background, early training, family life, musical works, honors, awards, and the various interpreters of Martin's music. A brief chronology of the main events in the composer's life prepared by Maria Martin follows and the volume concludes with a works list and discography.

B43.   Gaillard, Paul André. "Pour les 70 ans de Frank Martin."
         Schweizerische Musikzeitung. Revue musicale suisse 100
         (September-October 1960): 282-283.
         On the occasion of Frank Martin's seventieth birthday
         (September 15, 1960) the author declines to write the usual "eulogy"
         and instead elects to honor the composer through quotations, not
         only of Martin, but of many diverse composers including Bach,
         Mozart, Wagner, Bizet, Chopin, and others, concluding with a final
         quote from Frank Martin again.

B44.   Goldron, Romain. "Frank Martin, vingt ans après." Repères 11 (1985)
         In this unusual article, in which the title "Frank Martin, twenty
         years later," must certainly have been intended to read "ten years
         later," the author has compiled a list of five questions sent to younger
         active Swiss composers. Jean Perrin, Jean Balissat, Eric Gaudibut,
         Norbert Moret, Rudolph Kelterborn, and Armin Schibler were each
         asked to comment on the influence which Frank Martin had on their
         work, and on his impact upon Swiss musical life. While the
         responses vary, and are collectively inconclusive, each of the
         composers responded with utmost respect and affection for the
         unique contribution of Frank Martin to the music of Switzerland.

B45.   Gradenwitz, Peter. "Israel." Musical Times 110 (November 1969):
         1162.
         Highlighting a varied and outstanding Ninth Israel Festival, Frank
         Martin, appearing in Israel for the first time, conducted a program of
         his own works which included Der Cornet and the Petite symphonie
         concertante.

B46.   Graziosi, Giorgio. "Musiche di Frank Martin." Accademia filarmonica
         romana November 9, 1961.
         Writing in the program notes for a concert conducted by Victor
         Desarzens and Frank Martin, the author recalls the slow and gradual
         development of the composer from his early travel experiences
         outside of Geneva, and his somewhat late exposure to the
         mainstream musical developments in Europe during the early years of
         the twentieth century. From a background of Wagner and Franck,
         Martin developed a transitional style based on the harmonic bearings
         of Debussy and Ravel, absorbing also rhythmic impulses from
         Stravinsky and Bartók. This was followed by intense study, and
         confrontation with the twelve-tone theories of Schoenberg. By the end
         of the thirties, Martin had found his unique musical voice in an
         acclaimed work, Le Vin herbé, which employed modified serial
         procedures, combined with a harmonic structure that retained a sense
         of key feeling. Martin's late style then "In sostanza il compositore
         elvetico si tiene in una posizione mediana tra le innovazioni
         schönberghiane e la traduzióne;" "assumes a position midway
         between Schoenbergian innovations and tradition." In the description

of three Martin works that are included on the program, many of the characteristics just described are most evident here. The Etudes for string orchestra, the Violin Concerto, and the composer's most successful work, the Petite symphonie concertante, are each described in terms of how Martin employed his mature stylistic synthesis in the structure of each of the three pieces heard on this program.

B47.   Greene, David Mason. Greene's Biographical Encyclopedia of
        Composers. Garden City, NY: Doubleday, 1985.
        In this dictionary of basic biographical information, Martin receives a full two-column page which surveys the composer's stylistic traits, and his life and works in a chronological format.

B48.   Günther, Siegfried. "Frank Martin." [in German] Fono Forum 7
        (November 1962): 14-15.
        This is a survey of Martin's life and work, as defined through an examination of the musical works which the author organizes within three distinct periods in Frank Martin's creative life. "Aus dieser Synthese heraus sind die Merkmale seines Stiles zu verstehen: die Offenheit gegenüber dem Phänomen und den Erscheinungsformen des Polyphonen - seine Melodik, wie sie aus der gewonnenen Freiheit des ganzen Tonraumes profitiert - eine Harmonik, die bei aller Komplexivität mehr und mehr der verfeinerten Schlichtheit zustrebt - die Rhythmik, deren feine Abgewogenheit oft aus dem Worte herauswächst - die von der Zwölftönigkeit angereicherte Tonalität, welche in weitesten Schwüngen doch nicht die Basis völlig aufgibt und durch eine Verlangsamung der Modulationsgeschwindigkeit gekennzeichnet wird. "From this synthesis, the characteristics of his style may be understood: the openness to the phenomenon and the various forms of the polyphonic; his melodious style, which projects from his achieved freedom in the whole tonal sphere; a harmonic style, which through all complexity ever more strives for refined simplicity; the rhythmic style, whose fine balance often arises from the word (literary text); the tonality, enriched by the twelve-tone influence, which in its most buoyant vitality never completely abandons its basis, and which is characterized by a slowing down of the modulation speed." Finally the author reflects upon Frank Martin's frequently quoted essay on the responsibility of the composer (see M31) in the context of his and other Swiss composers' place in twentieth-century European music.

B49.   Gutscher, Manfred. "In der Musik gedeiht Schönheit. Zum Tode von
        Frank Martin." Musica 29 (January-February 1975): 57.
        This is one of many summary tributes to the life and death of Frank Martin. Here the path of development of Frank Martin as a composer is briefly reviewed, as beginning on a mainly impressionistic course, followed by a period of interest in and experimentation with rhythmic problems. During this time, he undertook what would

become a series of <u>Ballades</u> for various solo instruments with orchestral accompaniment, through which a lyrical nature is revealed. In mid-life, Martin embraced the serious study of the twelve-tone system, and began to employ the technique in his own works. From this experience was finally derived a stylistic synthesis in which he was able to employ twelve-tone melodies with traditional harmony. From this success the composer was able to extend the technique to embrace the larger forms of oratorio and opera. Thus, in summation, in passages of his music that strive for the monumental, one still experiences his sense of balance and form, and this constitutes the characteristic profile of Frank Martin.

B50.   Halter, Mary Frances. "The Major Choral works of Frank Martin." D.M.A. diss., University of Arizona, 1979.

    In a lecture recital document, the choral works <u>In terra pax</u>, <u>Golgotha</u>, <u>Le Mystère de la Nativité</u> and <u>Requiem</u> are examined, not only in terms of the composer's stylistic development, but also from the practical standpoint of the obstacles to be overcome in obtaining performance materials, and in the preparation of suitable translations of lengthy works from the original French texts. In the final chapter, devoted to the <u>Requiem</u>, the author analyzes its structural elements, with particular reference to Martin's use of serial devices derived from the system of Arnold Schoenberg. She concludes that "The difference between Schoenberg's ideas and Martin's use of them is: Schoenberg organized a row of sequential pitches that were locked into a set-system that has come to be associated with the treatment of the row; Martin, on the other hand, organizes a row of intervallic sequences that could be freely interchanged between tonality and atonality."

B51.   Hamilton, Iain. "Swiss Contemporary Music." <u>In European Music in the Twentieth Century</u>, 121-22. Routledge & Kegan Paul, London: 1957.

    After a brief essay on nationalism, or the lack of it in Swiss music, as well as its overall good and bad effects on all European music, the author identifies two outstanding Swiss composers, Arthur Honegger and Frank Martin. Martin's development as a composer and the development of his unique style is traced through an examination of a succession of works, demonstrating his modified use of the twelve-tone serial technique, and his insistent use of triads, especially minor triads, employed in a free and original way. Another Martin characteristic is the self-imposed problem of handling the textures of three or more layers, each self-sufficient, yet fused together in a masterful fashion. This characteristic is especially obvious and brilliantly successful in works such as the <u>Petite symphonie concertante</u> and the <u>Concerto for Seven Wind Instruments, Percussion and String Orchestra</u>. Like Honegger, Martin has been most successful with large choral works and with purely instrumental works. Unlike some other modern masters, chamber music has played a lesser part in the composing careers of both Honegger and Martin, as has music for the solo piano.

B52.   Herchenröder, Martin. "Der Tristanstoff in der Musik des 20. Jahrhunderts." Erste Staatsprüfung für die Lehrämter für die Sekundarstufe II und für die Sekundarstufe I. Musikhochschule Köln, der Universitat Köln, 1986. See: B223.

B53.   Hodges, Craig. "A performer's manual to the solo vocal works of Frank Martin (1890-1974)." D.M.A. diss., Southern Baptist Theological Seminary, 1983.
       The stated purpose of this dissertation is to produce a working guide for the use of singers and vocal teachers in the preparation of eight solo works by Frank Martin. Following preliminary chapters on the composer, each of the eight works is examined in detail that includes formal, textual and musical analysis, with translations and summary statements addressed to singer-performers in particular. A final chapter contains the author's concluding thoughts on Martin's vocal works addressing both stylistic and philosophical-theological concerns.

B54.   Hodges, Craig. "The Solo Vocal Music of Frank Martin." NATS Journal 43 (November-December 1986): 14-21.
       Based on the author's dissertation (see B53), this extended and detailed article identifies ten solo vocal works, and discusses the background, compositional style, and unique features of each. The last section of the article, which includes musical examples, explores the technical resources employed in the various works, and compares and contrasts how Martin's music relates to the particular texts chosen. A useful bibliography and discography are at the conclusion.

B55.   "Homage à Frank Martin." Feuilles musicales 6 (November 1953): 165-168.
       Reprinted in: Revue musicale de suisse romande 36 (1983): 29-31.
       In the formal presentation speech of the Musical Award of the City of Geneva, the unnamed speaker defines the problem that musical language has become more difficult and more complex in the twentieth century, and that, while musical production is now extremely abundant, only a small part of it is viable, because so few composers are able to produce solutions to the problems that new music is heir to. Frank Martin's achievement is that, having observed and studied the problem, he has also triumphed over it, bringing credit and high praise not only to himself but to the city of Geneva as well. To the question what does Martin's music bring to us, we are told that from Debussy we received lyricism, from Mussorgsky we communicate with the Russian soul, with Schumann we are put in touch with the most intimate emotional dreams, but from Martin's music we receive an expression of faith. This faith is not confined to the use of a religious text, "-mais parce que si un élan mélodique s'allonge au-delà des

simples symétries, s'ils'amplifie, se prolonge en de nouveaux élans, c'est qu'une foi le soutient - et tel est le comportement constant de la musique de Martin, comme il était celui de la musique de Bach et de Handel." "-because, if a melodic piece transcends simple symmetry, if it grows and extends into new worlds, it is because there is a faith sustaining it-and such is the constant and essential make-up of Martin's music, just as it characterized Bach's and Handel's works."

B56.   Hugli, Pierre. "Frank Martin, le Grand." <u>Gazette de Lausanne</u> 13 October 1984.

On the occasion of the opening of the Frank Martin Exposition (in observance of the tenth anniversary of the composer's death), the author chooses to confine his comments about the exhibition to a postscript, and to devote his article to an assessment of Frank Martin as a composer. He accurately points out that Frank Martin's name is almost never mentioned in didactic works on music. His independent position is difficult to classify and, thus, is often ignored. Yet it is the unique synthesis of Martin's French and Germanic background that creates a distinctive Martin sound, which, if not always instantly attractive to the casual listener, always rewards those who take the time to experience repeated listening. A review of Martin's development as a composer from his somewhat derivative early works to the total mastery achieved after his <u>Le Vin herbé</u> follows. The author sees Martin's work as less respected by musical theorists than by performing musicians, many of whom are world class artists. Most importantly, he believes that Frank Martin's music is not just a reflection of the mid-twentieth century, but that "...cette musique porte le signe d'une communication profonde, d'un message. Elle est souvent marquée par une forme d'austérité, qui veut exprimer l'essentiel, et nous amener à une quête implacable, sans s'attarder aux fioritures et sensualités superflues." "...his music carries a profound message. It often bears a mark of austerity which seeks to express something essential and to bring us a quest without lingering on the superfluous."

B57.   "Hundert Jahre Tonhalle Zürich. Festschrift zum Hundertjährigen bestehem der Tonhalle-Gesellschaft Zürich." Zürich: Atlantis Verlag, 1968.

Here is a detailed, statistical, chronological record of the history, development, and achievement of Zürich's concert hall, in a volume issued to commemorate its centennial. In addition to his <u>String Quartet</u>, which was commissioned for the centennial observance, Frank Martin is credited with twenty-five performances of eighteen different works, not including three additional works performed in the nearby opera house.

B58.   Hunziker, André. "L'itinéraire de Frank Martin." Coopération [Bâle] 6
        December 1984).
            The itinerary of the Frank Martin Exhibition is but one of three
        topics discussed by the author. Beginning with the Lucerne
        International Music Festival (on August 18, 1984), the traveling
        exhibition will be shown in a dozen Swiss cities and subsequently in
        other countries. The author stresses that the Exhibition illustrates
        what is perhaps the composer's greatest achievement: his role as
        mediator between the two most important cultures of Europe, the
        Latin and the Germanic. In achieving this the composer succeeded in
        reconciling the irreconcilable, the musical language of Ravel and
        Debussy with that of Schoenberg and the second Viennese school.

B59.   Jarocinski, Stefan. Orfeusz na Rozdrozu. Eseje o muzyce i muzykach
        XX wieku. [Orpheus at the crossroads. Essays on music and
        musicians of the 20th century] "Frank Martin," 279-282. Krakow:
        Polskie Wydawnictwo Muzyczne, 1983.
            In this volume, which explores the development of movements
        and trends in twentieth-century music, various composers are
        represented under the three designations of "protagonists" or
        "apostles" or "idealists and mediators." Frank Martin quite naturally
        fulfills the third category as the great mediator between Latin and
        Germanic elements of European art music. The composer's stylistic
        periods and major works are discussed in this brief essay.

B60.   Jaton, Henri. "Frank Martin at 70." Musical America 81 (January
        1961): 32, 111, 114.
            An interview at the time of the composer's seventieth birthday is
        combined with a consideration of Martin's Le Mystère de la Nativité,
        as presented in Saltzburg only a few weeks prior to the composer's
        birthday. Responding to direct questions, the composer indicates Le
        Vin herbé as the high point and pivotal work in his career, the one
        which set the course for all that would follow. He also admits to a
        preference for composing for the voice. Turning to the Saltzburg
        performance of Le Mystère, the first time in which the work was
        presented as a staged "opera" or theatre piece, it is judged to be a
        triumphant success. The composer concludes that "in my family all
        the Martins have reached full maturity late in life."

B61.   King, Charles W. "A Discography of the Music of Frank Martin."
        Association for Recorded Sound Collections Journal 14 (1982): 20-
        37.
            This discography was compiled before 1982 and has been
        enlarged, corrected and superceded by this volume.

B62.   "Klavierabend. Paul Badura-Skoda." Wiener Festwochen 1968 (May
        27, 1986).
            These are program notes for a recital by Viennese pianist Paul
        Badura-Skoda, in which Frank Martin's Fantaisie sur des rythmes

flamenco is performed by the pianist for whom it was written twelve years earlier, along with the Huit préludes which the pianist has championed and performed many times. After a brief sketch of the composer's background and career, the author quotes from Frank Martin writing about his interest in the rhythmic aspects of flamenco music, his desire to compose a piece that his daughter Teresa could dance to, and his need to provide a long promised new solo piece for Badura-Skoda. Then follows a description of the 1948 Preludes, which were written for, but never performed by, the legendary pianist Dinu Lipatti. The Eight Preludes are described as a compendium of Martin's composing skills.

B63.   Klein, Rudolf. "Frank Martin." [in German] Österreichische
          Musikzeitschrift 25 (October 1970): 642.
          This brief article is both an eightieth birthday tribute to the composer, and a postscript to Klein's 1960 monograph on Frank Martin (see B64). The author laments that the frequent performances of Martin's music during the sixties in Austria have now become rare and that many of the pieces of his mature years have yet to be heard in that country. It is recognized that, at this time, Martin is at the peak of his creative powers, and that his music is of lasting value. "Schöneres lässt sich wohl kaum von einem Komponisten sagen, als dass sein summum opus auch ein opus utile est. Möge es so bleiben!" "There is nothing more beautiful to be said about a composer than that his summum opus is also an opus utile. May it remain so!"

B64.   Klein, Rudolf. Frank Martin sein Leben und Werk. Wien:
          Österreichische Musikzeitschrift, 1960.
          This relatively brief monograph by the editor of Vienna's leading musical journal became the first Martin biography. It was a particularly important publication at that time when it was meant to acquaint the general (German-speaking) public and other musicians with the music of Frank Martin. Klein's book goes far beyond a simple recitation of his life and works. The biography is remarkably complete, including influences and heritages from previous generations, and, more importantly, probes deeply into Martin's aesthetic beliefs, his training and growth of his compositional style. At the same time, we gain insights into his performing and teaching career, his association with Swiss cultural organizations, his thoughts and concerns on the influence of Schoenberg's twelve-tone system on younger composers, as well as his own response to it. Finally, the composer's stylistic development is explored over the many years of his professional life. The remainder of the book examines, in some detail, individual major compositions up to and including Le Mystère de la Nativité. Missing are the final fourteen years of a long and creative life.

B65.   Klein, Rudolf. "Frank Martins jüngste Werke." Österreichische
        Musikzeitschrift 20 (September 1965): 483-486.
            Martin's biographer contributes this addendum to his 1960
        monograph (see B64) in which three new works--Monsieur de
        Pourceaugnac, Les Quatre eléments, and Pilate--are added, using for
        the most part Frank Martin's own commentary on each work. These
        commentaries have subsequently been collected in a volume called A
        propos de... commentaires de Frank Martin sur ses oeuvres (see M2)
        which the reader may consult to obtain the entire text. In Monsieur
        de Pourceaugnac, the composer explains his need to attempt an
        entire work in a comical vein after having composed so much serious
        music. This is done both as a relief and to test his own sense of
        comic wit. He then explains, in some detail, the various musical and
        theatrical devices employed to obtain the results he sought to achieve
        in the difficult task of setting to music the farce of Moliere. In Les
        Quatre eléments, the author comments briefly on the impressionistic
        quality of these orchestral pieces, and entrusts the remainder of the
        commentary to the composer, who describes his feelings and his
        approach to the four material elements which must be expressed in
        purely musical terms. The least familiar of the three works is the half-
        hour-long radio cantata Pilate, with a text taken from Arnold Gréban,
        which explores another facet of the Passion told from the point of
        view of Pilate. In this setting Jesus does not appear, and yet, by
        inference, he is always present. The author concludes that "...dieses
        Werk den Beginn der höchsten Erkenntnis und der reinsten
        Inkarnation lebenslang befolgter ethischer und asthetischer Ideale zu
        bedeuten." "...this work seems to signify the beginning of the highest
        understanding and the purest incarnation of ethical and aesthetic
        ideals followed for a lifetime."

B66.   Klein, Rudolf. "Frank Martin zum Gedenken." Österreichische
        Musikzeitschrift 30 (January-February 1975): 77-78.
            This is a brief memorial published just after the first anniversary
        of the composer's death. Here the author comments on Martin's
        relationship with the musical life of Vienna, where many of his
        important works were performed, and where he had personal ties to
        notable Viennese musicians. The Second Piano Concerto, composed
        for Paul Badura-Skoda, Maria-Triptychon, for Irmgard Seefried and
        Wolfgang Schneiderhan, and the world premiere of his opera Der
        Sturm are particular examples. As Frank Martin's first biographer, the
        author quotes from a gracious letter of thanks from the composer,
        and a second letter in which Martin describes his difficulties and
        successes in creating two new works for the celebration of the five-
        hundredth birthday of Erasmus in Rotterdam.

B67. Koelliker, Andrée. Frank Martin Biographie Les Oeuvres: evolution du style criture et expression musicale le musicien et les problèmes de la composition. Lausanne, Conservatoire de Lausanne, 1963.

A published thesis presents the life and work of Frank Martin in the most succinct outline form. Brief entries on individual works and topics such as "the musician and the problems of composition" are included. Most valuable is the classified bibliography which, although somewhat dated, contains many of the best articles by, and particularly about, the composer and his works.

B68. Lambert, Meinrado. "Frank Martin." [in French] Feuilles musicales 2 (May 1949): 25-28.

Prophetically, Frank Martin was recognized critically as an emerging talent to be reckoned with as early as 1913 on the occasion of the fifteenth Festival of the Association of Swiss Musicians. Further evidence of technical and expressive mastery was confirmed by his subsequent early works, such as Rythmes (1926) and Fêtes du Rhône (1927). Then followed a period of study and rhythmic experimentation with Jacques Dalcroze and with the twelve-tone system of Arnold Schoenberg. From this experimental period, the composer finally emerged with his Le Vin herbé, a setting of the Tristan legend from the novel of Joseph Bédier which, though written as a chamber oratorio, is now sometimes staged as an opera. This work was the beginning of Martin's reputation as an international composer, to be followed shortly by his critically acclaimed Petite symphonie concertante and the passion oratorio Golgotha.

B69. Lambrechts, Jean. "Jean Lambrechts' zoeklicht op: Frank Martin, begaafd en vooraanstaand toondichter." [Spotlight on Frank Martin, well mannered and premier composer] Limburg vandaag (November 15 1970): 61-62.

The article is based on conversations with the composer on the occasion of an eightieth birthday celebration, in which the composer responds to various questions about his own composing methods as contrasted with the direction taken by today's young composers. He also discusses his passion oratorio Golgotha as compared with those of Bach, his activities as a conductor, and his composition students, with particular reference to the direction taken by Karlheinz Stockhausen. Finally, the composer discusses musical traditions, the institutions that maintain and perpetuate a continuity of musical art, and his concern for those who would do away with the "old" to make room for the new and experimental.

B70. Lewinski, Wolf-Eberhard von. "Frank Martin." [in German] Musik und Szene 8 (1963-64): 6-8.

In this overview of Frank Martin's musical life, the emphasis is not on a chronological summary of works, but rather, it is an attempt to identify and define those elements which make this composer's works unique. The slow and painstaking creative process is cited, in which each piece represents the composer finding his own unique style without reference to changing trends going on all around him. This combination of study, performance, teaching, and experimentation finally resulted in the Petite symphonie concertante, in which a twelve-tone melody is employed in a manner which creates an extended tonal center, combined with the strikingly original sounds of solo harp, harpsichord, piano and double string orchestra to produce a work of great charm that has found a place in the repertoire. Martin has also contributed as an original thinker, wrestling with such topics as the problem of modern audiences coping with new music, writing sacred music in a twentieth-century environment, and the risks involved for a composer in avoiding both the avant-garde trends of the moment or an eclectic safe route precluding any significant originality beyond the immediate need of the present.

B71.   Litschauer, Franz. "Das Irrationale bei Frank Martin." Österreichische
         Musikzeitschrift 8 (March-April 1953): 95-97.
         In this unusual article, the author views the life and work of Frank Martin in philosophic terms. Despite the title, it is not so much the irrational but the synthesis of rational and irrational that defines the work of the composer. "Hier ist eine Synthese des Rationalen mit dem Irrationalen erreicht, hier sind die neuen Ausdrucksformen in dem Dienst einer tiefen geistigen schau gestellt." "Here a synthesis of the rational and irrational is reached. Here the new forms of expression are devoted to a deep spiritual vision." Recognizing that a "romantic view" of life had been destroyed in the turmoil of war and the emergence of new values in the twentieth century, in which a rationalistic approach has prevailed for some years, Martin is seen as part of the pendulum swing back toward spiritual and metaphysical values. There follows a letter from Martin to a pianist who had asked the composer for his thoughts on the Huit préludes. Martin responds that the pieces are written in such a way as to speak for themselves. The article concludes with a brief summary of some of the expressive devices that can be observed in various pieces, with particular focus on the Violin Concerto in which the author makes reference to the spiritual content that places it clearly in the sphere of the irrational.

B72.   Martin, Bernard. Frank Martin au la réalité du rêve. Neuchâtel: A la
         Baconnière, 1973.
         In a monograph that explores the personality, life and work of Frank Martin in symbolic and philosophical terms, the composer's nephew develops his argument around the premise that Frank Martin's work cannot be separated from Frank Martin the man, and it is this fact that gives unity to all that he created. The author relates a dream, experienced in the composer's youth, in which Martin and his teacher visit a wizard who claims to have the key to heaven but does not know how to use it. The wizard instructs the teacher to demonstrate how to use the key. Symbolically for Martin, in refusing the way of the wizard, he chooses to be himself and not to succumb

to the magic of an already revealed way. From this symbolic dream, the author explores Martin's lifelong concern for the role of the ethic and of the aesthetic in the creative process, and the responsibility of the composer to create beauty as an act of love. In subsequent sections, designated as interim correspondence, pure music, and perspectives, the author pursues in symbolic terms Martin's lyricism in setting to music verses of major poets. In addition, his spiritual concerns are revealed, both in the Passion of Christ (Golgotha) and in the depiction of love and hate, good and evil, anguish and hope as they emerge in the Tempest. The argument culminates in Martin's continuous response to the theme of death which is present in so many of his works. The author concludes that great mythical themes and symbols appear in Frank Martin's work by which he depicts that which is truly human. In his confrontation with these symbols, the composer was continuously discovering a part of himself that became a part of each musical work.

B73. Mengelberg, Karl. "Subliem IKON-concert." De Bel Laren N.H. November 30, 1965.

This is a very brief description of a recital given in Naarden where Frank Martin lived the last twenty years of his life, and in which the then seventy-five-year-old composer performed at the piano, assisted by the celebrated Dutch soprano Elly Ameling and flutist Pieter Odé. On the same program, the composer's wife, Maria Martin, a native Hollander, spoke about the composer's work. Included on the program in addition to works by Rameau and Purcell, were the composer's Trois chants de Noël, the Drey Minnelieder, the Huit préludes for piano and the Ballade for flute.

B74. Meylan, Pierre. "Musik und Musiker der französischen Schweiz." Musica 13 (July-August): 456-457.

In a survey article on the music of French-speaking Switzerland, the author identifies Frank Martin as the most important and most performed worldwide of Swiss composers. Martin's music is defined as a synthesis between Latin and Germanic traits. " ...sein Stil ist das Resultat meisterhafter Verschmelzung von Impulsen, die er im französischen Impressionismus, der Zwölftonmusik, der 'Motorik' von Bartók und Hindemith empfangen hat." "His style is the result of a masterful melting of impulses which are derived from French impressionism, the twelve-tone system and motoric rhythms of Bartók and Hindemith." Despite his French-speaking background, several of Martin's most important works were inspired by German literature. These would include Der Cornet by Rilke, Sechs Monologe aus Jedermann, with a text by von Hofmannsthal, the ballet on Cinderella, Das Märchen zum Aschenbrödel after the Grimm brothers, and the Schlegel translation of Shakespeare's The Tempest.

B75.   Mohr, Ernst. "Frank Martin." [in German] In Musik in Geschichte und
        Gegenwart V.8 1960, 1705-1709.
        In this entry for the major German language music encyclopedia,
        Frank Martin's professional life as a composer is meticulously
        documented from his family background since 1750 to his training as
        a musician, with particular attention to the major influences on his
        slowly developing musical style. Then follow the events that led to his
        breakthrough as a composer of international recognition. The
        composer's training with Joseph Lauber and his subsequent exposure
        to mainstream European modernism, particularly during a two-year
        sojourn in Paris, led to a series of compositions that reflect how he
        absorbed various outside influences, but continued to develop in his
        own independent manner. Rhythmic experimentation, folk rhythms,
        and melodies, along with the music of Debussy and Ravel, are
        reflected in works composed during the twenties. The study and
        application of Schoenberg's twelve-tone system are represented in
        works composed during the early thirties. After this period of
        searching and trial, the composer's evolving style found its first
        characteristic form in the secular oratorio Le Vin herbé. Martin's great
        sensitivity to the subtleties of language is reflected in Der Cornet and
        in the Sechs Monologe aus Jedermann, using texts by Rilke and Von
        Hofmannsthal. This was no small feat for the young composer,
        whose speaking language was French. In 1945 came the composer's
        most successful work, the Petite symphonie concertante, which in the
        shortest span of time was performed around the world, and
        established Frank Martin as an international composer. "Es gelang
        ihn, die dodekaphonische Technik mit seinem harmonischen und
        tonalen Empfinden in individueller Weise zu verbinden. Ohne sich der
        eigentlichen Reihentechnik im Schönbergschen Sinn zu bedienen,
        verwendet Martin häufig Zwölfton Melodien, die er mit einer nicht-
        funktionellen Dreiklangs-Harmonik in Bezichung setzt, wobei gerne
        eine homophone und eine polyphon sehr dichte Setzweise einander
        gegenüberstehen." "The composer has succeeded in combining the
        dodecaphonic technique with his harmonic and tonal feeling in an
        individual manner, without making use of the actual sequence-
        technique in a Schoenbergian sense. Martin frequently uses twelve-
        tone melodies, which he relates with a non-functional triad harmony in
        which a homophonically and polyphonically very dense network
        oppose each other." In addition to his music, the composer has
        shared his views about various issues in contemporary music in a
        series of noteworthy essays and lectures.

B76.   Möhring, Susanne. "Martin's Meditationen über Musik (zur Ethik und
        Asthetik). Staatlichen Prüfung für Musikschullehrer und
        Selbständige Musiklehrer." Köln, 1984. See: B223

B77.   Mollet, Pierre. "Le compositeur Frank Martin." <u>Messager suisse de France</u> 6 (September 1960): 15-16.

The author, a singer who first worked with Frank Martin in <u>Golgotha</u> at the 1952 Festival of Besançon, combines an affectionate personal reminiscence with an outline of some of the important influences and events of the composer's life. Mollet credits Martin's early training in a thorough knowledge of the Bible as a major contributor to the composer's success in writing large-scale choral-orchestral works with Biblical texts. In particular, he makes reference to <u>Golgotha</u> and <u>Le Mystère de la Nativité</u>, two works in which the author took part as soloist. Mollet concludes that Martin has achieved pre-eminence among his peers, but not without the price of many years of dedicated hard work.

B78.   "Musik zeigt schönheiten des Zusammenlebens." <u>Neue Züricher Nachrichten</u> 21 (December 1984).

In an article entitled "Music shows the beauty of living together in harmony," the author reflects on the traveling exhibition as presented in Winterthur, commemorating the tenth anniversary of Frank Martin's death. The author, as well as dignitaries at the opening ceremonies, recognizes the numerous ties between the composer and the city, but also recognizes that the scope of the exhibition embraces the totality of Frank Martin as both man and creative artist. After some description of the organization of the exhibits, the author turns his attention to a concert by the Collegium Musicum in which three major works were heard: the well-known <u>Petite symphonie concertante</u>, the <u>Jedermann Songs</u>, and appropriately, Martin's last work, the chamber cantata <u>Et la vie l'emporta</u>. In response to the program, the reviewer concludes that "...Wer der Schönheit solcher Musik nachspürt, ist dem menschlichen Zusammenleben auf der Spur." "...Whoever feels the beauty of such music is on the track of human being-together in harmony."

B79.   Oster, Otto. "Der Tristan-Mythos bei Joseph Bédier und Frank Martin." <u>Almanach der Gesellschaft ur Förderung der Münchner Festspiele</u> München: (1962): 28-30.

In a brief essay included with the program booklet for the first staged performance of <u>Le Vin herbé</u> (<u>Der Zaubertrank</u> in the German language), the author explores differences in the Tristan legend, as presented by Wagner with that of Bédier and Frank Martin. In particular, he points out how Martin is able to skillfully borrow from sections of Bédier's novel, beyond the three chapters on which the musical work is based, to provide clarity and continuity. The author concludes that "...Frank Martin war weise genug, den Fuss nicht über jene Grenze zu setzen, die den Strengen Stil des Oratoriums von dem romantischen Geiste des Musikalischen Theaters trennt." "...Frank Martin was wise enough not to put his foot over that border which divides the strict style of the oratorio from the romantic spirit of the musical theatre."

B80.   Overeem, H.M.J. van. "Ikon-concert met Frank Martin als middelpunt." Gooi-en Eemlander [Hilversum] 21 November 1965.

In this review of a chamber music concert sponsored by the Ikon Foundation, the author speaks to a public that seems to be unaware that the seventy-five-year-old Swiss composer was a permanent resident in Naarden where this recital was held. More importantly, he focuses on the artistry of Elly Ameling, soprano, Pieter Odé, flutist, and Frank Martin as both composer and pianist. Performed at this event were Martin's charming Christmas songs with obligato flute, Chants de Noël, the medieval German songs, Drey Minnelieder, and the virtuosic Ballade pour flûte. These brief pieces were supplemented by additional songs performed by Elly Ameling, and an intermission talk by Madame Martin on the composer and his music.

B81.   Paap, Wouter. "In memoriam Frank Martin 15-9-1890 (Genève) - 21-11 1974 (Naarden)." Mens en melodie [in Dutch] 30 (February 1975): 35-38.

The author, who has frequently written about Frank Martin, pays tribute to the composer, and surveys his creative output, with particular emphasis on the years that Martin lived in Holland and the works produced during the last decade of his life. Here then is a diary of Martin's creative activities from Les Quatre eléments (1964) to his final work E la vie l'emporta (1974), including some speculation about commissions that were never to be completed. Paap concludes that the Netherlands makes no claim on Frank Martin as being a Dutch composer, but is grateful that the Swiss composer found his new home congenial for creative work, and, in so doing, enriched the musical life of his adopted country.

B82.   Page, Tim. "Judging Composers: High Notes, and Low." New York Times 22 March 1987, p. 28.

Twenty leading musicians, including composers, performers and teacher-administrators were all asked to name one underrated and one overrated composer from the past. Flutist Ransom Wilson chose Frank Martin for his underrated category: ..."Every piece I've ever heard by him was good, but after his style was fully formed, it's hard to find anything that isn't a masterpiece."

B83.   Piquet, Jean-Claude. "Frank Martin." [in French] In Komponisten des 20. Jahrhunderts in der Paul Sacher Stiftung, 151-161. Basel: Paul Sacher Stiftung, 1986.

In a warm and loving but not sentimental tribute to Frank Martin, his lifetime friend and confidant speaks on the subject of Frank Martin as composer, as interpreter, but especially as humanist and man of culture. In fact, these three elements can only be temporarily separated because the search for his unique way led to the fusion of these elements. About a life described as an upward curve, the author says "...n'est seulement celle d'un musicien de profession. Elle

est bien davantage. Mais elle n'est pas celle seulement d'un philosophe ou d'un penseur. Elle est aussi davantage. Elle est vraiment, je crois, celle d'un homme, celle d'un humaniste qui se sent, simultanemént, héritier de la muse de l'artet de cellede la pensée."
"...it is not only that of a professional musician, it is much more. But it is neither only that of a philosopher or a thinker. It is also more. It is truly, I believe, that of a man, that of a humanist who considers himself, simultaneously, heir to the muse of art and the one of thought." And in conclusion he says: "L'essentiel de l'humanisme de Frank Martin réside finalement en cette idée si profonde, qu'il n'y a pas pour lui de prestation artistique valable sans la conscience et la responsabilité éthique de celui qui pratique un art, et, inversement, qu'aucune pensée humaine n'est valable qui se voudrait pure, ou, comme il dit, 'angelique,' dégagée d'une incarnation dans le monde sensible." "The essential of Frank Martin's humanity resides finally in this idea so profound that there is for him no valid artistic performance without conscious and ethical responsibility of the one practicing an art, and, inversely, no human thought is valid that pretends to be pure, or, as he says, 'angelic,' apart from incarnation in the real world."

B84.   R., J.-L. "L'univers d'un compositeur un peu photographe et trè tricoleur." Journal de Genève 10 November 1984.
    On the occasion of an Exposition commemorating the tenth anniversary of the death of Frank Martin, a special section of this newspaper was devoted to articles about the composer. In this brief article, the author describes how Frank Martin's lifestyle included an interest in photography, painting, gardening, as well as household chores, in addition to his professional career, and how these various facets of his life are accurately portrayed in the eleven sections of the exhibit.

B85.   Regamey, Constantin. "Cérémonie de collation du grade de docteur honoris causa à M. Frank Martin à l'Université de Lausanne." Schweizerische Musikzeitung. Revue musicale suisse 101 (November-December 1961): 381-386.
    As the title suggests, here is the presentation address given at the ceremonies conferring an honorary degree on Frank Martin at the University of Lausanne. The author, a fellow composer, delivers high praise for Martin's achievement, and thanks the composer for the models of highest quality which he has provided for future generations of aspiring Swiss composers to follow. The author reviews those qualities which he considers are the elements that make the works of Martin unique. Among these he uses value as an important word. For Frank Martin, the creative act is the joy of having fulfilled oneself in the created work, coupled with the need to share this joy with one's listeners. Regamey asserts that the secret of true creation resides in deep human sincerity that will submit itself to lucid criticism, and that innovation and sincerity are the qualities which permit the

artist to present new values to the world. At the conclusion, Frank Martin responds by expressing his astonishment that a center of higher learning would bestow such an honor on an artist. He briefly defines an artistic creation as one in which knowledge and intelligence are subordinate to another function of the mind. For lack of a better word he uses "judgment" or "choice." A work of art is a voluntary product of the mind, and becomes a living organism. It contains, simultaneously, elements of both the rational and irrational. Frank Martin finds reassurance that to some extent all creative activity is made up of a collaboration of these two elements.

B86.   Regamey, Constantin. "Les Éléments flamenco dans les dernières oeuvres de Frank Martin." Schweizerische Musikzeitung. Revue musicale suisse 116 (1976): 351-359.
        In the last several years of a long creative life, Frank Martin experienced a surge of creative activity in which he was composing more and at a faster rate than ever before. It is in these last musical works that two new influences are incorporated into his composing style: flamenco rhythms, and to a lesser extent, pop music. That the composer should be attracted to the rhythmic elements of flamenco dancing through his daughter Teresa, a professional dancer, is not surprising after a lifelong interest in rhythmic experimentation, and having worked closely with Jacques Dalcroze. These new influences are first discernible in the unique vocal work Poèmes de la mort for three male voices and three electric guitars. The use of electric guitar is thus an obvious influence of the pop culture. More important is the irregular flamenco rhythms employed in this same composition in the macabre "Ballade des pendus" (ballad of the hanged ones). At about the same time Martin was composing his Trois danses for oboe, harp, and string orchestra, in which each of the three movements employs rhythmic elements from specific flamenco dances. Flamenco elements appeared again in a solo piano work, the Fantaisie sur rythmes flamenco, composed for his daughter, Teresa Martin. A flamenco slow rhumba becomes the basis for this work. The author further explores the influence of flamenco-like rhythms in examining later works not intended for the dance. In these instances, it is not traditional rhythmic flamenco patterns, but asymmetrical rhythmic series, irregular and constantly repeated, that can be found in the Polyptyque and the "Dies Irae" section of the Requiem.

B87.   Regamey, Constantin. "Frank Martin est mort." Schweizerische Musikzeitung. Revue musicale suisse 115 (1975): 23-25.
        In this eulogy, representative of many such published expressions, the author, in great humility and affection, speaks on the subject of death as a central theme in the major works of Frank Martin. The composer's life was free of any morbid concern or anxiety over death and, on the contrary, he lived a joyous and creative life. It is Martin's personal simplicity, and his ability to have found a unique musical voice preserving the predominance of

traditional expressive means of melody, rhythm, and harmony within the mainstream of European art music, that assure him a place of honor. Among very few composers of our time "et cet homme très consciemment et très profondément ressentait son art comme un message." "This man very consciously and very profoundly feels his art as a message." In contrast to the serious mature works, there are earlier ones of great charm and gaiety that show another side of the composer's personality. In conclusion, there is the composer's final creative offering, commencing with his Requiem, in which Martin ponders his own death, and, in so doing, speaks to each of us about our own death. "Cette longue et lucide préparation à la dernière échéance, préparation dont le compositeur cherche à nous communiquer les résultats pour notre bien, est quelque chose d'unique dans l'histoire de la musique." "This long and lucid preparation for the final call, preparation in which the composer seeks to communicate the results for our own good, is something unique in the history of music."

B88.   Reich, Willi. "On Swiss Musical Composition of the Present." Musical
        Quarterly 51 (January 1965): 78-82.
            Professor Reich asserts that present day musical composition in
        Switzerland must be viewed from the unique background of a country
        with three language areas and the accumulated cultural traditions that
        are attached to each. Switzerland is seen as a country with highly
        developed musical resources, even in rural areas, but few creative
        artists of international rank. Frank Martin is the notable exception to
        this generalization. His musical influences and style are briefly
        surveyed, and his musical credo is expressed in an extensive
        quotation from the composer.

B89.   Richard, Georges. "Frank Martin (1890-1974) Personlichkeit und
        Aspecte seines Schaffens." [Personality and Aspects of his work]
        Luxemburger Wort August 1984.
            This review of performances of Frank Martin's music at the 1984
        International Music Festival in Lucerne is in the form of the author's
        reminiscences and reactions, both past and present, to Frank Martin.
        Recalling the strong impression of having first heard the Concerto for
        Seven Winds, Percussion and Strings in 1952, the author reiterates
        the basic tenets of Martin's working philosophy, that is, of his purpose
        "to write music which one can comprehend," and that "I expect of a
        work of art that liberation which beauty awakens in us." The author
        commends to his readers for further insights into the musical
        personality of the composer, the collected program notes in a volume
        called A propos de...commentaires. The festival performances include
        Maria-Triptychon, Le Mystère de la Nativité, and the early Piano
        Quintet of 1919. The author finds all of these performances richly
        rewarding, but confines most of his remarks to the staging of Le
        Mystère in a church environment which places some limitations on the

successful realization of three distinct spacial levels for heaven, earth, and hell.

B90.   Sabbe, Herman. "Frank Martin van metier tot inspiratie." <u>Vlaams Muziektijdschrift Maandblad</u> 23 (August-September, 1971): 195-200.

Here is an analytical essay in which stylistic evolution and development of the composer are meticulously documented, beginning with his early compositions that clearly demonstrate the influence of César Franck. Martin's earliest works reflect the ultra-conservative environment of turn-of-the-century Calvinist Geneva, where the young composer's formative years were spent. Further stylistic development came only when Martin left Geneva to spend some time in Rome and Paris where he experimented with writing works influenced by the style of Ravel. This was followed by a period of rhythmic experimentation. From increasing rhythmic freedom evolved greater melodic freedom, especially a freeing of the restrictions of diatonic melody. This move in the direction of chromaticism propelled Martin into the path of Schoenberg's twelve-tone system, which the composer studied thoroughly and used in his own way to build melodies in a semi-tonal framework. Martin saw chromaticism and diatonism as two musical tools that were almost opposites, both of which were needed for his expressive purposes. In a summary conclusion, the author finds that "in het ganse werk van Martin blijven de wezenlijke kenmerken konstant: de evenwichtige samenhang tussen de aangewende middelen onderling, tussen de melodie en het ritme en de harmonie, tussen de beweging en de klankkleur; en, b.v. in de afwisseling tussen de polyfonie en de homofonie, tussen complexiteit en eenvoud, de volledige overeenstemming van de aangewende middelen met de bedoeling." "In all the works of Martin, the essential characteristics stay constant: the balanced hanging together between the used forces amongst themselves, between the melody, the rhythm and the harmony, between the movement in the color of sound: and, e.g. in the interchange between the polyphony and the homophony, between complexity and simplicity, the total agreement of the forces used with the meaning."

B91.   Schäffer, Boguslaw. "Frank Martin." <u>W Kregu Nowej Muzyki</u> [All around modern music], 164-168. Krakow: Wydawnictwo Literackie, 1967.

This monograph by the Polish avant-garde composer assembles articles that had appeared previously in journals over a ten-year period (1955-1965) into a volume that explores the history and aesthetics of modern European music, with a particular focus on Polish composers and trends in contemporary Polish musical life. A portion of the book is devoted to summary articles on the life and works of some non-Polish composers including Frank Martin. In this article, the <u>Petite symphonie concertante</u> is examined in the context of Martin's use of twelve-tone techniques in his music.

B92.   Schibler, Armin. "Réflexions sur Frank Martin et la situation de son
        oeuvre dans l'histoire de la <<nouvelle musique>>." Repères (no.
        11, 1985): 103-105.
        Trans. as: "Gedanken zum Oeuvre von Frank Martin." Schweizer
        Musik-Padagogische Blätter [Zürich] (September 1986): 116-117.
        This essay responds to the question put to several Swiss
        composers on the tenth anniversary of Frank Martin's death
        concerning the importance of Martin's music within the history of
        modern music (see B44). Schibler looks at the question in modern
        psychological terms. He sees music and the other arts subjected to
        new researches of the human psyche in which emphasis is centered
        on individual parameters, such as color (Debussy) and rhythm
        (Stravinsky and Bartók), and in which composers of the second
        Viennese school developed, in music, the poly-layered complexity of
        expression reflecting a changing social structure. In focusing on
        individual components, there was a corresponding decline in
        emphasis on the formal aspects. Frank Martin's unique contribution
        as a second generation composer of new music was to achieve a
        synthesis of the new expressive means, while maintaining the ongoing
        tradition of European art music, thus achieving a re-integration of
        musical works into a unified whole.

B93.   Schönberger, Elmer. "Een jong componist van tachtig jaar."
        Preludium 30 (December 1970): 77-78.
        The title of this article, "A Young Composer, 80 years Old,"
        suggests a birthday tribute to the composer reviewing his
        accomplishments over the years. Instead, we "tune in" on a three-way
        conversation between the author (interviewer), the composer, Frank
        Martin, and performer-cellist Jean Decroos, who was soon to perform
        Martin's Cello Concerto with the Concertgebouw Orchestra. First, the
        concerto is discussed, and Jean Decroos describes how he
        discovered the work, and, subsequently, worked directly with the
        composer in preparing it for performance. The technical means of
        writing this work for solo cello and orchestra that permits the solo
        instrument to be heard at all times is also discussed. To the more
        difficult question of how he would assess his own place in the music
        of the twentieth century, the composer feels that others should have
        to answer this question. He believes that the avoidance of following
        what is momentarily fashionable has contributed an element of
        timelessness to his music. Both composer and cellist see their role
        as one of communicator with the listening public, and believe that
        some composers of our time have lost sight of this fundamental
        objective.

B94.   Schuh, Willi. "Kompositionsauftrage." In <u>Alte und Neue Musik Das</u>
<u>Baseler Kammerorchester (Kammerchor und Kammerorchester)</u>
<u>unter Leitung von Paul Sacher 1926-1951</u>, 51-56. Zurich: Atlantis,
1952.
        Writing in a volume commemorating the first twenty-five years of
the Basel Chamber Orchestra and its founder-conductor Paul Sacher,
the author contributes brief articles on ten European composers who
have written for the BKO, and whose works Sacher has often
championed through performances in many cities beyond those in
Switzerland. Writing about Frank Martin, the author goes beyond a
summary of works and dates, and, more importantly, shares excerpts
of letters between the composer and Sacher in which one learns
about the problems and concerns of the creative process as they
were experienced on a day-to-day basis. In particular, <u>Der Cornet</u>,
the <u>Petite symphonie concertante</u>, the <u>Ballade for Cello</u>, and, finally,
the <u>Violin Concerto</u> were discussed.

B95.   Skulsky, Abraham. "Frank Martin---a clear understanding of his ideals
of expression." <u>Musical America</u> 69 (August 1949): 8,18.
        In this article from 1949, the author is one of the first to
introduce to American readers, in some depth, the life and work and
thought of a composer whose reputation was just then coming to
international attention. The background of Martin's formative years in
Geneva, his early training, and his first compositions are surveyed,
followed by an examination, in some detail, of the composer's pivotal
work <u>Le Vin herbé</u>. Most valuable for English-speaking readers is a
detailed summary translation of the composer's frequently cited article,
<u>Responsabilité du compositeur</u> (see M31), in which Martin explores a
composer's responsibility for viewing his own work objectively, and in
determining the extent and limitations of this responsibility. Martin
perceives this objective post-mortem of a completed work as the
technique of inspiration, whereby a composer can benefit from this
examination in the creation of subsequent works. For the reader, the
formulation of these ideas provides an insight into Martin's process of
composing and his overview of the artist's place in modern society.

B96.   Slonimsky, Nicolas, ed. "Martin, Frank." <u>Baker's Biographical</u>
<u>Dictionary</u>, 7th ed., 1463-1464. New York: Schirmer Books, 1984.
        In this well-known reference of biographical entries, the author's
concluding summary is that "He succeeded in creating a distinctive
style supported by a consummate mastery of contrapuntal and
harmonic writing, and a profound feeling for emotional consistency
and continuity."

B97.   Stubin, Blanche. "L'univers d'un compositeur Le exposition Frank
Martin au Palais Wilson." <u>Le Courrier</u> [Genève] 26 November l984.
        In this review the author expresses her reaction to the eleven-
part exhibition on Frank Martin which was presented at Geneva's
Palais Wilson. From the written and pictorial displays one is able to

experience a whole lifetime of a Genevan who has achieved honor
and fame. Evidence of the thoughtful and loving attention which went
into the concept of this traveling exhibit reflects credit on Eugénia
Catala and Mme. Maria Martin, who brought it all together. They were
assisted by others who were closest to the composer during his
lifetime. In assessing Frank Martin in terms of his humanity, the
author believes that the quality of the exhibition reflects the image of
the man it honors: "l'image d'un homme noble, courageux et
authentique, qui se reflète dans son oeuvre, qui a sui triompher de
toutes les épreuves et qui, jusque face à la mort, garda sa lumineuse
sérénité." "It is the image of a noble, courageous and authentic man
who is reflected in his work, who was able to triumph over difficulties
and who, up until his death, never lost his luminous serenity."

B98.   Stuckenschmitt, H.H. Twentieth-Century Composers, Vol. II Germany
        and Central Europe. London: Weidenfeld and Nicolson, 1970: 175-
        182.
            In an unusually lucid account of the life and work of Frank
        Martin, the major choral and operatic works are presented in
        somewhat more detail. The article concludes with a description and
        summary review of the nativity oratorio Mystère de la Nativité.

B99.   Suter, Louis-Marc. "La polyrhythmie dans la musique de la première
        moitié du vingtième siècle, examinée à travers les oeuvres de vingt
        compositeurs. Ph.D diss., University of Berne, 1980.
            This dissertation on polyrhythms examines the use of the device
        by twenty composers during the first half of the twentieth century.
        Martin's association with Jacques Dalcroze and his lifelong interest in,
        and experimentation with, rhythms makes his inclusion among the
        twenty composers a logical choice.

B100.   Swol, Els van. "Het eclecticisme van Frank Martin." Mens en melodie
        35 (April 6, l980): 204-206.
            In this valuable essay the author rejects a definition of eclecticism
        that suggests either superficiality or opportunism, when applied to the
        music or compositional methods of Frank Martin. Rather, he assesses
        Martin's eclecticism as "...een erudiete synthese van tonicaliteit en de
        twaalftoons-techniek van Arnold Schönberg en Alban Berg, tevens van
        het duitse en franse idioom dat hem in zijn jonge jaren had
        aangetroken." "...an erudite synthesis of tonic-centered tonality and
        twelve-tone technique of Arnold Schoenberg and Alban Berg together
        with the Franco-Germanic idiom that he was attracted to in his early
        years." That Martin drew from the rich variety of sources that are his
        musical legacy is undeniable. There seems to be a natural tendency
        toward synthesis by composers from multi-cultural backgrounds, such
        as the Swiss and the Belgians. There follows a systematic and
        chronological survey of several of Martin's most important works, in
        which the author points out the elements that constitute this eclectic
        quality of synthesis. This extends from the impressionistic influences

found in early works, such as the Piano Quintet and the Quatre
sonnets à Cassandre, to the synthesis between classic sonata form
and twelve-tone technique in his Petite symphonie concertante, and to
the synthesis of modal diatonic and twelve-tone elements in the
beginning measures of the Cello Concerto.

B101.   Tappolet, Walter. "Briefwechsel mit Frank Martin." Musik und
        Gottesdienst 40 (1986): 11-13.
            As the title suggests, this is an exchange of letters between the
        author and Frank Martin, in which the composer is asked to
        contribute musical settings to texts that will be used in a new folk-style
        hymnal. Martin graciously declines on the basis of having already too
        many demands on his time and energy to undertake new projects. In
        addition, he points out that a true folkstyle of writing should come
        naturally, and not be a posture assumed for the moment to meet a
        particular requirement. Further correspondence contributes a note of
        sympathy to the composer on the death of his son-in-law, and also
        reports on a solution to musical settings of the hymn texts by fellow
        Swiss composer Willy Burkhard. Again, Martin responds with praise
        for the work of Burkhard, with only some reservation about the actual
        folk quality of the hymn settings.

B102.   Tappolet, Willy. "Frank Martin und die religiöse Musik."
        Schweizerische Musikzeitung. Revue musicale suisse 100
        (September-October 1960): 278-282.
            In this essay, the author attempts to define and clarify Frank
        Martin's position with respect to composing church music. In his
        early years as a young composer, Martin experienced a considerable
        difficulty, in which he recognized a dichotomy between the subjective
        artistic expression in the world of art music, and the strictly objective
        ecclesiastical uses for the church. From this position the question is
        raised: does the place and the context in which a work is performed
        decide the distinction between sacred and secular music? The author
        agrees with Samuel Baud-Bovy, who has also addressed this subject,
        that "...als religiös jede Musik bezichnet, die beim Hörer das Gefühl
        des Überirdischen auslöst, das Bedürfnis, an etwas zu glauben, was
        über ihn hinausweist, dann muss man ebensosehr die <<Psalmen-
        Sinfonie>> wie den <<König David>> in gleicher Weise wie den
        <<Messias>> oder die <<Missa solemnis>> als religiöse Werke
        bezeichnen." "...if one calls any music sacred which causes in the
        listener a feeling of spiritual matters, a desire to believe in something
        which points beyond him, then works such as Symphony of Psalms
        or King David must be identified as sacred works in the same way as
        Messiah and Missa Solemnis." Frank Martin believed that music used
        for the worship service should not call attention to the merits of the
        composer. Ideally, composers should remain unidentified, even
        though Martin realized the impracticality of putting this idea into
        practice. His strong and unresolved feelings on the matter led to his
        now popular Messe pour double choir remaining unperformed and

unpublished for many years (see W14). The impasse was finally
broken in 1944 by a commission from Radio Geneva to compose a
choral work to be broadcast on the Armistice day of World War II.
Martin responded by composing In terra pax, a short oratorio using
Biblical texts. Afterwards came the passion oratorio Golgotha, which
Martin composed on his own initiative. The success of these two
works led to additional commissions from Radio Geneva, which
resulted in the Pseaumes to commemorate the founding of the
University of Geneva by Calvin, and, finally, the nativity oratorio Le
Mystère de la Nativité.

B103.   Thijsse, Wim. "Frank Martin Een persoonlijke herinnering." Koor-en
         Kunstleven 29 (January-February 1975): 1-2.
             Writing in a publication directed to choral directors, the author
         offers a personal reminiscence, in which he shares his ideas and
         feelings in meeting and working with Frank Martin, and recalls a
         similar experience with the composer Darius Milhaud. The writer is
         particularly conscious that composing and the need to compose come
         before all else. Similarly, he sees in the composer a natural inclination
         to turn away from discussions of his own works in order to enter into
         a discussion about Bach. In addressing his remarks to Dutch choral
         directors, the author cites the Requiem and the earlier Five Songs of
         Ariel as outstanding works of the twentieth-century choral repertoire.
         Frank Martin's music contains a message: that death and renewal go
         hand in hand in music as in nature.

B104.   Trimble, Lester. "Some unexpected help for the 'romantic revival.'"
         Stereo Review 30 (April 1973): 80-81.
             In this record review, composer-author Trimble offers high praise
         for three works released together on the Candide label (see D50).
         Special attention is directed to the Harpsichord Concerto performed
         by Christiane Jaccottet, which the reviewer finds to be an outstanding
         piece of neo-classic writing, containing both depth and originality.
         While less enthusiastic, the author also finds pleasure in both the
         writing and the performance of Martin's Trombone Ballade and the
         Piano Ballade. He speculates that these pieces might well be an
         answer to the public's desire for a "romantic revival," without having to
         revive obscure nineteenth-century works.

B105.   Tupper, Janet Eloise. "Stylistic Analysis of Selected Works by Frank
         Martin." Ph.D. diss., Indiana University, 1964.
             The stated purpose of this dissertation is an examination of the
         stylistic development and compositional techniques of Frank Martin. It
         is important for being perhaps the first study in English that is an in-
         depth analysis of eleven of the composer's compositions, drawn from
         early, middle, and mature works. Employing, where appropriate,
         some of the analytical tools that have been developed by other
         theorists for studying modern music, the author examines the various
         elements of melody and phrase structure, harmony, meter and

rhythm, texture, form, and orchestration in considerable detail. As some writers have pointed out, Martin's music is often ignored by theorists and writers of textbooks on harmony and composition. However, and paradoxically, since this dissertation was written, there have been another two dozen formal papers on some aspect of Martin's music. This comprehensive analytic survey remains a valuable source despite the passage of years.

B106. Vestdijk, Simon. "Een groot experimentator (Martin)." De groene Amsterdammer 27 September, 1958.
Reprinted in: Muziek in blik. Amsterdam: De Bezige bij, 1960.
This analytical essay uses Frank Martin's Violin Concerto as the springboard to a detailed discussion of Martin's development as a composer. The composer's long years of study and experimentation with the craft of musical composition do not in themselves make him the "great experimenter." Instead, the success he ultimately achieves is in bringing together the disparate elements of neo-classicism (or neo-baroque), post Wagnerian chromaticism, and the twelve-tone system of Arnold Schoenberg. In achieving this, the author identifies what he calls "twelve-tonism" as distinct from both chromaticism and twelve-tone technique. This means the formation of a chromatic series of tones to form melodies, in which the rigid requirement of having exactly all twelve tones without repetition is relaxed, permitting the series to function within a harmonic basis. Thus, Martin sometimes employs a complete series of twelve tones as at the beginning of Petite symphonie concertante, or a modified series as in the Violin Concerto and other works, to serve his stylistic purpose. At other times, basic major and, especially, minor chords serve his expressive needs. One can recognize limitations in a style so balanced, refined and interdependent; yet Frank Martin has succeeded in endowing the Violin Concerto and many other works with the unmistakable Martin sound.

B107. Vestdijk, Simon. "Triomf der Harmonie (Martin)." De groene Amsterdammer 20 July 1957.
Reprinted in: Het kastje van oma. Amsterdam: De Bezige Bij, 1958.
This essay not only defines Frank Martin as a late bloomer, but links him with Franck, Bruckner, Wagner, and Janáček as composers whose musical development came with maturity, in sharp contrast to the Wunderkinder Mozart, Chopin and Mendelssohn. These works of composers who required many years to achieve mastery over the technical and formal aspects of their craft are credited with having the musical attributes of being well thought out, deeply emotional, and having religious significance and an inner freedom. At the same time, they often do not escape from the problems of form and technique. Frank Martin began serious study of the twelve-tone system after moving through several stylistic changes, only after his fortieth year. His inclination toward chromaticism, and fascination with the music of Debussy and Ravel, led to his finding a way of combining the new

freedom derived from chromatic series with an independently moving bass line. Thus he created a synthesis that permitted the composer to move into new areas of expressive freedom, while maintaining the tonal function of traditional harmony in a way that soon identified the unique Martin sound. All of the qualities associated with late developing composers, and Frank Martin's synthesis of harmonic and expressive elements, can be demonstrated in his Petite symphonie concertante, from the opening twelve-note melody, to the exhilarating march movement that brings the work to its conclusion.

B108.   Vicuña, Magdalena. "La vida musical en Suiza." Rivista musical chilena 11 (October-November): 52-58.
        In an article based on an interview with Swiss maestro Paul Kletzki, Chilean readers learn about the evolution of musical life in Switzerland, and about its important composers and musical institutions. Historically, Swiss composers of the late nineteenth and the twentieth century had no musical past, so their primary influences were culturally derived from neighboring musical cultures, that is, German and French. In order to establish their own identity, the Swiss German-speaking composers sought to free themselves from the influence of Weber and Wagner, while the French-speaking Swiss composers sought to escape the domination of Fauré and Debussy. The two composers to attain a world class status in achieving this are Arthur Honegger and Frank Martin, both of whom are from French-speaking Switzerland. Martin's development is unique in that his stylistic development has moved from German influence to French influence, and culminated in a synthesis of the two in his modified use of the twelve-tone system.

B109.   Vink, Fija. "Frank Martin, Nederland en de kritiek een onderzoek naar de receptie von de muziek von Frank Martin in Nederland (1946-1974)." Ph.D. diss., University of Utrecht, 1987.
        This is a critique about how Frank Martin's music was received in the Netherlands during the years in which the composer resided there, 1946-1974.

B110.   Vlad, Roman. "Frank Martin." [in Italian] Le Rassegna musicale 24 (1954): 36-47.
        Composer-musicologist Vlad places Frank Martin in the context of his position with respect to other composers that were active during the fifties. In so doing, he identifies a composer who has found it necessary to find his own way, and who has slowly evolved a style that does not fit comfortably into any defined stylistic group. Thus, Martin has risked alienating the musical establishment on all sides. Frank Martin's unique position is seen as the result of his conservative Suisse Romande background, and the equally conservative formative influences of his early musical training. His artistic turning point came only after a period of study and travel that led to Paris, and exposure to the international musical scene. Finally,

there had to be a coming to grips with the Schoenbergian school, if only on his own terms. The author traces the course of Martin's creative output through three distinct periods: an early formative and largely derivative style, followed by a difficult experimental period, in which he attempts to employ the twelve-tone system in his works. Finally, with his Le Vin herbé, he achieved a breakthrough into a mature style in which he was faithful to the concept of tonality, however tentatively. By employing the twelve-tone system, often modified--primarily to the melodic elements in his music--Frank Martin succeeded in achieving a compromise within conflicting stylistic diversities that exactly suited his artistic nature. Despite the risks of compromise and overrefinement that are inherent in his style, the best works clearly demonstrate that the risks have been worth taking.

B111.   Vlad, Roman. "Frank Martin." [in Italian] In Modernità e Tradizióne nelle Musica Contemporea, 236-249. Torino: G. Einaudi, 1955.

The author's 1954 article on Frank Martin is incorporated into this larger work (see B110).

B112.   Vlad, Roman. "Influsso della dodecafonia su compositori che non ne adottano integralmente il metodo." [The influence of the twelve-tone system on composers who do not entirely take over its method.] in Storia della dodecafonia, 175-181. Milano: Suvini Zerboni, 1958.

In a book that explores the historical development of the twelve-tone technique, and the contribution and techniques employed by various serialists, the author places Frank Martin into the chapter on composers who have not adopted the twelve-tone system fully into their composing technique. Martin's only organ work, the Passacaille, is briefly analyzed to show how, by employing modified serial rows, he is able to retain harmonic elements tied to traditional harmony. The author points out the danger that exists for a composer who writes in a style that is neither strictly adherent to the twelve-tone system nor to traditional harmonic practice. Despite this risk, it is the pieces that succeed that give hope that composers today, and in the future, may not be lost in a system of sterile and formal abstractions.

B113.   "Die Welt eines grossen Komponisten." Nordschweiz Baseler Volsblatt 23 April 1985.

Another review of the traveling exhibition pays tribute to Frank Martin on the tenth anniversary of his death. The review describes the exhibit held in the University Library in Basel, which features plexiglass panels with written or pictorial documents of both Martin's private and professional life. Unique in the exhibition is the audio and video equipment which permit visitors to hear most of the composer's works, plus a video presentation of his Requiem and a twenty-minute film. The comprehensive exhibition was designed and put together by Eugénia Catala and Mme. Maria Martin.

B114. "De Wereld van Frank Martin (1890-1974)" Mens en melodie 42
(October 1987): 486.
This is a brief survey of the Exposition on the life and work of
Frank Martin which began on the tenth anniversary of the composer's
death in Switzerland, and is concluded with this final presentation in
the Hague. Martin's impact on the musical life of Holland and his
overall contribution to European art music are considered, along with
a summary of the special events taking place as a part of this tribute
to the composer.

B115. Whittall, Arnold. "Review of Books: Un compositeur médite sur son
art." Music and Letters 59 (1978): 496-498.
This review assembles Frank Martin's most important writings
about music, including his own. Over a forty-year span, the
composer reveals his evolving, though remarkably consistent,
response to the directions and experiments taking place in twentieth-
century music. Martin's path of synthesis, a reconciling of the twelve-
tone system with a traditional tonal base, created difficulties and a
need for explanation of how he both opposes Schoenberg's theory of
atonality, while, at the same time, he employs serial techniques to
enhance his own musical expressivity. His most valuable writings
would seem to be those concerned with aesthetics rather than
analysis. The composer's responsibility, the importance of words with
music, and sacred music in the twentieth century are some of the
topics which Frank Martin pondered on, and that he addressed
repeatedly over the years in speeches, lectures, letters, and essays.
This became a most valuable insight into the mind of a creative artist
spanning the early and mid-twentieth century.

B116. "Die Zauberhafte Klangwelt Frank Martins." Basellandschaftliche
Zeitung [Liestal] 24 April 1985.
The traveling exhibition commemorating the tenth anniversary of
the death of Frank Martin is presented in Basel as the "Magical world
of the sound of Frank Martin." After acknowledging the contribution of
several individuals, especially Basel's Paul Sacher, whose collaboration
with Frank Martin produced several important works, there is a brief
description of the exhibition and its catalog. As a special event
paying homage to Frank Martin there is a performance of his Le Vin
herbé, the work that started Martin toward international recognition as
a major composer. The performance under conductor Räto Tschupp
is judged to be outstanding, and in every way worthy of the special
occasion for which it was presented.

B117. "Zwanzig Jahre Collegium Musicum Zürich. Die Konzerte des
Kammerorchesters Collegium Musicum Zürich 1941-1961."
Here is a volume produced to commemorate the first twenty
years of Zürich's Collegium Musicum and its founder-conductor Paul
Sacher. In addition to essays on the orchestra and its conductor,
there are chronological lists of the programs, and a separate listing by

composer. Frank Martin is represented by seven works during this period including the world premiere of his Petite symphonie concertante and the Ballade pour violoncelle. See: W76, W87

Titles

Ballade pour flûte

B118.   Mooser, Robert-Aloys. "Frank Martin: 'Ballade pour flûte et orchestre'
(Genève, 30 November 1939)." In Regards sur la musique
contemporaine 1921-1946, 336-339. Lausanne: F. Rouge, 1946.
   In a brief review written during the same year of its premiere, the
author describes the Ballade as requiring virtuosity on the part of the
flutist with a strong sense of rhythm. At the same time the piece
contains a serious inner feeling that lends itself to the expressive
characteristics of the flute. Intended to be played with piano
accompaniment, an orchestral accompaniment has been arranged by
Ernest Ansermet. The article was written before Frank Martin's own
version with string orchestra appeared in 1941. See: W51

Ballade pour piano

B119.   Mooser, Robert-Aloys. "Frank Martin Ballade, pour piano et orchestre
(Genève, 22 fèvrier 1945)." In Regards sur la musique
contemporaire 1921-1946, 408-412. Lausanne: F. Rouge, 1946.
   Using a form favored by eighteenth-century French musicians,
Frank Martin has fashioned a series of works for diverse instruments,
each with its own unique characteristics. Formal liberty and extreme
contrast of sentiment are characteristic of the genre. The author sees
the Piano Ballade written in 1939 as a work that indicates an end to
Martin's period of self doubt and searching for his own voice.
Comparing the Piano Ballade with the composer's [1st] Piano
Concerto and his Symphony, the writing has clarified itself and taken
a definitive shape. The music expresses a conflict of feelings,
sometimes elegiac, at other times dramatic. The listener cannot help
but react. "Comment, au reste, celle-ci ne réagirait-elle pas, soumise
à des impressions si fortes et si diverses! Comment ne se laisserait-
elle pas troubler, dès les premières mesures, par l'exaltation toujours
grandissante du thème angoissé, si concentré et si chargé
d'expression, que le clavier chante au début de l'oeuvre dont il
semble bien être, en quelque sorte, l'élément générateur!" "There is a
theme of anguish in 'Ballade' which becomes more and more intense;
the keyboard seems to express this anguish at the beginning of the
work and it also seems to be the work's generating element!" Despite
the free form in which it is cast the Piano Ballade is not disjointed.
Episodes are united by thematic links which allow the piece to remain
an organic whole.

Ballade pour saxophone

B120. Pfannensteil, Ekkehart. "Frank Martin Oldenburg." Musica 20 (March-
       April 1966): 68.
            This is a very brief review of the German premiere of Frank
       Martin's Ballade for Saxophone, string orchestra, piano, and
       percussion. Using the title and free form of ballade, which the
       composer particularly liked, he has created a rhapsody reminiscent of
       old folk ballads. Characteristics which one associates with the music
       of Frank Martin are present here: economy and reserve, total tension
       with dodecaphonic writing that remains tonally connected, and
       harmony and tonal colors that fascinate and hold the attention of the
       listener throughout. Soloist Hans Weinrich played masterfully and
       conductor Karl Rudolf demonstrated skillfully his commitment to this
       new work.

Ballade pour violoncello

B121. Regamey, Constantin. "Ballade pour violoncelle et orchestre (1949)."
       In Musiques du vingtième siècle presentation de 80 oeuvres pour
       orchestre de chambre, 160-162. Lausanne: Editions du Cervin,
       1966.
            In what proved to be a total of six works for various instruments
       and written primarily for the international competition in Geneva, the
       composer named each of them Ballade, to emphasize the fact that
       each is cast in a free formal structure that eschews the traditional
       sonata-allegro form that is most often the basis of a concerto. For
       Martin, the title was not intended to suggest literary or romantic
       meanings. In electing a free formal structure, Martin does not mean a
       lack of formal structure. The intent of each of these pieces was to far
       exceed the utilitarian requirement of providing a bravura contest piece.
       Instead, the composer sought to display the instrument's most
       expressive qualities by revealing its most unique and individual
       characteristics. For the Cello Ballade the composer chose to
       emphasize the nostalgic and mournful quality of its sonority, and he
       has created a deeply felt work of unrelieved melancholy that finally
       ends on a note of resignation.

B122. "Tortelier introduces Frank Martin's Ballade." Musical America 72
       (December 15, 1952): 24.
            French cellist Paul Tortelier is the soloist with Thomas Scherman
       and the Little Orchestra Society in presenting the U.S. premiere of the
       Ballade for Cello and Orchestra. The music is tonal but very
       chromatic and contains pages of "haunting beauty and great
       originality" if also some passages of rather routine development.

Concert pour clavecin

B123.   Ansermet, Ernest. "Concerto pour clavecin et orchestre." [program
        notes] Orchestre de la Suisse Romande (November 2, 1953).
        In program notes for a concert by his Suisse Romande
Orchestra with harpsichordist Isabelle Nef as soloist, Ernest Ansermet
compares and contrasts Martin's Petite symphonie concertante with its
soloistic role for the harpsichord with this new concerto. He advises
the listener to expect a more intimate and concentrated work in which
the orchestra must of necessity play a discreet role to permit the
soloist to be properly heard. Frank Martin's total mastery of the
instrument results from having played it himself, and as the conductor
states "...à lui-même il marque à chaque oeuvre nouvelle un nouveau
degré de liberté et de maîtrise de son langage." "...he also stamps
each new work with a new degree of freedom, of mastership of his
language." The two-movement work consists of a classical symphonic
allegro, while the second movement combines the role of slow
movement and finale into one which also contains a Bach-like
cadenza for the soloist.

B124.   "In my Opinion - The London Concert World: Leppard Orchestra."
        Musical Opinion 78 (May 1955): 455.
        George Malcolm was soloist in the British premiere of the
Harpsichord Concerto of Frank Martin with Raymond Leppard
conducting his Leppard Orchestra. The reviewer sees flaws in the
writing, but finds it still sufficiently interesting and attractive to hope for
additional performances.

Concerto I pour piano

B125.   Moore, David W. "Martin: Piano Concertos: no. 1 (1933-34); No.2
        (1968-69); Ballade for Piano and Orchestra (1939)." American
        Record Guide 50 (November-December 1987): 51-52.
        In reviewing the first recording of Martin's neglected and almost
forgotten First Piano Concerto, the author is provided with the
opportunity by their inclusion on the same disc, to compare and
contrast the work with the Ballade and the Second Concerto. In
performances by the young Swiss-Italian pianist Jean-Françoise
Antonioli (see D51, D54, D26), the reviewer finds the First Concerto
less instantly recognizable stylistically as a work of Martin, and with
some passages that recall Hindemith. For some listeners, the First
Concerto may be the most attractive of the three. The middle piece,
Ballade, is the longest of the six works given this title for as many
solo instruments. It is in one movement with several contrasting
sections. The final Second Concerto written for and championed by
Viennese pianist Paul Badura-Skoda is a brilliant virtuoso piece
containing all of the elements that have become associated with
Martin's musical style, including extended solo passages for several

instruments including the saxophone. The author finds that "this fluent and lovely work is a distillation of his musical language."

B126.   Mooser, Robert-Aloys. "XIVe Festival de la Société internationale de musique contemporaine (Barcelone, avril 1936)." In Regards sur la musique contemporaine 1921-1946, 263-264. Lausanne: F. Rouge, 1946.

This is a review from the International Society for Contemporary Music Festival of 1936 held in Barcelona where the First Piano Concerto of Frank Martin was performed for the second time with Ernest Ansermet conducting. The Swiss reviewer gives high marks to Martin's Concerto, finding in it a richness of invention, intense rhythmic animation, and a soundness of structure that provides for both unity and diversity. The musical language of the composer is judged to have acquired both a flexibility and dexterity not shown to this degree in his previous works, and the concerto while requiring considerable virtuosity has explored the area of integrating the solo piano into the fabric of the total orchestral sound.

Concerto II pour piano

B127.   Badura-Skoda, Paul. "Genesis of a Concerto." Music Journal 30 (November 1972): 10-11.

Badura-Skoda, for whom the Second Piano Concerto was written and who gave both the European and American premieres, describes in detail how the work came to be written. His relationship to the composer, both professionally and as friend and regular guest in the Martin home, is shared with insights into Martin's working methods and his ability to assimilate musical ideas from other composers such as A. Scarlatti and Haydn in such a way that they become entirely Martin's. The composer-performer relationship extends beyond composition into rehearsal and performance, the two subsequently collaborating in a recording of the work (see D52).

B128.   Bartenstein, Hans. "Deutsche Erstaufführung von Frank Martins 2. Klavierkonzert in Freiburg." Das Orchester 20 (January 1972): 16.

Frank Martin's Second Piano Concerto was written for pianist Paul Badura-Skoda and dedicated to the Wiener Gesellschaft der Musikfreunde. The Viennese premiere, however, did not take place as planned, and the premiere took place in the Netherlands. This review concerns the first German performance in Freiburg in which Badura-Skoda was again the soloist. In describing Martin's music, the author identifies it as "...Musik, in der sich hohe Geistigkeit und sprühende vitalität glücklich verbinden." "...music in which high spirituality and sparkling vitality find their happy connection." This description seems apt to describe the concerto which begins with brilliant passages constructed from a twelve-tone row, and later develops a fugato with hard driving syncopated rhythms. The middle movement has a contrasting passacaglia-like movement, while the spirited scherzo finale, demonic in character, makes the greatest technical demands on the soloist. Badura-Skoda, who has made this concerto his own, was able to fulfill the virtuosic demands of this brilliant work with great distinction.

B129. Dellinger, Michael Eldon. "An Analysis of Frank Martin's Second Piano Concerto." D.M.A. diss., Ohio State University, 1985.
        This detailed analysis of Frank Martin's Concerto no. 2 for piano and orchestra is in five chapters which explore, in turn, the form of each movement, the prevailing scheme of pitch organization (analytical approach of Allen Forte), meter--tempo and rhythm, texture and the preeminence of homophony. Finally, there is an investigation of performance considerations.

B130. Hartzell, Eugene. "Badura-Skoda: Martin Premiere." High Fidelity/Musical America 21 (April 1971): MA20.
        The Second Piano Concerto written for Paul Badura-Skoda and dedicated to the one-hundredth anniversary of the Society of Friends of Music in Vienna had its first performance there with Paul Badura-Skoda as soloist and with Joseph Krips conducting. The three-movement virtuosic work is constructed from minor triads and skillfully employs melodic tone row elements into a basic tonal orientation. The concerto has structural strength underpinning its surface brilliance, and makes an immediate impression of strength.

B131. Klein, Rudolf. "Frank Martins neue Klavierkonzert." Österreichische Musikzeitschrift 26 (February 1971): 98-99.
        The author who is also Martin's first biographer, in reviewing the Vienna premiere of the Second Piano Concerto, points out that Frank Martin's music was often performed in Vienna during the forties and fifties to the acclaim of a usually conservative audience, but has received less attention since the sixties. The Second Piano Concerto, written for the Viennese pianist Paul Badura-Skoda and dedicated to the centennial of the Gesellschaft der Musikfreunde building in Vienna, actually received its premiere in Schveningen (The Netherlands) but was enthusiastically received at its belated Vienna premiere. The difficult concerto is composed in the twelve-tone technique, but as the author says "...die genügend Raum für traditionelle Elemente, wie Erfindung eines Themas und dessen Verarbeitung, Rhythmus, Form und vor allem Tonalität, gewährt." "...leaves room for the traditional elements such as the development of a theme and its rhythmic form and tonality." The prominent use of the saxophone is seen as an effective device. The author perceives that "Elemente deutscher Kontrapunktik treffen auf solche französischer Klangfreude und aus der Ferne grüssen Ravels Klavierkonzerte als Urahnen." "Elements of German counterpoint meet French joy of sound and in the distance there are Ravel's piano concertos as ancestors." The generally restrained Vienna audience received the new concerto with jubilation.

B132. Sagmaster, Joseph. "Frank Martin 'Concerto No. 2 for Piano and Orchestra.'" <u>Cincinnati Symphony Orchestra</u> [program notes] (April 7-8, 1972): 480-482.

On the occasion of the American premiere of the <u>Second Piano Concerto</u> by Paul Badura-Skoda with Thomas Schippers conducting, (see W126), the author quotes the composer where he describes the concerto as "a synthesis of the linearity of Bach, the declamation of Monteverdi, and the polychromaticism of Debussy." Expanding this definition, the author describes it as "a combination of the linear or horizontal aspect of counterpoint, as contrasted to the vertical or harmonic aspect; together with the bold and strongly chordal style of the Italian Renaissance master, and the Frenchman's use of the chromatic scale in which the music is developed from two or more different tonal starting points." The result is a difficult to play bravura concerto in the grand manner, and exactly what the pianist who commissioned the work asked for. A brief technical description of each movement follows.

B133. Vermeulen, Ernst. "Holland Festival 1970." [in Dutch and English] <u>Sonorum Speculum</u> 43 (Summer 1970): 1-17.

Here is a comprehensive if brief review of the many musical events of the 1970 Holland Festival in which Frank Martin's <u>Second Piano Concerto</u> received its world premiere by the Viennese pianist Paul Badura-Skoda. Politely described as distinguished and refined, the concerto is called typical, with familiar musical devices from Martin's other concerted works very much in evidence.

B134. Welbourne, Todd G. "A Comprehensive Performance Project in Piano Literature with an Essay on Frank Martin's Second Piano Concerto. D.M.A. diss. University of Iowa, 1981.

This doctoral essay examines in critical detail the structural, stylistic, and performance aspects of the <u>Second Piano Concerto</u>.

Concerto pour sept instruments à vent et orchestre à cordes

B135. Ansermet, Ernest. "Concerto pour sept instruments à vent et orchestre à cordes." [program notes] <u>Orchestre de la Suisse Romande</u> (March 22, 1950).

Conductor Ernest Ansermet describes Martin's new concertante symphony in which the major wind instruments of the orchestra: flute, oboe, clarinet, bassoon, horn, trumpet, and trombone are the solo concertante against string orchestra. In addition, the tympani are assigned solo material. A unique feature of the three-movement work is that, unlike common practice, the theme is not simply passed from one solo instrument to another, but each instrument introduces its own thematic material in turn, particularly in the first movement. The slow movement of melody over an ostinato figure can, according to Ansermet, bring to mind an aria by Bach, although the musical materials are quite modern. In the finale, the solo instruments are, for the most part, heard playing together rather than separately, and the work concludes in a rousing lively fashion.

B136. Borowski, Felix. "Concerto for Seven Wind Instruments, Timpani, Percussion and String Orchestra." Chicago Symphony Orchestra Program Notes (October 25, 1951): 17, 19, 21, 23.

Composer-critic Borowski, writing about Frank Martin and his Concerto for Seven Wind Instruments, borrows from Abraham Skulsky (see B99.) and Herbert Peyser who wrote in the NY Philharmonic program notes of the American premiere. From these three sources we learn something of Martin's background and works from his early years, more about his compositional methods from Martin's own writings, also quoted, and finally a brief formal description of the three movements of the Concerto.

B137. Regamey, Constantin. "Concerto pour sept instruments à vent, timbales, batterie et orchestre à cordes (1949)." In Musiques du vingtième siècle presentation de 80 oeuvres pour orchestre de chambre, 162-163. Lausanne: Editions du Cervin, 1966.

Building on the success of his Petite symphonie concertante, Frank Martin has gone several steps further in the same direction by employing seven orchestral winds, plus the timpani, instead of plucked strings in a modern concertante concerto again with string orchestra. Each of the seven wind instruments has solo thematic material which emphasizes the individual characteristics of the instrument. They are heard individually, especially in the first movement, and in various combinations as soloists, and at times are absorbed into the sonority of the entire orchestra. Within the three-movement work there exists a certain feeling of "Angst," never entirely dispelled in the first two movements, which then resolves in the final movement into a brilliant and joyful cascade of sounds leading to a conclusion which vacillates between a scherzo and a march.

B138. "Szell and Serkin Offer New Concerto by Frank Martin." Musical America 71 (January 15, 1951): 13.

The U.S. premiere of Frank Martin's Concerto for Seven Wind Instruments, Tympani, Percussion and String Orchestra was presented in a series of three concerts with George Szell conducting the New York Philharmonic (see W87). The Concerto is compared and contrasted with the composer's earlier Petite symphonie concertante, and is said to be better in some ways: "The hearer cannot fail to be taken by the rare nobility and restraint of Martin's lyricism and the accomplished manipulation of its sonorities." However, the author perceives the Concerto to be less original in its formal structure.

B139. Vestdijk, Simon. "Kaleidoscoop der blazers (Mozart, Martin)." De
       groene Amsterdammer January 12, 1962.
       Reprinted in: De Symphonieën van Anton Bruckner en andere essays
       over muziek. Amsterdam: Uitgeverij de Bezige Bij, 1966.
            This is an essay that explores the ambiance of the multiple wind
       instrument concerto in examining Mozart's Sinfonia concertante,
       K.Anh. 9 (K.297b) along with Frank Martin's Concerto pour sept
       instruments à vent, timbales, batterie et orchestre à cordes. Here is
       seen the virtuosic element in a double meaning of both brilliant color
       and brilliant interaction between the instruments. The wind
       instruments are so strikingly individualistic in their tone colors as to set
       them uniquely apart from the strings that combine so completely as to
       form a sound that sometimes doesn't distinguish between them.
       Despite the extreme contrast between early Mozart and mature Martin,
       each in his own way reaches listeners through the skilled manipulation
       of the unique tonal colors of wind instruments employed in such a
       way that the listener becomes involved and moved. It is not important
       that in Martin's concerto one will not find a single melodic phrase that
       could be mistaken for one of Mozart's lovely melodies, yet the
       twentieth-century master exploits the resources of multiple wind
       instruments in a way that touches the receptive listener on its own
       terms. Each composer presents to the audience a kaleidoscope of
       musical colors, the distinctive sound of each of the wind instruments,
       sometimes separately, in combinations, or all together, and in sharp
       relief to the accompanying strings of the orchestra.

Concerto pour violon

B140. "Composers Corner." Time 59 (May 26, 1952): 82.
            Frank Martin's Violin Concerto, as premiered by Joseph Szigeti
       with Ernest Ansermet conducting, received an ovation with five curtain
       calls. "With a musical language reflecting aspects of both Debussy
       and of Schoenberg, the Violin Concerto conveys a sense of worth
       and tragedy." The expatriate Swiss composer lived and worked
       quietly in the Netherlands to insure sufficient privacy to pursue his
       composing activities.

B141. "Editorial Notes." Strad 67 (June 1956): 43.
            This is a brief and negative reaction to Frank Martin's Violin
       Concerto. The editor admits to a minority opinion, but finds the
       Concerto lacking in musical substance and repetitious of the
       composer's other works.

B142. Harrison, Jay. "New York Music Scene." Musical America 84
       (January 1964): 35.
            This is a review of the New York Philharmonic performance of
       Frank Martin's Violin Concerto played by Tossy Spivakovsky who
       played the piece "producing silken sounds that fell graciously on the

ear." The concerto as a whole is seen as lacking in strength of musical ideas which seem to exist as if in a vacuum.

B143. "Modern Symphony Orchestra." Musical Opinion 76 (May 1953): 455.
This review of the first London performance of the Violin Concerto by Frederick Grinke with the Modern Symphony Orchestra conducted by Arthur Dennington suggests that, despite its level of dissonance, it is recommended as a more accessible work for the listener than some of Martin's other works. "...this concerto which is notable for fastidiously wrought texture, novel coloration, ingeniously varied rhythms, and highly individual yet eminently playable solo writing."

B144. Peyser, Herbert F. "Concerto for Violin and Orchestra." New York Philharmonic Program Notes (November 13-14, 1952,)
The American premiere of the Violin Concerto, with violinist Joseph Szigeti, and Dimitri Mitropoulos conducting, brought Martin's new concerto to America after successful performances in Paris and elsewhere. Quoting from the composer's own words and other reviewers we learn that Martin set out to write a concerto in the grand manner and that he incorporated elements from his preceding work, the choral Ariel Songs, into the concerto with both a melodic motif and its element of mystery which permeates the work. The expressive freedom employed in writing this large work is seen as Martin's final breakthrough from the overly conservative and reticent style of writing employed in earlier works.

B145. Regamey, Constantin. "Concerto pour violon et orchestre." In Musique du vingtième siècle Presentation du 80 oeuvres per orchestre de chambre, 164-165. Lausanne: Editions de Cervin, 1966.
The Violin Concerto written at the time the composer had just completed his 5 Ariel songs in preparation for undertaking the complete Shakespeare play, The Tempest, is strongly influenced by the composer's germinating Ariel music. The concerto represents to some extent a return to the Martin of the Ballades, with more overt use of the impressionism. Throughout the work the composer sought to emphasize the "fantastic," to create a mysterious and enchanted atmosphere appropriate for Shakespeare's fantasy island. Thus the lengthy first movement can be described as poetic, the second contains melancholy elements, and the third has an atmosphere of capriciousness. The author concludes that "le Concerto possède non seulement une unité d'atmosphère extraordinairement èvocatrice, mais également une ètonnante cohèrence dans le discours." "In spite of the vagueness of its melodic themes, and despite the impression of its structure which is malleable according to the composer's wishes, the concerto has an extraordinary unity of atmosphere and an astounding coherence of discourse."

B146. Schuh, Willi. "Violinkonzert." In <u>Von neuer Musik Konzert und</u>
<u>Opernwerke Musikfeste, Personlichkeiten</u>, 58-59. Zürich: Atlantis,
1955.
The <u>Violin Concerto</u> is seen as further proof that Frank Martin
has arrived as a composer in full command of his creative energies
and is now demonstrating his ability to work in the larger forms of
purely instrumental music. The spiritual origin of the concerto derives
from the fantasy world of Shakespeare's <u>Tempest</u>, and employs in the
first movement thematic material from the composer's recently
completed <u>Ariel Songs</u>, although something of the spirit of Prospero
permeates the entire work.

B147. Shaw-Taylor, Desmond. "The Arts and Entertainment: Frank Martin."
<u>New Statesman and Nation</u> 45 (January 17, 1953): 63.
This favorable review of Frank Martin's <u>Violin Concerto</u> is
subordinate to a discussion about the composer's style of writing
which is seen as so controlled and refined that it fails to attract the
attention it deserves from musician and listener alike. The <u>Violin</u>
<u>Concerto</u> is perceived to be an example of these qualities in that it
lacks a crowd-pleasing display of virtuosity, yet contains real beauty
and substance for the patient and attentive listener.

B148. Shaw-Taylor, Desmond. "Music." <u>New Statesman and Nation</u> 44
(August 30, 1952): 236.
Joseph Szigeti introduces the Martin <u>Violin Concerto</u> to
Edinburgh Festival audiences with Vittorio Gui conducting the Royal
Philharmonic. The concerto makes a strong impression despite a lack
of exhilaration, which is seen as a characteristic of this composer's
refined taste and restraint in using a harmonic language that brings to
mind the music of Fauré and Roussel. The second movement is
judged to be one of the most successful of its kind in modern music.

B149. "Szigeti Introduces Martin Concerto." <u>Musical America</u> 72 (December
1, 1952): 22.
A mixed review of the American premiere in which many beautiful
moments to listen to and a grateful vehicle for violinists to play are
seen as insufficient to balance a lack of harmonic direction or
rhythmic propulsion. The new concerto is one which will benefit from
additional performances.

Concerto pour violoncelle

B150. Ansermet, Ernest. "Frank Martin: 'Concert voor violoncel.'"
<u>Concertgebouworkest</u> [program notes] 9-10 December 1970.
In the briefest essay, Ansermet plunges the reader into the
complexities of Frank Martin's composing techniques, pointing out
how the composer has in the <u>Cello Concerto</u> used twelve-tone series
at times, but that they are used as a melodic line within a quasi-tonal

framework. In fact, all of the elements which Martin uses have a tonal basis. Each of the three movements of the concerto are then described briefly.

B151.   Dale, S.S. "Contemporary Cello Concerti XXIV: Henry Dutilleux and Frank Martin." Strad 85 (January 1975): 561-569.
   This double review speculates on the decline of contemporary French music after about 1939 and the lack of performing experience in Britain by composers of the caliber of Dutilleux. Similarly, the lack of outstanding native composers from Switzerland is seen as a factor in the relatively late arrival of Martin's Cello Concerto to London, as performed by Pierre Fournier. Despite its infrequent performances, the reviewer concurs with Ernest Ansermet who called it "a prodigious work, particularly the slow movement, which is a tour de force unequaled since the time of Bach himself."

B152.   Delden, Lex van. "Succes voor celloconcert van Martin." Parool [Amsterdam] 10 December, 1970.
   In a concert by the Concertgebouw Orchestra conducted by Bernard Haitink, Frank Martin's Cello Concerto performed by Jean Decroos receives its Netherlands premiere. In a program with Beethoven and Bruckner, fellow composer Lex van Delden devotes his review mostly to praise for Martin's concerto. The author sees that in this work, "...zowee de innige lyriek als de ritmische speelsheid, die er naast elkaar aan bad komen, zijn doortrokken van een elegische sfeer die aan Martins nogal chromatische harmoniek is toe te schrijven." "...both the intrinsic lyricism as well as the rhythmic playfulness, juxtaposed, is permeated with the elegiac sphere attributed to Martin's chromatic harmony." The performance by Decroos and Haitink was one of intense conviction, fiery glow, and wonderful tone production.

B153.   Murray, Bain. "Fournier: Martin Cello Concerto." High Fidelity/Musical America 18 (January 1968): MA9-10
   Pierre Fournier with George Szell and the Cleveland Symphony present the first performance in America of Frank Martin's Cello Concerto (see W120) written for the French cellist in 1965-66. The concerto begins with an elegy played by the cello alone, setting a somber atmosphere that is never completely dispelled even in the final movement marked "savage and rough." Despite a jaunty tarantella, solo material for the saxophone, and impassioned writing for the strings, the Concerto is seen as being expressed in cool emotions that may be a detriment to popular acceptance.

B154.   Samama, Leo. "Frank Martin en zijn 'Violoncelconcert.'" Praeludium 43 (December 1984): 3-4.
   Reading about the Cello Concerto in the Concertgebouw magazine, the reader experiences a three-way commentary with quotations from Frank Martin's 1966 essay "Responsabilité du Compositeur" (see M29) and other writings, summary statements

about Martin's compositional style and his life in Holland by the author, and finally remarks by the cellist Jean Decroos, derived from an interview with the author. From this exchange we learn about the background and difficulties experienced by Frank Martin in writing this concerto commissioned by Pierre Fournier. From the author we learn something of Martin's compositional style and his career with emphasis on his years spent as a Swiss composer living in the Netherlands. At the conclusion the soloist and principal cellist of the Concertgebouw Orchestra talks about his relationship with Frank Martin. First he discusses working with the composer in preparing the earlier Ballade for cello and his subsequent discovery of the Cello Concerto and its preparation for performance with the Concertgebouw. The cellist finds this concerto especially well written for the instrument and accessible to listeners despite its complexities.

B155. Seelmann-Eggebert, Ulrich. "Paul Sachers vierzigstes Jubiläum Uraufführungen von Frank Martin und Albert Moeschinger." Zeitschrift für Musik 128 (March 1967): 94-96.
　　　In a concert honoring Paul Sacher's fortieth year as conductor of the Baseler Kammerorchester, two new works by Swiss composers are dedicated to and performed by Paul Sacher and his orchestra. They are Albert Moeschinger's Consort for Strings and Frank Martin's Cello Concerto with Pierre Fournier as soloist. The concerto uses an orchestra that makes effective use of the harp, saxophone, and percussion instruments in support of the solo cello and includes music that ranges from the purest diatonic to the densest chromaticism. The three-movement work begins with a long solo passage for the cello followed by an allegro movement. The second movement has the festive manner of a sarabande and the finale, marked vivace, is dominated by syncopated rhythms. The author points out that just as in the Violin Concerto, one could hear echoes of Ariel's music from Der Sturm. Likewise, in the Cello Concerto, there are echoes of the composer's later opera, Monsieur de Pourceaugnac.

Der Cornet

B156. Meester, Magda de. "Frank Martin "Die Weise von Liebe und Tod des Cornets Christoph Rilke." Rijksuniversiteit, Gent 1983. See: B223

B157. Meylan, Frank. "Der Cornet." Record liner notes from Jecklin Disco 539.
　　　For the 1972 recording of Der Cornet (see D64), with Ursula Mayer-Reinach, contralto, and the composer conducting, the author summarizes the unique achievement of Frank Martin in creating a work which in its sensitivity to Rilke's poetic lines in the German language manages to create an endless variety and contrast that neither overwhelms the poetry nor fails to sustain interest throughout the hour-long work. Thus in twenty-three strophes the composer is

able to create a sound imagery that exactly parallels the verses which depict a wide range of events and emotions. Martin's music mirrors with subtle restraint the mood, action and emotion of each strophe. "Es war auch ein Wagnis, einen Text, der zwischen beschreibenden Bildern mehrere Personen handeln und sprechen lässt, einer einzigen Solostimme auzuvertrauen. Dieses Wagnis hat Frank Martin mit unvergleichlicher Könnerschaft gemeistert." "It was a daring undertaking to trust a text which balances descriptive episodes and the actions of multiple characters to a single solo voice. Frank Martin mastered this bold venture with incomparable knowledge."

B158. Meylan, Pierre. "'Der Cornet' de Frank Martin. Poème de Rainer Maria Rilke." Feuilles musicales 6 (November 1953): 175-181.

This extended essay on Der Cornet is both a review, touching on its strengths and weaknesses, and an analysis of aspects of its structure. It is also an overview of Frank Martin's vocal compositions and how this work relates to both past and future works by this composer. Much has been written concerning Frank Martin's choice of literary works of undisputed quality to make into musical settings, and, more importantly, his absolute fidelity to the author's text, making little or no changes for personal or musical reasons. In Der Cornet the composer assumes great risks in attempting a work in its original German language when his anticipated audience would be French-speaking. In addition, the lengthy narrative is entrusted to a single voice accompanied by chamber orchestra that makes challenging demands on the soloist both musically and artistically. To the familiar question raised with musical settings of great literature, that the work is sufficient unto itself and that it needs no musical setting, the composer indicates that he hopes his music will help to enlarge the perspective of non-German readers, thereby making the poem more accessible to them. To this rambling narrative prose-poem that encompasses the widest spectrum of contrasting elements--loneliness, military camaraderie, fear, nostalgia, awaking love, combat and youthful death--the composer adopts his musical sensitivity to words and his consummate skill in writing for the chamber orchestra to move rapidly from one brief episode to the next. Only the cheerful wit of the Cornet seems to escape the composer, but it is when the young soldier reveals his soul that the composer's inspiration reaches its highest peak. As in Rilke's poem so, too, in Martin's music, the elements of melancholy, mystery, and death are ever present even in the happiest scenes. For Frank Martin, then, "Avant In terra pax et Golgotha, symboles de la foi en la bonté des hommes et en la toute-puissance de Dieu, il fallait que fut accomplie cette épopée du désespoir, ou la mort est le salaire amer de toute jeunesse et de toute vie." "...before [writing] In terra pax and Golgotha, symbols of faith in the goodness of man and in the omnipotence of God, he had to complete this epic of despair, in which death is the bitter payment for all youth and all life."

B159. Mooser, Robert-Aloys. "Frank Martin 'Die Weise von Liebe und Tod des Cornets Christoph Rilke' (Genève, 5 juin 1946)." In Regards sur la musique contemporaine 1921-1946, 446-450. Lausanne: F. Rouge, 1946.

    Der Cornet is a prose poem from Rilke's youth that combines four fundamental themes that appear frequently in his poetic works: youth, love, heroism, and juvenile death. In setting this narrative poem to music, Frank Martin experienced the difficult problem of creating cohesiveness in a rambling, episodic work which explores the widest possible ranging of emotions from the recollections of a mother who feels from the heart, to fear on the part of the juvenile hero, to drunken feasting and the awaking of a new love, to death in battle and mourning. Each episode is expressed in the briefest verse and moves quickly to the next. Martin, using only the solo contralto voice with chamber orchestra, has succeeded in drawing the work together, changing moods quickly and remaining always faithful to the poet's text. The hour-long work draws the listener into the drama from the opening dramatic lines and holds one's attention throughout, so skillful is the writing for voice and orchestra. "Frank Martin nous offre ici une version musicale aussi pénétrante qu'achevée au fond et à la forme." "Frank Martin presents us with a musical version that is both penetrating and complete in essence and in form."

B160. Schuh, Willi. "Der Cornet." In Schweizer Music der Gegenwart, 135-142. Zürich: Atlantis, 1948.

    Der Cornet along with Le Vin herbé and Sechs Monologe aus Jedermann form a trilogy by Frank Martin which closely connects both ideas and musical style. Each work places music of great quality and sensitivity at the service of great poetry. Each is based on legendary stories, or contains elements of a legendary character. Each is meticulously faithful to the poet's text, with only minor alterations or omissions. In each work Martin employs his declamatory vocal style and a harmonic basis of modified tone rows undergirded by strong tonal relationships. Of the three, Der Cornet presents the greatest challenge to the skills of the composer, who has set to music all but three of the twenty-six stanzas. The length and constantly changing moods of the narrative, along with the juxtaposition of rhythmical prose and rhymed verse, all present obstacles for the composer. Martin's creative imagination casts these narrative prose poems as a modern trouvère and assigns this role to the solo alto voice with chamber orchestra. Metrical, rhythmic, and intervallic connections are drawn together in a subtle manner. Polyrhythm and polymeter play an important part as does Martin's penchant for employing pure triads side by side with serial procedures. The chamber orchestra is used skillfully to achieve variety, to set and change moods, and even to assume a dominating role at times, but it is always used as an expressive means to the end of projecting the poetry. If the wishes of the poets had always been followed, the world would be infinitely poorer for the loss of Schubert's setting of Goethe, Maeterlinck's

Pelléas by Debussy, and to the list may be added Rilke's Cornet as
realized by Frank Martin.

B161.   Schuh, Willi. "Drei Uraufführungen." Schweizerische Musikzeitung.
Revue musicale suisse 85 (1945): 83-86.

This is a review of three first performances presented by Paul
Sacher and the Collegium Musicum, Zürich, and the Baseler
Kammerorchester in which Frank Martin's Der Cornet is performed
along with Paul Müller's Sinfonia für Streichorchester and Willy
Burkhard's Violinkonzert. In this triple review, Der Cornet receives by
far the primary attention of the reviewer. The author pays tribute to
Paul Sacher for his musicianship, but especially for his role as catalyst
between composer and performer and listener. Similarly, he sees in
Frank Martin the ideal musical mind to set to music Rilke's prose
poem containing such widely contrasting elements as joy, sadness,
combat, festivity, love, and death in a rapidly changing sequence.
Great skill is required to devise a unified formal structure and to
create a vocal line that is sensitive to the meter of Rilke's verse. The
reviewer describes how Martin is able to achieve these ends in a
setting of twenty-three songs for alto voice, and the skillful but
restrained use of a chamber orchestra that both accompanies and at
times carries forward the action of the narrative. Professor Schuh
sees that Rilke's Cornet has gained by this musical setting from the
tension between the legendary distance of its historical narrative and
the eternal truths of human emotions that apply to this or any other
generation.

B162.   Snook, Paul. "Martin: Der Cornet - Ballad of the Love and Death of
Christophe Rilke." Fanfare 1 (May-June 1978): 57-59.

In reviewing the recording by Ursula Mayer-Reinach with the
composer conducting, the reviewer defines Martin's music as a blend
of Ravel and Schoenberg. Der Cornet along with the Jedermann
songs are seen as Martin's two vocal masterworks. Martin's refined
sensitivity to Rilke's text and his restrained use of a chamber
orchestra accompaniment enable him to make both dramatic and
musical sense of the prose poem using only a single soloist in a work
that seems to require larger musical resources. "In fact, it's not going
too far to assert that his music endows the story with a
persuasiveness, an emotional resonance, and a universality of
reference which enhance the power of the original text."

Drey Minnelieder

B163.   Klein, Rudolf. "Drey Minnelieder von Frank Martin." Österreichische
Musikzeitschrift 16 (October 1961): 492-493.

Written for the occasion of the Viennese premiere and performed
by Irmgard Seefried and Erik Werba, the Minnelieder is Frank Martin's
first composition following his Le Mystère de la Nativité for which the

composer had deliberately altered his style to create a simple and naive quality for the nativity play. In these songs of a middle-high German text, Martin succeeds in creating a setting that projects the listener into the Middle Ages, yet employs modern means to achieve it. "Martins Musik ist immer, und ganz besonders in diesen stillen Liedern, so erfunden, so erfühlt, sie kommt aus so reinen Empfindungsbezirken..." "Especially in these gentle songs, Martin's music is always so discovered, so felt, that it can only be understood by the listener from this level of sensitivity."

Et la vie l'emporta

B164.   Benary, Peter. "Frank Martin: 'Et la vie l'emporta.'" Schweizerische Musikzeitung. Revue musical suisse 115 (November-December 1975): 325.
        This is a review of the premiere of Martin's last musical work, the chamber cantata Et la vie l'emporta (see W141), conducted by Michel Corboz with soloists Claudine Perret, alto, and Philippe Huttenlocker, bass, with a small chorus and instrumental ensemble. The half-hour-long work is in three parts and begins with a text by Zundel. The middle movement is called Combat, which the composer adapted from the third verse of Luther's Christ lag in Todesbanden, but which is derived melodically from an old German song Der Grimanig Tod mit seinen Pfeil. A concluding Offrande is from a letter erroneously attributed to Fra Angelico. The composer uses the greatest economy in these settings both musically and in the small resources required to perform them. "Frank Martins Schwanengesang ist ein Bekenntniswerk, reich an klanglichen Schönheiten und überzeugend in seiner kompositorischen Faktur." "The Schwanengesang of Frank Martin is a work of confession, rich with beauty in sound and very convincing in its compositional structure."

B165.   Martin, Maria. "Genèse d'une cantate. Entstehung einer Kantate. Genesis of the chamber cantata <<Et la vie l'emporta>> (1974). Jacket notes for Erato ERA 9137.
        Reprinted in: A propos de ...commentaires de Frank Martin sur ses oeuvres, 234-237. Neuchâtel: A la Baconnière, 1984.
        In tri-lingual program notes for the 1975 recording of Et la vie l'emporta (see D79), Maria Martin describes the circumstances surrounding the composer's last composition. Inseparably linked to his final illness, the cantata on human suffering begins with a text by Maurice Zundel which was supplied with the commission and to which the composer added a section from Martin Luther set to a traditional German folk melody, and a final text from a letter wrongly attributed to Fra Angelico. Strongly motivated by the theme of human suffering and the beauty of the poetic texts with which he was working, the composer was able to overcome the obstacles of his failing health to bring the piece to near completion. Maria Martin concludes that "...we

can consider the end of 'Offering' as a last salutation from him to his fellow-men, the brethren whom he loved. He dedicated this prayer to them with all the warmth of his soul, pouring out in the music which bears it to them his art and all his love."

Erasmi monumentum

B166. Amerongen, Alex von. "Première Frank Martin bij Erasmusherdenking RPhO." NW. Rott. Courant 28 October 1969.
       In a newspaper account of the first performance of Erasmi monumentum performed by the Rotterdam Philharmonic, we learn that the composer was offered and accepted a commission to compose a work commemorating the five-hundredth anniversary of Erasmus only after two native Dutch composers had declined. In each of the three movements of the work for organ and large orchestra, Martin took a characteristic Erasmian viewpoint as a starting point in creating a work to pay homage musically to the memory of Erasmus. In the first section, "homo pro se" is depicted as a free-thinking individual who remains loyal to his principles against narrow-minded fanaticism and new ideas and behavior. Musically the role of the free man is assigned to the organ while the orchestra represents the antagonists. The second movement, a scherzo, represents ironic waggishness from "Laus stultiae" and, in the final section, the organ and orchestra represent peace and war respectively. This movement is drawn from Erasmus' "Querela pacis." The composer and performers were rewarded with a standing ovation at the conclusion of this unusual work.

B167. Werker, Gerard. "Erasmi monumentum." Mens en melodie 24 (December 1969): 379.
       In a review of the premiere of Martin's Erasmi monumentum, the piece is described as a symphonic triptych in which different aspects of Erasmus' personality are represented by musical symbols, rather than, as may have been expected, by a setting of selected passages set to music for voices. In the first section, "Homo pro se," we learn how Erasmus maintained control over his own personality in a confused society. The middle section is a scherzo reflecting good humor, while the final section, "Querela pacis," depicts Erasmus confronted with the conflicts of war and peace, violence and tolerance that ends in a chorale-like apotheosis. Uniquely, the organ becomes the voice of Erasmus in this occasional work to commemorate the five-hundredth anniversary of the birth of Erasmus in Rotterdam.

B168. Wolvekamp, W.H. "Feestconcert Rotterdams Philharmonish Orkest." Trouw [Amsterdam] 28 October 1969.
       Writing in an Amsterdam newspaper, the author describes the festival concert that took place in Rotterdam on the previous day as part of a celebration of the five-hundredth birthday of Erasmus. The

focal point of the program was the world premiere of a new work by Frank Martin especially commissioned for the event. Erasmi monumentum is scored for organ and large orchestra, and is in three movements each representing aspects of Erasmus' personality as reflected in his writings. In the first movement called "Homo pro se," or man for himself, the organ represents the man (Erasmus), and has an unchanging sound pattern. In the second, called "in praise of folly," the main theme is one of fun and humor and uses some special effects. The impressive third part, called "Querela pacis," or complaint of the peace, depicts the contradiction between war and peace and concludes with a chorale expressing the victory of peace. The concert featured Jean Fournet conducting the Rotterdam Philharmonic with the composer and many dignitaries in attendance. Strangely, the organist, Arie Keijzer, is not identified.

Etudes pour orchestre à cordes

B169. "Etudes for String Orchestra." BBC Symphony Program Notes (October 7, 1959): 7.
　　　　A concert at London's Royal Festival Hall was conducted by Ernest Ansermet. A brief raison d'etre is as follows: "The work...consists of an overture followed by four studies each of which sets a specific technical problem to test and exhibit the orchestra's virtuosity..."

B170. "Frank Martin, 'Etudes per orchestra d'archi, Universal-Edition, Wien." Rassegna musicale 28 (September 1958): 240.
　　　　This review is a response to the publication by Universal-Edition of Frank Martin's Etudes for String Orchestra. Despite the title, the reviewer finds these pieces to be didactic mainly in providing challenges for the composer to resolve, rather than being experimental in terms of extending the technical limitations of string players. The work consists of an introductory overture which introduces rhythmic elements of both a detached and a legato section which leads by extension to the first etude. The composer calls it "for the connection of links," in which a chromatic motif is passed back and forth between sections of the orchestra, a device that requires great skill and care to execute smoothly. Then follows a movement exploring every possible type of pizzicato. The third movement is an exercise in sustained legato playing by divided violas and cellos, after which the work concludes with a brief fugal study. Despite this description couched in technical terms, the composer has given both audiences and string players a pleasing, brilliant, and lively addition to the literature for string orchestra.

B171. Regamey, Constantin. "Etudes pour orchestre à cordes." In
Musiques du vingtième siècle Presentation de 80 oeuvres pour
orchestre de chambre, 166-168. Lausanne: Editions du Cervin,
1966.
In this essay, the author, after quoting briefly from the
composer's previously published program notes (see M17), examines
in some detail each of the four etudes that make up this work for
string orchestra. The author first makes the point that, unlike avant-
garde composers, Martin does not seek to enlarge to maximum the
spectrum of colors that the string instruments are capable of, but
rather is concerned with technical problems involving the collective
development of a string ensemble. The work then is examined in
terms of the technical problems which the composer has set forth for
the orchestra to resolve. The piece commences with an overture
whose main purpose is the expressive display of the orchestra playing
together, and whose thematic material leads into the first etude
subtitled "series of sketches." The challenge is the execution of a
rapid melodic line passed from one section of the orchestra to
another, which the composer calls "links." A second study explores
every possible variety of pizzicato playing within an ensemble. A third
study is for only violas and cellos divisi and is an exercise in
expressive intensity and legato ensemble playing. The final section is
a complex fugal study where several different kinds of music develop
simultaneously on various parallel levels and become a problem of
sonorous equilibrium between diverse elements. The work concludes
with a coda containing only perfect chords, a surprise element after
the polymodal complexities which have preceded it.

B172. Reich, Willi. "Ein neues Orchesterwerk von Frank Martin." Melos 24
(February 1957): 57-58.
Here is an enthusiastic review of the first performance by Paul
Sacher and his Basel Chamber Orchestra of Etudes for String
Orchestra (see W102) in which the composer's own description of the
piece is utilized. The four "studies," which follow an introductory
prelude for full orchestra, explore the "connection of links" or
transitions from one section of the orchestra to another, all possible
forms of pizzicato, "sostenuto" or sustained playing from divided violas
and cellos, and finally present a fugal study. The reviewer predicts
that the success of the premiere will lead to its rapid acceptance into
the repertoire worldwide.

B173. Wouters, Jos. "Frank Martin." [in Dutch] Preludium (April 1959): 121-
123.
One seldom encounters the word etude as a title in orchestral
concerts. The term traditionally is applied to study material not
usually heard outside the practice studio, and is always directed
toward gaining technical proficiency on a single instrument. Even the
concert etudes of Chopin, Liszt, and Debussy limit themselves to the
resources of the piano alone. By extension, Frank Martin, who by his

own admission found inspiration in musical problem solving, has enlarged the concept to embrace the resources of the modern string orchestra. In so doing, and again by his own admission, the composer has created a work which provided technical challenges for himself far more than enlarging the technical boundaries of string players. The work consists of an overture for the ensemble to sound together, and sets the stage for four challenging sections to follow. These consist of a movement of making smooth transitions within sections of the orchestra, a movement to exploit all means of pizzicato, a sostenuto exercise for divided lower strings, and a final fugal study. Once mastered, it is a pleasure for performers and listeners alike.

Fantaisie sur des rythmes flamenco

B174. Benary, Peter. "Internationale Musikfestwochen." Schweizerische Musikzeitung. Revue musicale suisse 114 (November-December 1974): 351-352.

This is a summary article of some of the events taking place at Luzerne's International Music Festival in which an afternoon program is devoted to music and a lecture by Frank Martin. The focal point of this program is a first performance of the composer's Fantaisie sur des rythmes flamenco (see W139), a solo piece for piano and flamenco dancer performed by pianist Paul Badura-Skoda and the composer's daughter Teresa Martin, a professional dancer. "Die Flamenco-Fantasien zeigten Martins Fähigkeit, rhythmische Vitalität und Einfallsfulle in die Tanztypen (Rumba u.a.) einzufügen. Klaviersatz mit iberischen Klangkolorit auf durchaus unbillige Art zu verbinden ..." "The Flamenco Fantasy shows Martin's ability to bring rhythmic vitality and a fullness of ideas into the dance types (rhumba and others), and to connect the piano part with Spanish sound color..."

Five Ariel Songs

B175. Geraedts, Jaap. "Shakespeares 'Storm' als opera Martins a.s. Wereldpremière." Haagse Post 14 January 1956.

Despite its title, this preview of Frank Martin's opera Der Sturm was written before the premiere and concerns itself primarily with the opera's antecedents. We learn that the composer's one Symphony was a first inspiration derived from Shakespeare's fantasy play, to be followed by the 5 Ariel Songs for a cappella choir. This, in turn, was followed by the Violin Concerto which uses a theme from and captures some of the mystery of the Ariel Songs. Each of the five songs which are incorporated into the opera with only slight modification is then described in some detail that relates the technical means employed to the poetic imagery of Shakespeare's text.

B176.   Haberlen, John B. "Conversations with Felix de Nobel." Choral
        Journal 17 (April 1977): 17-20.
            In an August interview conducted during the eighth Vienna
        Symposium for Choral Directors in 1976, the author elicits a list of
        favorite choral compositions from the now retired director of the
        Netherlands Chamber Choir. A discussion follows on Frank Martin's
        Ariel Songs. De Nobel describes how the Ariel Songs were written for
        his choir, and that he had exclusive performing rights to them for
        fifteen years. Most valuable, perhaps, is a description of differences
        between the manuscript and the version published fifteen years later.

Golgotha

B177.   Appia, Edmond. "Musical Life in Switzerland: a Study in Diverse
        Heritages." Musical America 69 (September 1949): 6.
            In an article which surveys the musical life of Switzerland,
        Martin's Golgotha is singled out for its distinction. Unlike the passion
        music of Bach and others, the figure of Christ is illuminated while all
        of the other participants remain in the background. "A work of
        magisterial scope, Golgotha is written in a style and language that are
        admirable for their originality and power, and contain many pages of
        altogether overwhelming beauty."

B178.   Baud-Bovy, Samuel. "Sur le Golgotha de Frank Martin."
        Schweizerische Musikzeitung. Revue musicale suisse 90 (1950):
        252-255.
            In writing about Golgotha, Baud-Bovy, who prepared and
        conducted the first performance, asserts that Martin himself should
        have written this article, and quotes a lengthy passage from Martin's
        essay Responsabilité du compositeur (see M31). Here the composer
        describes how the work came to be written, and his objectives in
        writing a passion for contemporary audiences. The remaining section
        succinctly describes with musical examples some of the technical
        devices employed in composing the work. The use of serial
        technique compares a passage in Golgotha with one in Petite
        symphonie concertante and shows how Martin uses it as the bass to
        a harmonic progression. A further example demonstrates the use of
        irregular rhythmic scheme based on early Bulgarian folksong, in which
        the composer skillfully combines archaism and modernism to create a
        language "without time." Finally, to the argument that the work lacks
        the unity and classical perfection of the Petite symphonie concertante,
        the answer lies in the setting of the text. This unity and cohesion is
        necessarily located outside of the music in the words which permit the
        work as a whole "...donner une expression nouvelle aux thèmes
        éternels de la mort, de l'amour, de la souffrance et de la joie." "...to
        give new expression to the eternal themes of death, love, suffering,
        and joy."

B179. Bruyr, Jose. "'Golgotha' de Frank Martin." Feuilles musicales 6 (November 1953): 173-175.

    In this essay, the Passion is seen as, not only dominating the liturgy from its beginnings, but dominating religion itself. From the fourth century the Passion was a part of the liturgy. From the twelfth century its dramatic characterizations were assigned to specific voices in plainsong. Its evolution led to settings by individual composers. The first important ones are credited to Heinrich Schütz. Passion motets followed in which the outstanding composers of the renaissance period enriched the musical settings of the passion. This movement culminated in the masterful settings of J.S. Bach. Following Bach, the genre of passion music waned, with a renewal of interest taking place in the twentieth century. In our own time, it is the Swiss Frank Martin who has re-interpreted musically the timeless passion of Christ for modern society. In so doing, Martin made some innovations. While the general outline of the Bach passion is retained, the composer prepared his own libretto from the gospel narratives, and created a commentary on the events of the passion by using texts from St Augustine's Confessions and his Meditations. These, in effect, replaced the chorale hymn tunes used by Bach in which the listeners were able to take an active part. In Martin's Golgotha, the entire work is both a meditation and a prayer. The listener's attention is focused entirely on the person of Jesus, but, unlike the passions of Bach, he is not asked to actively participate in the musical drama. The author concludes that "et le Golgotha de Frank Martin ou l'on entend s'arrêter le coeur d'un Dieu, est bien, tout compte fait, l'un des sommets de la musique de ce temps." "And the Golgotha of Frank Martin, where one hears the heart of a God stop beating, is eminently, when all is said and done, one of the summits of the music of this era."

B180. Cowell, Henry. "Current Chronicle." Musical Quarterly 38 (1952): 291-294.

    In reviewing the New York premiere of Golgotha, composer Henry Cowell finds the work "sufficiently impressive to belong among those few works deservedly called great." The author then demonstrates with musical examples how Martin's work can remain stylistically baroque while combining devices borrowed from Mozart and Beethoven in the treatment of his motifs and their extensions with some dissonances that clearly speak with a twentieth-century voice. The work is lacking a genuine fast movement. However, this is seen as only a minor flaw in a major work.

B181. D'Amico, Fedele. "F. Martin - 'Golgotha.'" IV Sagra musicale umbra [program notes] (September 29, 1949): 3-6.

    In an article ostensibly concerned with the passion oratorio Golgotha, the focus is much more on Martin the composer, and how the particular events of his environment and development have produced a work such as Golgotha. The author takes pains to review the events of Frank Martin's career, with particular emphasis on his slow and deliberate development from the musical world of César Franck to that of Schoenberg. The author believes that it is this long period of careful assimilation and patient experimentation, coupled with the composer's humility, that has led him away from the cult of personality. The author sees Martin's role as an attempt to define a general climate of European culture and civilization, "...l'esigenza di definire un generale clima di cultura e di civiltà, attentamente vagliato e investito da una segreta commozione umanistica." "...a climate that is attentively sifted or weighted and invested with a secret humanistic urgency." To make a critical judgment on either this particular work, or on Martin's output as a whole, is deemed to be premature. To attempt a modern setting of the passion by varied means that are simple enough for immediate comprehension, yet speak in the language of our time, is seen as a bold move by a composer in full control of his creative resources. Like Bach's Passions, the religious position of Golgotha is orthodox, i.e. the drama of the Passion is inseparable from its glorious resolution in the resurrection. Martin has once again demonstrated that he eschews the cult of anxiety to embrace the profession of hope and faith.

B182.   Gatti, Guido M. "Current Chronicle." Musical Quarterly 36 (January 1950): 129.
Frank Martin's passion oratorio, Golgotha, is a work which incorporates elements of nineteenth-century romanticism and the twentieth-century declamatory style of Debussy, and beyond, to create a piece that is free flowing throughout, achieving a synthesis of these musical elements to create a unique new setting of the passion.

B183.   "Golgotha." Musical Opinion 79 (January 1956): 199.
At the British premiere, conducted by Sir Malcolm Sargent with the BBC Chorus and Orchestra, this reviewer, while acknowledging high points of beauty and originality, finds the work as a whole lacking contrapuntal and rhythmic interest, with long and arid recitatives which fail to sustain the listener throughout the lengthy work.

B184.   Hutchinson, Robert Joseph, Jr. "Twentieth Century Settings of the Passion: an Opusculum on the Powerless God." Ph.D. diss., Washington University, 1976.
This dissertation examines, compares, and contrasts four passion settings written in the twentieth century. Selected for this study are Ernst Pepping's Passionsbericht des Matthäus (1950), Krzysztof Penderecki's St. Luke's Passion (1966), Max Baumann's Passion (1959), and Frank Martin's Golgotha (1945-48). The author presents this study in the context of the contemporary theological climate, and demonstrates how each composer's response to the passion

interacted with modern Biblical criticism and with his own personal experience to shape the form and substance of each of the four settings. The final chapter is devoted to the motivations of each of the composers to make a setting of the Passion, and some of the problems which they encountered.

B185.   Kolodin, Irving. "Music to My Ears. New Work of Martin...." Saturday Review 35 (February 2, 1952): 33.
The first performance in New York of Frank Martin's Golgotha by the Dessoff Choirs is seen as "a choral work in the line of Berlioz, Debussy, and Honegger, which will stand out as a landmark for a time of trifles." Strengths are perceived in the tonal organization of the solo, choral, and orchestral elements which are handled in a fresh and convincing manner. The work is also seen as having a certain static quality in its harmonic scheme, and a lack of contrapuntal texture. Additional performances are needed to arrive at a true evaluation of the work.

B186.   "Martin's Golgotha." Newsweek 39 (January 28, 1952): 86-87.
Following on the heels of New York premieres of the Petite symphonie concertante and the Concerto for Seven Wind Instruments, Tympani, Percussion and String Orchestra, Paul Boepple and his Dessoff Choirs presented the first American performance of the passion oratorio Golgotha. The large work, drawn from the Gospels and selected writings of St. Augustine, received a polite but cool response from New York critics. The exception was composer-critic Virgil Thomson who wrote that "Martin's Golgotha had a grandeur of dramatic expression rarely encountered in our century's composition for massed choral and orchestral affectives."

B187.   Melroy, Mardia. "Frank Martin's 'Golgotha.'" D.M.A. diss., University of Illinois, 1988.
Focusing on the passion oratorio, this thesis first discusses the composer and surveys his choral music as a whole. Golgotha is then examined in detail, followed by additional chapters containing an analysis of style and matters pertaining to performances, followed by a summary of the author's conclusions. A useful translation of Martin's important article, "Le compositeur moderne et les textes sacrés" (see M12), concludes the dissertation.

B188.   Meylan, Pierre. "Le 'Golgotha' de Frank Martin." La Revue internationale de musique 9 (1950-1951): 274-281.
The strengths and weaknesses of Martin's passion oratorio are examined sympathetically and in some detail in this extended critical-analytical essay. Martin had first to deal with the initial problem of preparing a text and choosing the direction and focus of both text and music. The composer chose to work from the gospel narratives and at the same time inserted meditative passages from St. Augustine, not unlike the passion music of Bach. Quite unlike Bach,

however, Martin chose to eliminate a part for most of the characters as well as for the narrator, focusing on the person of Jesus throughout. Proceeding section by section, the author finds the "Last Supper" section the least successful for lack of rhythmic variety, but praises other sections for their beauty and the unexpected originality of some parts, as, for example, the extreme simplicity with which he depicts the death of Christ. The author then examines the composer's compositional style with particular reference to his modified twelve-tone writing and the chromatic elements which are carefully understated in Golgotha. Overall, the work is remarkable for its synthesis of classical and modern expressive means, both vocally and instrumentally. Within the orchestral music are passages written in a style to remind one of Bach. Elsewhere there is a reminder of early organum, while in still other passages there are intervals and chords depicting the music of Debussy. Despite passages of rhythmical and even harmonic repetitiveness, Martin has fashioned a modern setting of the passion that reaches out to even non-initiated music listeners with extraordinary persuasive force. The author concludes that Martin's work "elle trancende la musique pour devenir un témoignage de piété et de foi dont la valeur universelle ne fait aucun doute." "...transcends music and becomes a testimony of piety and faith whose universal value exists without a doubt."

B189.   Moser, Hans Joachim. "Die Passion von Schütz bis Frank Martin." In Musikalische Formen in historischen Reihen, 16 (2-40).
Wolfenbüttel: Möseler, 1967.
   This anthology volume traces the development of passion music chronologically from its preliminary or pre-history period (1400-1650), particularly in Germany, to the major settings of Schütz and Bach, and continues on into the present century with Ernst Pepping and Frank Martin. Beginning with the Passion being chanted or intoned by the clergy, the form gradually developed in terms of the assignment of parts to other voices and to the use of polyphonic settings. In sixteenth-century practice, there was a dramaturgical-responsorial with choral-setting type and a motet-like through-composed type, sometimes in Latin, sometimes in German. Further development in the seventeenth century introduced the aria as employed by Bach and Handel with greater use of instrumental resources. In the twentieth century, Frank Martin's setting of the Passion entitled Golgotha is set in French and uses both the gospel narratives and contemplative passages from St. Augustine, which carries forward in time stylistic affinities with Heinrich Schütz's Cantiones Sacraes and the great passions of J.S. Bach. In Martin, the full resources of the modern orchestra and compositional devices ranging from twelve-tone elements to a repeated ostinato on B-A-C-H are used; yet the work relates in sound and form and creates a continuity with the great passion music of the past.

B190. Paap, Wouter. "'Golgotha,' oratorium van Frank Martin." <u>Mens en</u>
       <u>melodie</u> 13 (July 1958): 215-217.
       In writing about the Dutch premiere of <u>Golgotha</u>, the author
compares Frank Martin's inspiration from Rembrandt's etching "The
Three Crosses" with that of Honegger and Claudel responding to
wood engravings by Holbein. In describing the work, the author
emphasizes how the composer was able to combine the traditional
structure of the passion oratorio with some innovations that focus the
passion on the person of Christ with greater intensity by omitting or
reducing the characterization of other figures. The evangelist as
narrator is omitted, with this function assigned to soloists or choir.
Meditative sections as in the passions of Bach are drawn from
sources other than the gospel narrative, and in this instance Martin
uses passages from St. Augustine. The intensity of sorrowing
expressed here becomes one of the most moving parts of the score.
"Augustinus' Meditatie over het Goddelijk Lam, waarmede het eerste
deel besluit, is een van de diepstbespiegelende religieuze koorwerken
uit de hedendaagse muziekliteratuur, terwijl het tegelijkertijd sterk tot
de verbeelding spreekt." "Augustine's Meditations regarding the Holy
Lamb, with which the first part ends, is one of the most deeply
contemplative religious choral works from modern music literature."
The Holland premiere, although using a non-professional choir, was
able to overcome the considerable difficulties in learning this new
music, and to communicate in a way that left no doubt about the
success of this premiere. The author concludes that "Martin heeft met
zijn <u>Golgotha</u> een religieus kunstwerk van deze tijd geschapen, dat
met de schoonste muzikale Passievertolkingen uit het verleden op één
lijn geplaatst mag worden, en het behoeft geen betoog, dat alleen een
begenadigd kunstenaarschap hiertoe in staat is." "Martin has created
a religious work of art of this time with <u>Golgotha</u> that can be placed at
the same level as the most beautiful Passion-oratorios of the past."

B191. Robertson, Alec. "Golgotha." <u>BBC Symphony Concerts Programme</u>
       <u>notes</u>" (November 9, 1955).
       In program notes for the British premiere of <u>Golgotha</u> presented
by Sir Malcolm Sargent conducting the BBC Orchestra and Chorus
and sung in an English translation by Basil Douglas, the author
surveys succinctly Frank Martin's development as a composer with
particular notice given to his earlier vocal works and to the unique
way in which he has utilized elements of the twelve-tone system while
retaining a link with traditional tonality. In this modern setting of the
Passion, Martin uses passages from St. Augustine's <u>Confessions</u> and
from his <u>Meditations</u>, in addition to the gospel narrative. He does not,
however, follow the pattern of the great Lutheran passions of Bach
and others except in the overall outline. The role of the evangelist is
omitted. Instead, the gospel narratives are entrusted to various
soloists and sometimes to the low voices of the chorus. Then follows
an explication of each numbered section that includes the text and
sometimes a musical incipit in which both the action of the passion

drama and a description of some of the musical devices used to
achieve the desired result are included.

B192. Rochester, Mark. "Frank Martin at Golgotha. Frank Martin's
compositional technique as shown by his passion oratorio,
Golgotha." Master's thesis, University of Wales, 1976.
　　This examination of Golgotha, organized under the broad
headings of Frank Martin, the man and his music, explores the
background and structure of the passion, and Martin's approach to
making a modern setting. Then follows a detailed analytic description
of the harmonic and thematic elements, and how they are employed
in this modern passion setting.

B193. Rostand, Claude. "'Golgotha,' oratorio de Frank Martin." Contrepoints
No. 6 (1949): 161-164.
　　In an article addressed to French readers, the author states that
Frank Martin's music is not well-known in France due partly to the
misconception that his writing is difficult and impenetrable. This is
viewed as particularly unfortunate in that among twentieth-century
composers Martin's inspiration and the technical means which he
employs are direct, natural, and speak to the heart. Golgotha is seen
as a culmination of a long evolutionary stylistic search, in which the
composer has not so much sought a goal, but rather sought the
means to achieve his goal. The oratorio consists of two parts divided
into ten sections. The author describes each section pointing out its
strengths and the structural unity of the work section by section. In
conclusion, Golgotha is seen as avoiding the common pitfalls
associated with passion music, that is, wordy and noisy emptiness
that fails to communicate. In Martin's passion "La declamation y est
presque toujours traitée avec un sens profond de la langue, et les
couleurs, tant harmoniques qu'instrumentales, utilisées avec une
remarquable économie pour un rendement maximum, y sont d'une
invention et d'une subtilité prodigieuses." "There is always a profound
sense of language in this work, and the colors, harmonic and
instrumental, which are utilized in a very economical way and yet
render the maximum, constitute a prodigious subtlety and creativity."

B194. Schuh, Willi. "Frank Martin 'Golgotha.'" [in German] In Von neuer
Musik Konzert und Opernwerke Musikfeste, Personlichkeiten, 55-57.
Zürich: Atlantis Verlag, 1955.
　　Writing in 1950, Professor Schuh pays tribute to Frank Martin as
a master having both spirituality and the humanity to successfully
create, in the shadow of J.S. Bach, a new setting of the Passion
capable of engaging the interest of professional musicians, and, at the
same time, become a deeply moving musical experience to any
sensitive listener. In this concentrated presentation of the passion
story, the composer focuses entirely on Jesus, and, unlike Bach's
passions, does not develop other characters. Of especial interest is
the unifying force of the final chorus in each of the two parts. The

first concludes with a stirring chorus of sinners, while the finale, beginning with the homophonic cry "O death where is thy sting?," develops a powerful polyphonic gloria concluding finally with "essential and sovereign light" from the Exsultet (office of Holy Saturday).

B195.   Stuckenschmitt, H.H.   "Zürich Honors Anniversary of Swiss Tonkünstlerverein."   Music America 70 (October 1950): 10.

Sharing an oratorio program with Willy Burkhard, Frank Martin's Golgotha is presented in Zürich in a program commemorating the fiftieth anniversary of the Schweizerische Tonkunstlerverein. Contrasted to the passions of Bach, Martin's Golgotha is a dramatic presentation rather than an epic one and "a modern branch grafted onto the tree of nineteenth-century romantic religious music."

B196.   Tappolet, Willy.   "Golgotha oratorio de Frank Martin."   Schweizerische Musikzeitung. Revue musicale suisse 89 (1949): 262-263.

The essay is both a response to, and an explanation of, the facts surrounding the composition of Golgotha. It is also an enthusiastic review of the premiere. Again referring to the composer's own comments (see M22) about the circumstances and motivation in writing a modern passion, the author further compares and contrasts the work to the Passions of J.S. Bach. While similar in overall layout, that is the alternation of airs, texts, and choruses, Martin eliminates the role of the evangelist, creating an extremely concentrated version that focuses almost completely on the person of Christ, the only part to have a distinct sung role. The musical elements of Golgotha incorporate all of the technical devices that Martin has used in his previous works, and skillfully blends new sounds and harmonies with archaic musical devices to create his unique and powerful work. The author praises the first performance and scolds the audiences of Geneva for their lack of interest in a native son.

B197.   Terzian, Alicia.   "Frank Martin: 'Golgotha.'"   [In spanish] Teatro Colon (October 14, 1968).

In the program notes for performances in Buenos Aires of Golgotha conducted by Wilhelm Brückner-Rüggeberg, and assisted by the composer who journeyed to Argentina to participate, the author describes the evolution of the tonal function in music through the nineteenth century and its gradual expansion through greater chromatic freedom that led eventually to its collapse into atonality and the development of serialism. Frank Martin's own search for a personal style is described through quotations from his articles and essays in which he traces his development that is strongly influenced by the harmonic language of César Franck, through a style period of only diatonic writing, to more dissonant and rhythmically complex writing, and finally to the twelve-tone system. From this point there remained only to re-introduce tonal elements in combination with the new-found freedoms achieved through serial techniques, that made it possible for the composer to discover his unique musical voice.

Following a summary outline of Martin's composing career, the article concludes with a brief section-by-section description of the passion oratorio for the benefit of listeners hearing the work for the first time.

B198.   Thomson, Virgil. "Dessoff Choirs." New York Herald Tribune 19 January 1952.

Composer-critic Virgil Thomson, along with fellow composer Henry Cowell (see B180), is altogether more enthusiastic about the New York premiere of Frank Martin's oratorio Golgotha than most of the remaining New York critics. Thomson found in the work, after a tentative beginning, that "from there to the end, its varied musical invention and expressive emotional content seemed inexhaustible, unendingly powerful, and fresh." The author sees in Frank Martin a composer with a real gift for the stage and an uncommon skill in setting words to music. Both oratorio and opera seem to be genre that Martin's gifts are especially well suited for.

B199.   Winkler, Gerhard E. "Frank Martin: 'Golgotha.'" Salzburger Festspiele 1986 (August 11, 1986).

Writing in the program notes for the 1986 Salzburg Music Festival, the author states that Switzerland's neutrality has stimulated the development of a rich choral culture after World War II, and that some of the most important twentieth-century oratorios were produced there. The most important of these choral composers was Frank Martin, whose In terra pax was actually commissioned to be performed on armistice day (1945). Following this came the passion oratorio Golgotha in which the composer, inspired by Rembrandt's etching, The Three Crosses, created a new setting of the passion that speaks in a twentieth-century voice, but maintains a strict simplicity in its scoring that lets its powerful choruses and long meditative sections reach out to a general audience. Two main features become evident in this work: the importance of harmony over melody, and the carrying role of the rhythm. All of Golgotha is characterized by chromatic successions of melodies and triads demonstrating Martin's unusual way of employing twelve-tone techniques within a tonal framework. The two central parts of the work are the crucifixion scene, with its somber homophonic minor chords, and the Last Supper, which employs major chords throughout. Unlike traditional settings of the Passion, Golgotha spans the week from Palm Sunday to Easter evening in order to bring the allegory of pure light to its highest peak.

B200.   Zwol, Cornelis van. "'Golgotha' oratorium van Frank Martin." [in Dutch] N.C.V.R. - Gids [Hilversum] (21 March 1970.)

Writing in the radio guide publication for Dutch radio, the author describes an interview with Frank Martin in which his wife Maria Martin, a native of Holland, acted as interpreter and conversation partner. At this event it was announced that the passion oratorio Golgotha had been recorded and that it had been awarded the Grand

Prix. The author borrows from Martin's previously published comments on his own approach to writing sacred music in which he acknowledges the direct inspiration and impetus he had received from Rembrandt's etching, the Three Crosses. In conclusion Martin observes that the Three Crosses is probably Rembrandt's strongest work, while similarly the author asserts that Golgotha is probably Martin's strongest work. The composer has composed music of his own time for a setting of the timeless Passion in a manner that links it with Schütz's Kleine geistliche Konzerte and the passion music of J. S. Bach.

Huit préludes pour le piano

B201. Billeter, Bernhard. "Die <<8 Préludes>> für Klavier." In Frank Martin ein Aussenseiter der neuen Musik. Frauenfeld: Huber, 1970 130-133.

In his important analytical book (see B14), Professor Billeter describes Martin as a remarkable pianist who contributed much to the musical life of Switzerland through his performances of chamber music and by recitals with cellist Henri Honegger and others. At the same time, Martin always used the piano not only for its own unique expressive purposes but also as part of a larger musical statement in other works, rather than in composing works for his own performance. Contained in the Preludes is a summary of all of the technical and expressive devices that appear in his mature works. This includes the use of unusual combinations of triads as in the Second Prelude; the B-A-C-H motif in the eighth Prelude and elsewhere; a relationship to Chopin's Second Prelude in Martin's third; rhythmic counterpoint in the fourth Prelude with rhythmic figures borrowed from outside of the western musical tradition, and, finally, a contrasting canon in the sixth Prelude employing chromatics and narrow tone sequences. The piece concludes with a rousing virtuosic rondo.

B202. Burge, David. "Contemporary Piano: Frank Martin's Eight Preludes." Contemporary Keyboard 6 (March 1950): 58, 60.

In a succinct article complete with musical examples, composer-pianist David Burge makes a compelling case for Frank Martin's Huit préludes. Here he discusses the elements of metric rhythm, ostinato, and formal structure, and he comments on each prelude in turn. "These pieces skillfully embody all of his thought concerning the musical, stylistic, and technical possibilities of the piano. The variety of moods and striking timbral contrasts make the twenty-minute set attractive for both performer and listener."

B203.   Corleonis, Adrian. Jacket notes. Veronica Jochum, pianist. <u>Eight</u>
         <u>Preludes</u> by Frank Martin and <u>Seven Short Pieces for the</u>
         <u>Cultivation of Polyphonic Playing</u> by Ferruccio Busoni. Laurel LR-
         135, 1986.
             In program notes for keyboard works by Martin and Busoni (see
         D119), the similarities of the two composers whose lives are separated
         by only a generation are clearly focused. Both men were influenced
         in a major and lifelong way by the music of Bach; both maintained a
         spiritual conception of art; both maintained an integrity that required
         many years to reach their ultimate mature style; and, in addition, both
         composers achieved a certain success in reconciling Germanic and
         Latin elements in their music, while each felt the heavy responsibility of
         maintaining a continuity with past European history and a need to be
         a vital link in its perpetuation. Martin's <u>Huit préludes</u> in their brevity
         tend to obscure the extraordinary wealth of invention invested in each
         of them. The author briefly describes each Prelude analytically, and
         concludes by a similar description of each of the Busoni pieces.

B204.   Grier, Christopher. "<u>Edinburgh International Festival Program</u>" (August
         25, 1971).
             In a recital which also includes Mozart's <u>F Major Sonata, K.332</u>
         and Beethoven's <u>Op. 111 Sonata</u>, Claude Frank performed the <u>Eight</u>
         <u>Preludes</u> of Frank Martin. Asserting that pianists like to play them and
         that audiences like to hear them, the author explains: "because they
         reflect a subtle and civilized creative mind, one which sensitively
         balances the past and the present and which demonstratively relishes
         the sound of the piano. ...each [prelude] of which possesses a
         special flavour, deriving from rhythmic, melodic or harmonic properties
         stressed throughout its length."

B205.   Simmons, Walter. "Eight Preludes." <u>Fanfare</u> 8 (May-June 1985): 243-
         244.
             In a review of Martin's <u>Huit préludes</u> by pianist Yolanda Liepa,
         the author in fact compares her performance with that of five others
         including a reading by the composer (see D105) in which he finds no
         recording without shortcomings, but ranks Ms. Liepa at the top of the
         list. The curious history of the now forty-year-old <u>Preludes</u> (which
         were written for, but never performed by Dinu Lipatti) is that over the
         years, there have been over a dozen recordings by as many pianists,
         but that they remain uncommon on recital programs. Despite this
         lack of general acceptance, "the <u>Eight Preludes</u> are enormously varied
         in mood, texture, and technical requirements, while they are unified by
         subtle motivic relationships."

B206.   Tanner, André. "Les Préludes pour piano de Frank Martin." <u>Feuilles</u>
         <u>musicales</u> 3 (1950): 60-61.
             The <u>Huit préludes</u> were written for the celebrated pianist Dinu
         Lipatti, whose failing health and untimely death prevented his ever
         performing them publicly. In this commentary, prepared for Radio

Lausanne to accompany a broadcast performance by Denise Bidal who gave the first performance of the work, the author indicates that the Preludes are of particular interest for being the composer's first major work for solo piano. The author sees a difficulty for the listener in hearing a new work in that one's pleasure in listening is derived partly from allusionary value, which one derives from prior associations with familiar music. In hearing a Prelude by Bach, the listener can relate to the music of the Passions, while a Debussy Prelude alludes to the sound world of Pelléas. In Frank Martin's Preludes the allusion is derived from the sound world of the Petite symphonie concertante and works which followed. The Preludes are seen as a near perfect balance of the basic elements of melody, harmony, and rhythm. In so doing the composer can introduce new and attractive rhythms while maintaining rich and expressive harmony. These Preludes are perceived as a latter-day return to romantic expressiveness in keyboard writing, largely abandoned by Stravinsky, Bartók, Hindemith, and other twentieth-century masters. The composer has achieved this by successfully combining elements of both Germanic and French musical cultures.

In terra pax

B207. "In terra pax Frank Martins Oratorium in Zürich." Neue Züricher Zeitung (December 27-28, 1980): 47.

A revival of In terra pax on a Christmas-time concert was performed by Edmund de Stoutz conducting the Zürich Chamber Orchestra and Chorus. The oratorio, composed as a work to be performed on the armistice day of World War II, uses a text drawn from the Old and New Testaments. In this performance, Bach's one-movement choral cantata no. 50, Nun ist das Heil und die Kraft, is inserted after the second part of Martin's oratorio. The reviewer, while recognizing the complementary nature of the two works, still feels that the music of In terra pax is better served by being uninterrupted in its natural flow. The selection of soloists and the carefully prepared performance are deemed to be outstanding.

B208. Klein, Rudolf. "Frank Martin und sein Oratorium 'In Terra Pax.'" [program notes] 2. Jugend Konzert der Münchner Philharmoniker (December 6, 1979): 4-8.

In program notes for a performance of In terra pax, a portion of the author's monograph, Frank Martin, sein Leben und Werk, is used (see B64). This, in turn, draws from Martin's own writing in which some of the topics the composer often addresses are quoted or summarized: What is meant by "understanding" a piece of music; the difficulty for audiences in comprehending a new piece of music; the importance of using musical settings of words as a bridge to assist the listener; and, finally, Martin's attitude toward writing religious music. It was the strong conviction of the composer that, in addition to reaching an audience through words, a sacred text needs a collective character. Because modern society is not built on a religious base of at least general agreement, it is no longer possible to compose such a work in our time. This impasse was resolved by the unique circumstances of a radio commission to compose a work for the armistice of World War II. Here, at last, in response to the tragic war was a unique moment of religious collective consciousness, which swept away all religious differences and provided the composer the opportunity he needed. The work itself divides into four sections, and the writing strives for a simplicity aimed at attracting the largest possible audience. The article concludes with a summary of some of the musical devices that Martin used to achieve this objective.

B209.   Mila, Massimo. "In terra pax di Frank Martin." Rassegna musicale 28 (March 1958): 41-42.

In writing about a performance of In terra pax in Torino some thirteen years after its premiere, the author finds much to admire in the short oratorio written to commemorate the termination of World War II. He is particularly impressed by the clarity and structural divisions of the work in which the composer strived to compose music that would be easily comprehended by the largest possible audience. The four Biblical sections depict war and divine anger, petitions for forgiveness, Christ's passion and redemption, and, finally, divine peace. The work achieves these ends by a variety of skillful means including the use of unison choruses as well as more complex double chorus, canon, and even twelve-tone elements in a passacaglia passage which begins part three. In terra pax is a clearly defined and noble work, free from the atmosphere of French impressionism, which can be heard in other works by this composer, and which speaks in a language that is contemporary but not avant-garde.

B210.   Paap, Wouter. "Groningen: Het oratorium In terra pax." Mens en melodie 17 (1962): 225-226.

Commissioned by Radio Genève as an oratorio to be performed on the armistice day of World War II, this "occasional piece" was broadcast over all Swiss radio stations on May 7, 1945. Using a text drawn from both the Old and New Testaments, Martin composed a work for five soloists, chorus and orchestra lasting about forty-five minutes. In terra pax is divided into four sections: the first deals with humanity's dark and warlike nature; the second deals with guilt; a third section introduces the figure of Christ; and a concluding section calls for a new earth with lasting peace. The reviewer has high praise for both the deeply spiritual composition and for the performing forces at Groningen under conductor Charles de Wolff.

B211.   Paychère, Albert. "In terra pax, oratorio breve de Frank Martin."
Schweizerische Musikzeitung. Revue musicale suisse 85 (1945):
272-273.

Albert Paychère describes how In terra pax came to be written
as a commission from Radio Genève to commemorate the end of
World War II with a work of serious artistic value to be performed on
the day of the armistice. Frank Martin put aside other composing
projects and devoted himself to writing an oratorio worthy of this great
solemn but rejoicing occasion. Using texts from the Old and New
Testaments, the work divides into four complete sections in which are
depicted the pain and horrors of war, followed by petitions that ask
for mercy. A third section is the annunciation of Him whose life and
death would redeem sins. Finally, there is an invocation of a new city
where mourning and suffering will be abolished. The work ends on a
Sanctus. Using the traditional resources of oratorio: vocal soloists,
mixed chorus, and small orchestra, the composer uses a wide variety
of musical devices ranging from chorus in unison to complex
polyphony, the use of consonant chords, elements of twelve-tone
writing, and regular and irregular canon, all of which produce a unified
whole. "Dans la forte unité du style, tout s'ordonne en une admirable
variété de formes, témoignage d'imagination et de totale maîtrise du
musicien." "In the strong unity of style, all is ordered in an admirable
variety of forms, testimony of imagination and of total mastery by the
musician."

B212.   Shigihara, Susanne. "In terra pax Anmerkungen zu Frank Martins
Oratorium." Beiträge zur Geschichte des Oratoriums seit Händel.
Festschrift Günther Massenkeil zum 60. Geburtstag, 514-532. Bonn,
Voggenreiter Verlag, 1986.

This is an extended analytical essay on Frank Martin's In terra
pax in which the unique circumstances of its composition as a work
to celebrate the end of World War II are briefly summarized. Martin's
extraordinary sensitivity to language and his profound respect for the
literary texts which he chooses to set to music preclude any
significant alterations on his part. He did, however, devise means of
shortening passages to solve problems resulting from a strict
adherence to the text. The author identifies several such text
alterations which the composer employed in adapting various
passages from the Bible to form a cohesive work. These consist of
single words or phrases altered for rhythmic purposes or to identify
with the ending of the war, or yet to achieve greater precision and
finally to produce a text which conveys the message he wished to
express, i.e. the portrayal of war and the joy which an end to
hostilities produces, coupled with the necessity of forgiveness among
nations as well as individuals, without which true peace can never be
achieved. Unlike the musical setting of a finished literary work of
recognized high quality, In terra pax posed unique problems. The
composer needed to fashion a text drawn from the Bible in which no
single continuous text was suitable. As a commission for Radio

Geneva it needed to be confined to about forty-five minutes. The composer felt strongly the need to create a work accessible to the largest possible audience of listeners, not just veteran concertgoers. He achieved this with melodic unison choruses and familiar passages of scripture, while at the same time he produced a work of complex formal structure in which the four parts of the work have a unifying and interrelated structure of three sections superimposed over the four which the author describes in detail with musical and textural examples. "Zu bedauern ist nur, dass 'In terra pax,' weder von seiner inhaltlichen Aussage noch von seiner musikalischen Ausstrahlungskraft her veraltet, in unseren Konzertprogrammen nicht längst heimisch geworden ist." "It is only regrettable that In terra pax, obsolete neither in its content message nor in its musical charisma, has not yet become a part of our regular concert programs."

B213.   Webster, Elizabeth. "New Paths for the Three Choirs. Music and Musicians 9 (November): 11.
         Britain's famous Three Choirs Festival (Worchester, Gloucester and Hereford cathedrals) inaugurates the 1960 season with new and unfamiliar works which include Frank Martin's In terra pax, a work commissioned to be performed on the actual armistice day of World War II. The reviewer finds the piece disappointing with a sparsity of actual choral writing, a clumsy text, and a sense of prevailing gloom.

Inter arma caritas

B214.   Ehinger, Hans. "Für das Rotz Kreuz komponiert." Neue Zeitschrift für Musik 124 (December 1963): 491.
         This is a brief review of a program commemorating the centenary of the International Red Cross in which three especially commissioned pieces are performed for the first time in a performance conducted by Ernest Ansermet. Opening the program was an eight-minute work, Inter arma caritas by Frank Martin. Then followed Benjamin Britten's Cantata misericordium, and the concluding work was Postludes by Witold Lutoslawski. Martin's brief orchestral score begins with warlike sounds that gradually resolve into a forgiving mood and finally a sublime mood.

B215.   Schule, Bernard. "Zeitgenossische Musik im Dienst des Roten Kreuzes." Schweizerische Musikzeitung. Revue musicale suisse 103 (1963): 302.
         Here is a review of three musical compositions written for and presented at the festivities commemorating the centennial of the International Red Cross. Along with Benjamin Britten's Cantata misericordium and Witold Lutoslawski's Three Postludes, Frank Martin's Inter arma caritas received its first performance. The short symphonic poem for full orchestra depicted musically the horrors of war; then in a separate section for strings, pain and mourning were

expressed; and, finally, there emerges a chorale leading to a victorious finale.

Maria-Triptychon

B216. Delden, Lex van. "Martins drieluik: grote natuurlijkheid." Parool [Amsterdam] 25 February 1971.
        Composer-critic van Delden finds both Martin's new work Maria-Triptychon in its Amsterdam premiere, and the composer himself to be endowed with "grote natuurlijkheid" "great or direct naturalness." The piece was commissioned by soprano Irmgard Seefried and her husband, violinist Wolfgang Schneiderhan. It consists of three Marian anthems: "Ave Maria" and "Magnificat" both sung in German to the text of Luther's Bible, and the first half of the "Stabat Mater" sung in the original Latin. The elegiac lyricism of the "Ave Maria" is followed by the less successful "Magnificat," that retains much of the elegiac quality established in the "Ave Maria." In the concluding "Stabat Mater," the sorrowful drama steadily increases to achieve a march-like quality of exceptional expressive impact, highlighted by the orchestra's ability to convey the "whiplashing" that is mentioned in the seventh verse (tercet) of the text. Elements of the harmonic language also remind the listener of Martin's earlier Jedermann Monologues.

B217. "Frank Martin: 'Magnificat.'" Schweizerische Musikzeitung. Revue musicale suisse 108 (September-October, 1968): 342.
        This brief review is also an analysis of the premiere of Magnificat which was soon to become the middle section of Maria-Triptychon, the final version of this work. The reviewer describes how the composer required a number of years to find a text which met the unusual requirement of a work for soprano and solo violin. Finally, using the Biblical translation of Luther, he chose the Marian anthem which permits the violin to be heard as an alter ego to the human voice. A description of some of the technical devices used concludes the article.

B218. Pijnenburg, Piet. "Maria-triptiek oogst ovatie." Volkskrant [Amsterdam] 25 February 1971.
        A brief review of Maria-Triptychon in its Amsterdam premiere identifies the two artists who commissioned the work, soprano Irmgard Seefried and her husband, violinist Wolfgang Schneiderhan, who perform with Eugen Jochum conducting the Concertgebouw Orchestra. The reviewer admires the contrast between the "Ave Maria" and "Magnificat" movements, but finds the middle movement to be of lesser inspiration than the two outer sections. Both soloists and the new composition were warmly received by the public.

B219.   Vranken, Toon. " 'Maria-triptiek' fraaie muziek van Martin." De Tijd
[Amsterdam] 25 February 1971.
In a newspaper review entitled "Maria Triptychon, beautiful music
by Martin," the author explains the origin of this work as a commission
by Viennese soprano Irmgard Seefried and violinist Wolfgang
Schneiderhan for the Magnificat alone, which they premiered in 1968.
The composer later agreed to make this the center of a triptych.
Although the author finds it strange to have two sections in the
German language while the "Stabat Mater" remains in the original
Latin, he nevertheless finds the song with violin obligato score
fascinating, and the music and inspiration of Frank Martin strong. The
performance by the artists for whom it was written, with guest
conductor Eugen Jochum leading the Concertgebouw Orchestra,
proved to be an outstanding occasion of "beautiful music by Martin."

Messe

B220.   Brevet, Françoise Pulfer. "Frank Martin et sa 'Messe pour double
choeur.'" Ecole Normale de Lausanne, 1979. See: B223

B221.   Glassman, Robert V. Jr. "À Choral Conductor's Analysis for
Performance of 'Messe pour double choeur a cappella' by Frank
Martin." D.M.A. University of Wisconsin, Madison, 1987.
Here is, perhaps, the first English language doctoral analysis of
the early Mass which has previously been more often performed, but
less often written about than many other works by Martin. Included
here, in addition to a section on analysis, is a summary of the unusual
background of the Mass, along with an examination of Martin's
attitude toward writing music to sacred texts.

B222.   Hager, Adr. "Bureaubade van Martin na veertig jaar geopend." Trouw
[Amsterdam] June 25, 1973.
In a concert presented by two of Holland's finest choirs, the
Nederlands Kamerkoor and the NCRV Vocal Ensemble, conducted by
Marinus Voorberg, the focal point of the evening is the 1922-26 Mass
by Frank Martin. The composer, then a permanent resident in
Holland, attended the concert and is quoted as hoping that the fifty-
year-old work may offer something convincing and beautiful. The
reviewer believes that Martin has succeeded in producing a work of
"...is van een aangrijpende melodische schoonheid, zeer ingetogen en
overwegend gedragen van karacter, met een verfijnde klankkleur, die
zo typerend is voor het werk van Martin." "...gripping melodic beauty,
very introverted and heavy of character, with a refined tone color
typical of Martin's works."

B223. Henke, Rosel-Maria. "Frank Martin und seine 'Messe für zwei
vierstimmige Chöre a cappella (1922).'" Staatlichen Prüfung für
Musikschullehrer und Selbständige Musiklehrer. Köln, 1978.
Here are included a group of formal papers in French, German,
and Dutch that are included to remind English-speaking readers of the
fact that while not often cited nor easy to obtain, these research
documents do exist and should not be overlooked. The subject areas
are usually identified by title. See: B52, B76, B156, B220, B260, B285,
and B310

B224. Strategier, Herman. "Frank Martin: mis voor twee gemengde koren."
Gregoriusblad 99 (March 1975): 6-10.
In this article, the curious history of Martin's Mass is described
both by the author and with quotations from a letter on this subject
from Maria Martin, widow of the composer. The unknown,
unperformed, and unpublished Mass completed in 1926 was finally
premiered in Hamburg in 1963 by Franz Brunnert, conducting the
Bugenhagen-Kantorei (see W14). It was a performance in 1970 that
led to publication by Bärenreiter in 1972, some fifty years after the
work was completed. Madame Martin explains that for many years
Frank Martin considered his religious compositions too personal to be
judged on purely aesthetic grounds and chose to consider them as
being only between God and himself. This impasse in the
composition of sacred works was finally resolved by the need for a
work to celebrate the end of World War II, and Martin's belief that only
a text from the Bible on the theme of forgiveness could meet this
need. Subsequently, several large choral-orchestral works on sacred
texts occupied the composer for many years. The article concludes
with musical examples that demonstrate homophonic and polyphonic
passages and the way they trade off on various phrases. The author
concludes that this work represents a high point in musical settings of
the mass in the twentieth century, and that for the listener it contains
its own stylistic unity despite the time lapse in its actual composition.

B225. Vantine, Bruce Lynn. "Four Twentieth-Century Masses: an analytical
comparison of style and compositional technique." D.M.A. diss.,
University of Illinois, 1982.
The author presents an examination of masses by Frank Martin,
Poulenc, Stravinsky, and Hindemith, all of whom at some point in their
composing career were associated with the designation neo-classicist.
He compares and contrasts the four settings and explores the
difficulties each composer experienced in seeking new expressive
means.

Monsieur de Pourceaugnac

B226. Ehinger, Hans. "Frank Martins heitere Oper nach Molière." Zeitschrift
        für Musik 124 (June 1963): 243.
        In an enthusiastic review of Frank Martin's operatic setting of
        Molière's Monsieur de Pourceaugnac, the reviewer observes that one
        thinks of Frank Martin as the very serious composer of religious
        oratorios and vocal works concerned with death. Looking back in
        Martin's composing career, however, one finds his first opera on
        Shakespeare's Tempest which contains elements of both comedy and
        farce. Many years earlier there was the theatre piece La Nique à
        Satan. The difficult task of setting Moliere to music is seen to have
        been achieved by a skillful combination of singing, both recitative and
        aria, with passages of spoken dialogue alone and utilizing a small
        orchestra with important parts for piano and harpsichord. Although
        the play has been shortened somewhat, the text remains absolutely
        faithful to Moliere throughout. A unique aspect of Martin's opera is
        that it demands singers who are good actors and that have good
        speaking voices. The premiere on April 23, 1963 (see W114) enjoyed
        a grand success.

B227. Helm, Everett. "A self-mocking opera by Martin." New York Times
        112 (June 30, 1963): 9.
        Molière's farce, Monsieur de Pourceaugnac as set to music by
        Frank Martin, was presented at the 1963 Holland Festival. The
        composer has stated that his attraction to the play was an urge to
        explore his own comic talents utilizing even the most serious aspects
        of his composing style in a form of self-mockery. "Despite a high
        level of performance and frequent audience-pleasing comedy scenes,
        the music becomes a deterrent, slowing down and complicating the
        story, and is without any great distinction in itself."

B228. Lüttwitz, Heinrich von. "Frank Martin und der Baron Ochs." Musica
        (1964): 75-76.
        In a review of the German premiere of Frank Martin's opera
        Monsieur de Pourceaugnac presented at Duisburg, the reviewer finds
        it not equal to previous presentations in Geneva and Amsterdam.
        There is a striking plot similarity between Molière's play and Richard
        Strauss's opera, Der Rosenkavalier, in which the rich elder is thwarted
        in his attempt to marry the youthful heroine by means of skillful
        intrigues, and the young lovers are finally united at the happy ending.
        The reviewer finds the work lacking in humor and fantasy and objects
        to such a variety of effects as an Alpine yodeler or familiar tunes such
        as Funiculi-funicula. He further finds a lack of antic give-and-take
        especially at the finale. Despite these reservations, the production
        and performances were skillfully done with generous applause for the
        composer who was present, as well as for the participants.

B229.   Neukirchen, Alfons. "Duisburg." Opera 15 (April 1964): 261-262.
The first German production of Monsieur de Pourceaugnac
proved to be a disappointment despite what the reviewer calls
"graceful and charming music which mirrors the pattern of speech,
and in turn leads to a high-spirited, richly interwoven contrapuntal
finale." The failure is perceived to lie in the loss of "tempo" of the play
when adapted to singing, and to elements of Molière's play such as
scorn and malicious hostility which could only be adequately
conveyed by inflections of the speaking voice.

B230.   Posthuma, Klaas. "Holland: June 15-August 15. Monsieur De
Pourceaugnac." Opera 14 (October): 81-82.
The world premiere of Frank Martin's opera on Molière's
Monsieur de Pourceaugnac on June 15, 1963 (see W114) received a
cautiously positive review. The author sees Martin's music as
"disappearing into the background most of the time," and believes that
the music becomes an element to make comprehension of Molière's
French more difficult. An outstanding cast of singing actors and
Molière's comedy bring the evening to a successful conclusion.

B231.   Sénéchaud, Marcel. "Switzerland: Molière to Music." Opera 14
(August 1963): 546-547.
In this brief review, the author summarizes the lack of success
by various composers in operatic settings of Molière. Similarly he
finds Martin's Monsieur de Pourceaugnac ultimately a bore despite an
outstanding musical and theatrical production.

B232.   Tappolet, Willy. "Frank Martin: 'Monsieur de Pourceaugnac.'"
Schweizerische Musikzeitung. Revue musicale suisse 103 (May-
June, 1963); 152-153.
In writing about the first performance in Geneva's Grand Théâtre
of Frank Martin's latest opera on Molière's Monsieur de
Pourceaugnac, the author devotes most of his attention to the work
itself. Acknowledging that Frank Martin has consistently set to music
only literary works of the highest quality, Molière's farce represents a
continuation in this direction. While elements of humor appear in the
composer's previous opera Der Sturm and in the Nativity play Le
Mystère de la Nativité, this is the first attempt at a completely comical
work. The bare plot outline of Molière's comic story has a striking
similarity to Strauss's Der Rosenkavalier. Musically, they have nothing
further in common. Consistent with his great respect for a literary
text, the composer rejects a librettist's re-write, and sets to music
almost the entire text with only minimal alterations. Of greatest
interest is how the composer would solve the manifold problems of
setting to music Molière's fast and witty dialogues with various
regional dialects and sometimes with bitter and stinging satire. Martin
has met the challenge with a variety of devices intended to provide a
lively flowing diction. In so doing the story is carried by recitative that
is varied and punctuated by spoken dialogue, by arioso, and

sometimes by aria. The orchestra likewise contributes with music that is transparent, subtle, and with unexpected rhythms and colors, but with a restraint that never covers the singers. Martin's tonal language is always comprehensible and reminds one more of Ravel than of Stravinsky. The strong cast of performers and the many touches of musical and theatrical humor ensure a successful premiere of this unusual operatic work.

Mystère de la Nativité

B233.   Bernheimer, Martin. "The New Saltzburg." American Record Guide 27 (October 1960): 101-102.
    This article reports on the newly constructed Festspielhaus in Saltzburg with its enormous stage rivaling Radio City Music Hall. The new hall may create as many problems as it solves in the presentation of the more intimate settings required for Mozart's operas. A new work utilizing to good advantage the theatre's mammoth stage is Frank Martin's Le Mystère de la Nativité in which scenes of earth, heaven, and hell are literally depicted at three different spacial levels. The reviewer, however, finds the music unequal to the production, having long stretches that tend to bore, and he is further put off by winged angels and wire-haloed saints believing that it raises questions of taste, no matter how stylish the production may be.

B234.   Brunner, Gerhard. "Saltzburg stages 'Cosi' and Martin opera." Musical Courrier 162 (October 27, 1960): 27.
    In the briefest of terms, the Mystery of the Nativity in its premiere staging in Saltzburg is judged to be too cinemagraphic in effect to serve the lofty ideals of the text. The reviewer is more favorably disposed to Martin's music than to the production as a theatre piece. The Berlin Philharmonic in the pit with excellent soloists and chorus conducted by Heinz Wallberg insured an outstanding production.

B235.   Clark, Andrew. "Lucerne: Martin Revived." Opera 35 (November 1984): 1222.
    To commemorate the tenth anniversary of the composer's death, the Lucerne Festival has produced a "staged" performance of Le Mystère de la Nativité in the Jesuiten Kirche on August 28, 1984. "The score is dominated by outstandingly beautiful choral writing and instrumental obbligatos." The entire work is enhanced by the reverberating acoustics of the church setting.

B236.   Downes, Edward. "Modern Musical Mystery on the Birth of Christ." New York Times 28 August 1960, 109, 9.
    Le Mystère de la Nativité, originally an oratorio commissioned for Swiss Radio, is given a spectacular production as a showpiece for Saltzburg's new Festspielhaus. The lavish production is seen to

overwhelm the somewhat modest music which is dominated by vocal melody of a modal cast. The telling of the Nativity story lacks the dramatic energy needed for operatic projection, the music remaining largely contemplative and lyrical.

B237. Downes, Edward. "Reports: Early Autumn - Saltzburg Debuts."
Opera News 25 (October 29 1960): 18.
The new and gigantic stage of the Festspielhaus in Saltzburg is the setting for the premiere of Frank Martin's oratorio Le Mystère de la Nativité as a fully staged work. Despite the three-level depiction of earth, heaven, and hell, the author finds the music lacking in sufficient individuality and dramatic energy to match the theatrical spectacle of its staged presentation.

B238. Frias, Leopoldo. "Buenos Aires Colon Premiere of Frank Martin's Oratorio." Music Magazine 164 (February 1962): 36.
Le Mystère de la Nativité had its well-received Latin American premiere at the Teatro Colón in a performance which included four soloists from the European premiere: Elly Ameling, Eric Tappy, Andre Vessieres, and Derrick Olsen.

B239. Gardiner, Bennitt. "First London Performance of a Great New Oratorio." Music and Musicians 9 (December 1960): 20.
The title of this article tells all except the identity of Frank Martin's oratorio Le Mystère de la Nativité, as heard in its London premiere in concert form.

B240. Gardiner, Bennitt. "Frank Martin - an Outsider?" Musical Events 26 (July 1971): 6-8.
The title of this article translates in part the title of Bernard Billeter's book, Frank Martin, Wirkung und Gestalt: un Aussenseiter der neuen Musik (see B14). This article is not so much a review of the book, but a summary statement of Frank Martin's musical life with particular emphasis on his Le Mystère de la Nativité described as the most outstanding and probably most enduring work. The article concludes with a summary statement on Martin's strongly developed sense of a composer's responsibility toward music and its audience, a subject that he has written and lectured on frequently during his long career (see M29).

B241. Helm, Everett. "Festival in Decline? Two Diverse Views." Musical America 80 (October 1960): 28.
The reviewer asserts that the opening of the new Festspielhaus with its gigantic stage has become a disservice to the more intimate operas of Mozart, the Saltzburg Festival's raison d'être. On the other hand, making the best possible use of the new facility, Frank Martin's Le Mystère de la Nativité is being presented as a staged work for the first time. The music, however, is found to be not strong enough or sufficiently interesting to match the sumptuous production.

B242.   Klein, Rudolf. "Le Mystère de la Nativité von Frank Martin."
         Österreichische Musikzeitschrift 14 (December 1959): 502-507.
         Writing a short time prior to the premiere of Le Mystère, the
author describes his article as a comprehensive appreciation of the
work. It was based on Le Mystère de la passion, a work from 1450
by Arnoul Gréban, which was designed to be performed over a
period of four days and contains nearly 35,000 verses. From this
gigantic mystery play, Frank Martin selected portions from the
Prologue and the first day to become his Le Mystère de la Nativité, a
work which depicts the events of the birth of Christ up to and
including the presentation to Simeon in the temple. Although written
in response to a commission from Radio Geneva for a Christmas
oratorio, Martin quickly saw the potential of the work for a staged
presentation and wrote detailed instructions as to how it should be
presented. Martin expressed the idea that a staging should be
inspired by paintings and stained glass windows of the fifteenth
century, but that this concept should not result in the literal copying of
every detail. Musically, Le Mystère is unique in its simplicity. From
the composer's Pour une mise en scène du Mystère de la Nativité, we
learn that Martin attempted to portray in his music facets of the action
such as mysticism, human sensitivity, devilish impudence, but also
simplicity. The work calls for nine soloists singing multiple roles, small
and large chorus, and men's choir, with full orchestra. When staged,
three levels of heaven, earth, and hell are depicted and require special
spacial separation. Despite its lack of operatic convention, Le Mystère
as a stage work becomes something of a modern period piece.

B243.   Klein, Rudolf. "Saltzburg 1960: Rückschau und Ausblick. Frank
         Martins Mysterium." Österreichische Musikzeitschrift 15 (September
         1960): 436-438.
         Despite some facets of the production that leave much to be
desired, the grand production of Frank Martin's Le Mystère de la
Nativité in the new Festspielhaus in Saltzburg is an undisputed
success. The reviewer takes issue with a translation from old French
into old German that makes the text incomprehensible to audiences
fluent in either or both languages. A further flaw is that, in creating
this translation into old German, the quality of late medieval epic
influenced by French love lyrics is lost and becomes instead a nativity
play of German-peasant baroque. Using outstanding soloists and the
Berlin Philharmonic, Martin's noble music comes across directly in its
simplicity to the listener and succeeds in creating a work that triumphs
over its staging and sweeps aside all other problems in presenting
this nativity play.

B244.   Marcus, Michael. "Music at home and abroad. The LPO." Music and
         Musicians 9 (February 1961): 24-25.
         On the occasion of the first performance in Britain of Frank
Martin's Le Mystère de la Nativité the oratorio is sung in English by
the London Philharmonic Choir and Orchestra. The reviewer finds this

performance lackluster and the music insufficient without the added interest of staging to sustain the work throughout its entirety.

B245. Marcus, Michael. "Opera and Concerts at Saltzburg Festival." Music and Musicians 9 (October 1960): 14-16.
      The staging of Frank Martin's oratorio Le Mystère de la Nativité in the newly reopened Festspielhaus utilizes the spacious new theatre to optimum effect despite the intimate nature of the nativity scene. The three levels of heaven, earth, and hell were, in fact, actually depicted at three different levels. Martin's intent to capture both the musical and visual atmosphere of the fifteenth-century text by Arnoul Gréban was notably achieved. While the work has moments of unevenness, its staged version with appropriate costumes and stylized staging enhances the effect suggested by stained-glass church windows which the composer sought to achieve.

B246. "Le Mystère de la Nativité." Opera 12 (February 1961): 129-130.
      The London premiere of Le Mystère sung in English by the London Philharmonic Orchestra and Choir is described by this reviewer as ultimately a bore. He finds the straightforward tonal or modal harmonization insufficiently interesting to support the length of the work.

B247. "Le Mystère de la Nativité de Frank Martin." Gazette de Lausanne 30 June 1962.
      After a performance of Le Mystère in Zürich the reviewer says "...la beauté d'une musique qui est problement la plus inspirée de notre époque. Dès la première scène, nous avons été empoignée et pourtant d'une suprème liberté, exprimant une grandeur de conception et une genérosité de sentiments qui sont d'un prince de la musique." "...the beauty of this music is probably the most inspired of our time. From the first scene, we were gripped by tense and finely wrought writing which nevertheless moves in supreme liberty, expressing a grandeur of conception and generosity of feeling which are those of a prince of music." The author further states that difficulties experienced in an earlier performance with the stylistic differences of the writing for heaven, earth, and hell that appeared to lack musical continuity were totally resolved by the outstanding performance in Zürich.

B248. Porter, Andrew. "Martin's New Oratorio." Musical Times 102 (February 1961): 91.
      Responding to the first British performance of Le Mystère in English, the author finds it a difficult work to make a judgment on, due to a different impression received from the score than from the performance. He concludes that the work suffers from a stiff and angular text in English while it has many beautiful and flowing phrases in the original French. A tentative conclusion is that, although uneven, the score contains passages of great beauty, and that judgment

should be deferred until there is an opportunity to hear the work performed by distinguished French artists.

B249. Rayment, Malcolm. "The Mystery of the Nativity." [Program Note] (December 13, 1960): 9-12.

Here are program notes for the British premiere of Le Mystère de la Nativité, performed in its oratorio format with an English translation by George Barker and conducted by Jaroslav Krombholc leading the London Philharmonic Chorus and Orchestra. The author first discusses Frank Martin's conducting style and his use of modified tone row procedures in several works that have been performed in Britain, if not notably the Nativity music. In discussing the background of the medieval mystery play and the work of the poet Arnoul Gréban, from which Martin derived the text, the author quotes an extended passage from the composer's own commentary written for the premiere by Radio Geneva. Again, in discussing the work as a staged presentation, Martin's notes provide an insight into how the composer visualized a staged production. The large-scaled oratorio requires nine soloists performing multiple parts as well as full orchestra and chorus. Following the medieval concept of representing heaven, hell, and earth, Martin achieves this by writing a different style of music for each. This concept is enhanced further when the work is staged at three different levels. Unlike more recent settings of the Nativity story, the medieval plays contained humorous elements in which the poet combines the comic with the horrific. The work is inspired by, and attempts to create a feeling for, the tableau of stained-glass windows from the fifteenth century. Musically, however, the work is expressed in modern terms, and does not attempt to re-create a literal medieval setting. The composer asks only that producers and designers have an understanding of, and a feeling for, the period.

B250. "Reports from Festivals." Canadian Music Journal 5 (Autumn 1960): 43.

This is a brief overview on the Saltzburg Festival and the premiere of Frank Martin's Le Mystère de la Nativité presented for the first time fully staged as an opera. The reviewer finds that "Mr. Martin's fine-boned, eclectic treatment of Arnoul Gréban's fifteenth-century mystery play was given a production so superb that at times it carried the idea forward more effectively than did the music."

B251. Stevens, David. "Le Mystère de la Mysteré." Opera 13 (autumn 1962): 53.

In a brief but enthusiastic response to Frank Martin's Nativity piece in its staged premiere, the reviewer sees the work as "an almost child-like retelling of the birth of Christ, easily accessible, too, in its tonally-based musical idiom..." The three levels of earth, heaven, and hell are enhanced visually by the staged presentation.

B252. Storrer, William Allin. "Cambridge Feast." Opera News 27 (February
       2, 1963): 31.
            The American premiere of Martin's Le Mystère de la Mysteré by
       the Harvard Glee Club and the Radcliffe Choral Society took place in
       Carnegie Hall on December 16, 1962 (see W103.). The author faults
       the work as being too long in the middle and closing sections, and
       lacking more comic relief from the quartet of devils.

B253. Tappolet, Willy. "Le Mystère de la Nativité von Frank Martin."
       Schweizerische Musikzeitung. Revue musicale suisse 100 (1960):
       107-109.
            In his response to a request for a new work by Radio Genève,
       Frank Martin wished to move in a different direction and produce a
       new and happy work. His search for a suitable text led him to the
       gigantic religious folk drama of the fifteenth-century poet Arnoul
       Gréban. Gréban's Mystère de la passion, intended for a performance
       of four days, contained many stories from the scriptures. Martin was
       attracted to Gréban's deep piety and naivete, and to his irregular
       poetic meters and often clumsy dialogues. From Gréban's massive
       work, Frank Martin selected portions to produce a nativity play
       extending from the Annunciation to the Presentation in the Temple.
       Le Mystère de la Nativité exists in three spacial levels of heaven,
       earth, and hell, which offered Martin the unique opportunity to
       compose appropriate music for each level, and which became a
       compelling reason for the work to be staged. As the author states,
       "Die in zwölf Bilder oder Episoden aufgeteilte Hundlung verlegt auch
       Martin in 'drei Klangsphären,' in drei verschiedene harmonische
       Klimas..." "...the twelve episodes are put into three sound spheres, in
       three different harmonic climates..." The music of heaven is usually
       modal and homophonic. Chromatic dissonance is employed in the
       earth scenes. Twelve-tone and grotesque sounds which often are
       distorted music from the other levels are employed in the scenes of
       hell. Le Nativité requires nine soloists, large and small choirs, large
       orchestra, and sufficient space for the three levels to be portrayed.
       As always, Frank Martin remains faithful to Gréban's text in which he
       has produced a unique nativity play seemingly inspired by medieval
       stained-glass windows. First performed as an oratorio for radio, the
       work was presented the following year at the Saltzburg Festival as a
       fully staged opera and again was a triumph for Frank Martin.

B254. Thomas, Ernst. "Martin's 'Mysterium von der Geburt des Herrn.'"
       Zeitschrift für Musik 122 (March 1961): 112-113.
            In this review of the first performance of Frank Martin's Le
       Mystère de la Nativité sung in the German language and presented at
       Wuppertal, the question is raised and explored as to whether or not
       the oratorio should be presented as a staged work. As a theatre
       piece, the reviewer finds Martin's work to be a kind of hybrid between
       scenic oratorio and true lyric theatre. The music is very noble but
       reticent and lacking in dramatic force. The composer's absolute

fidelity to the original text is seen as an obstacle to obtaining a successful theatre presentation. Despite these reservations, the presentation on three distinct physical levels (heaven, earth and hell), while difficult to achieve, proved to be a notable success, as was the improved clarity of the translated text. The composer, who was present for the performance, was rewarded by an outstanding production at the Wuppertal Theatre.

B255.   Walter, Franz. "'Le Mystère de la Nativité' de Frank Martin." Schweizerische Musikzeitung. Revue musicale suisse 100 (January-February 1960): 44-45.

In a review of the premiere of Le Mystère (see W104), we learn of the composer's desire to write a Christmas work, a commission by Radio Geneva to provide the means, and a previous experience with Arnoul Gréban's Mystère de la passion from a play directed by Martin's sister Pauline in the past. All of these elements come together with the composer's inspiration to create Le Mystère de la Nativité. Frank Martin was attracted to the fifteenth-century poet's long-winded mystery play by its slightly naive versification, but especially by the vividness and sharply defined personalities of its many characters. The quartet of devils, each uniquely defined, is contrasted with Mary, the incarnation of both human and divine grace. Even the various shepherds emerge as clearly defined personalities. A further appeal, typical of the genre, is the depiction of events on three different spacial levels, that is heaven, earth, and hell. This element provided the composer with the opportunity to compose music of three contrasting types for his oratorio, and in so doing, the visual elements became even more clearly delineated, thus leading to the work's presentation as a staged opera. In depicting the three levels, Martin has used modal writing with sequences of perfect harmony often containing no thirds to illustrate heaven. Earth is represented by a kind of tonal dodecaphony, and an atonal style which is sometimes a distortion of elements from the heaven and earth music is used to depict hell. At the same time, as in the earlier Golgotha, the music assumes a simplicity and clarity that are untypical of much of the composer's complex chromaticism, and risks a certain obvious repetitive formula that nevertheless contributes to the overall expression of serenity. The large musical resources required are used skillfully with a large chorus that comments on the action as in ancient Greek dramas, and a small mixed chorus represents the angels with a small men's chorus to represent the lesser devils. In addition, there are nine soloists performing multiple roles. The premiere in Geneva's Victoria Hall proved to be an outstanding success.

B256.   Witteman, Wim. "Frank Martin en zijn 'Mystère de la Nativité.'" Gregoriusblad (December 1968): 231-233.

Before a discussion of Le Mystère de la Nativité, we are shown in the most succinct summary how Frank Martin as a developing composer parallels the experience of César Franck and Anton

Bruckner in only achieving their mature style after age fifty. In addition, each was coming from a strong religious background, and each had been influenced greatly by the music of Wagner. For Frank Martin the critical experimental period of the early and middle thirties led to an extended use of chromaticism embracing elements of the twelve-tone system developed by Arnold Schoenberg, but in a manner that employed the system horizontally or melodically while retaining a tonal base. From this point in his career Martin was able to carry forward the European tradition of oratorio, and after Le Vin herbé, In terra pax, and Golgotha he was particularly well qualified to undertake the large-scale nativity play with a text from Arnoul Gréban's Mystère de la passion. In this morality play from the fifteenth century, Frank Martin was able to utilize the convention of frequently changing scenes, such as heaven, earth, and hell in a manner that permitted him to compose contrasting music for each locale. Despite a simplification of his musical style to fit the subject and the character of a mystery play, we still may recognize characteristics of the composer's musical style: the pedal-point, a slow "Tristan"-like reaching of the climax in the accompanying strings, and the chromatic construction of melodic lines. Although the dramatic and illustrative music and the effective use of chaotic sounds to depict devilish scenes demonstrate great skill on the part of the composer, it is his lyrical gifts in writing for the chorus that place the oratorios of Martin among the finest works in this genre produced in the twentieth century.

La Nique à Satan

B257. Gaillard, Roger. "Le souffle du diable." L'Hebdo No. 11 (March 19, 1982): 46-48.
    "The breath of the devil" is about both the restoration of an old theatre (Théâtre du Jurat in Mézières, Switzerland), and the resurrection of an old musical play, Frank Martin's La Nique à Satan, not seen since its Geneva premiere in 1933. The theatre is described in some detail along with the concept of performing plays in rural villages, the plays produced there over the years, and the difficulty of maintaining the theatre in a postwar economy. Finally, there is an enthusiastic plan for its restoration. A part of this overall plan is a revival of La Nique à Satan (Thumbing your nose at Satan), a fantasy musical theatre piece by poet Albert Rudhardt and composer Frank Martin. In 1933 the play was identified in a politically negative way by both factions during troubled times and failed with a financial loss for its creators. It is hoped that this humorous and light-hearted musical fantasy, full of parody, will enjoy a popular revival that will permit its musical and theatrical values to be heard and enjoyed by today's audiences.

B258.   Mermoud, Robert. "La résurrection de la Nique à Satan, trente ans de petit pas." Revue musicale de suisse romande 35 (1982): 68-71.

Robert Mermoud takes justifiable pride in his considerable part in reviving the musical theatre piece La Nique à Satan, a collaboration of poet Albert Rudhardt and composer Frank Martin, which had not been heard since its initial performances in 1933. The author describes how he discovered the piece in the offices of Editions Henn, the Genevan music publisher, and the efforts required to get the work before the public. This was accomplished by first performing selections with his choirs. Later, a radio version was prepared but then rejected. Finally, after many difficulties, a full revival took place in which some of the original cast from twenty years previous took part, most notably Pauline Martin, sister of the composer, in the key role of the witch.

B259.   Tappolet, Willy. "La Nique à Satan." Schweizerische Musikzeitung. Revue musicale suisse 73 (1933): 310-311.

The poet Albert Rudhardt and the composer Frank Martin have devised a theatre piece consisting of three acts and eleven scenes called La Nique à Satan (Thumbing your nose at Satan). It is a satiric and fantastic fairy tale which has some elements that remind one of the Pied Piper story, and which utilizes groups of children as an important part of the action. The work, scored mainly for wind instruments, contains eighteen songs. Two of these are traditional folk songs, the remainder are composed by Frank Martin. Despite its affinity to music hall entertainment, the piece is seen as a well-crafted quality work which is superior to the usual fare that Genevan audiences have become accustomed to hearing.

B260.   Vaney, Jean-François. "La Nique à Satan." Lausanne, Ecole Normale de Lausanne, 1976. See: B223

Ode à la musique

B261.   Haller, Charles. "Création a Bienne de L'Ode à la musique, de Frank Martin." Feuilles musicales 15 (October 1962): 102-103.

In this review of the first performance of Ode à la musique, the author tells us Frank Martin chose the text of Guillaume de Machaut, written in old French, because the short verses and variety of episodes seem to invite a musical commentary which, in turn, can be as varied as the poem itself. In a composition lasting less than ten minutes the composer achieves a remarkable variety through flexible rhythms which exactly fit the prosody and in a tonal framework that moves freely into various keys and employs stylistic elements of various periods, including a passage that reminds us of organum with its fifths and octaves. "Cette richesse d'ecriture, tout en servant le poème de Guillaume de Machaut, permet de rendre un hommage fugitif au style de diverses époques, un peu commesi le maître avait voulu synthétiser les éléments qui ont illustré son art." "The richness of this music uses Guillaume de Machaut's poem and also pays hommage to the style of various periods, as if the master had wanted to synthesize the elements which illustrate his art."

Passacaille

B262. Aprahamian, Felix. "Frank Martin." Music and Musicians 19
(December 1970): 44-48.
A thorough but succinct survey of Frank Martin's life and musical works is placed in the context of his conservative Swiss background. The influences, both personal and musical, which shaped his development are introduced along with the major works of each stage of Martin's career. The Passacaille for organ is analyzed in some detail as an example of the composer's ability to combine the twelve-tone system with the traditional form of the passacaglia. The author asserts that "Martin's name must be added to those musical geniuses who have proved their ability to use absolutely primary harmonic colours in a new and completely personal manner."

B263. Billeter, Bernhard. "Das Orgelmusikalische Schaffen der Gegenwart."
In Orgel und Orgelmusik heute, 64-85. Stuttgart:
Musikwissenschaftliche Verlags-Gesellschaft, I968.
In a lecture followed by questions and discussion, the author identifies two distinct types of compositions being written for the organ in our time. These are identified as avant-garde music represented by composers such as Ligeti, Kagel, Messiaen, Schoenberg, and Krenek, and neo-baroque style as represented by composers such as Distler, Pepping, Micheelson, Reda, and Walcha. Billeter then acknowledges the limitations imposed by the liturgical function of the organ as an instrument of the church: short duration, accessibility to amateurs and technically easy to play. Most composers who write for these limitations produce work that is not outstanding, and good composers tend to fulfill commissions with rather ordinary works, often below their usual standard. Inextricably linked to compositional style is the change or reform in organ building, most pronounced in Holland and Scandinavia, least affected in France. Some composers dislike the lack of clarity that comes from octave doublings, notably Schoenberg and Hindemith. Likewise, Frank Martin, who wrote only one solo organ piece, believed that for this same reason his Passacaille did not sound satisfying on the organ, and he subsequently re-scored it for both string and full orchestra.

B264. Mengelberg, Karel. "'Passacaglia' van Martin." Het Vrije Volk
[Amsterdam] 2 March 1967.
In a Concertgebouw Orchestra concert conducted by Eugen Jochum, the full orchestral version of the Passacaille, a piece first

composed for solo organ and later transcribed for string orchestra, is heard in Amsterdam for the first time, some five years after its premiere. Both critical and public praise is bestowed on Frank Martin for a work constructed with consummate mastery, and it is believed to be also a work of special importance to the composer who returned to it to produce three versions.

B265. Morehen, John. "Frank Martin's Passacaille." Musical Times 114 (October 1973): 1049-1051.
Morehen analyzes Frank Martin's only work for solo organ, from which the composer later prepared versions for both string and full orchestra. The work consists of a passacaglia or ground bass theme and also an independent "main theme." These two melodic ideas, sometimes modified, are explored separately and/or together in a series of twenty-seven variations. The orchestral version is examined closely for both registrational ideas and structural clarity based on the composer's subsequent thoughts in the revised versions.

B266. "Ein neues Werk von Frank Martin." Melos 20 (December 1953): 360.
In a brief review of Passacaille for string orchestra, the author curiously makes no mention of the work's origins as a 1944 piece for solo organ (see W67). Nevertheless, this string orchestra version is praised as an enrichment of the literature for strings. The author further speculates as to whether the work was intended for school or amateur orchestras.

B267. Peterson, John David. "Frank Martin's Passacaille for Organ." Diapason 67 (May 1976): 6,11.
The author presents a detailed analysis, intended to interest and assist organists in preparing the work for performance. He takes the reader through the twenty-seven variations, sometimes in groups or several at a time, meticulously comparing the organ score with Martin's versions for string and full orchestra (see W99 & W117). Specific suggestions for the performer are inserted at various points. The author asserts: "...the Passacaille is unique in the organ literature. The structure is severe; the harmonies at time acrid, at times lush; the sense profound - the work is one of the glories, not just of this century, but of all music for organ."

B268. Regamey, Constantin. "Passacaille pour orchestre à cordes." In Musiques du vingtième siècle presentation de 80 oeuvres pour orchestre de chambre, 150-153. Lausanne: Editions du Cervin, 1966.
The Passacaille for string orchestra is the second of three versions of this work written in 1944 for organ solo. As its title suggests, this is a set of variations on a theme repeated continuously in the bass line. In addition, Martin introduced a second theme which sometimes became the basis for variations as well. The Passacaille, using modified tone rows, permits the composer to employ a series of

ingenious variations that range from rich and lush romanticism to harshly dissonant and many shades in between. In its instrumental format, the work reminds one of the composer's Le Vin herbé.

B269.   "Review of Music." Music and Letters 37 (October 1956): 419-420.
    Frank Martin's Passacaille is briefly reviewed with several other organ works. The reviewer asserts " that the treatment is wonderfully varied, but the narrative is closely argued, and a judicious mixture of contrapuntal and harmonic treatment keeps the music developing organically to the end. A masterpiece, the work of a genius."

B270.   Vlad, Roman. "Frank Martin, 'Passacaille per organo,' Universal Edition, Wien." Rassegna musicale 27 (September 1957): 249-250.
    In this article the author assigns the Passacaille for organ to the list of works written in Martin's fully mature style, having been written during the same year in which the composer began composing his most successful work, the Petite symphonie concertante. In this work is seen an example of Martin's use of modified or altered tone rows, in which the composition employs a double exposition that is expressed in two variants of eleven tones, the integration of which results in the entire chromatic series. This serial mutation resulting in a synthesis between serial procedures and traditional harmonic practice is a basic characteristic of this and many subsequent works by Frank Martin.

Petite symphonie concertante

B271.   Adams, Byron. "Part I: Concerto for Violin and Orchestra. Part II: Frank Martin's 'Petite symphonie concertante:' an analysis." D.M.A. diss., Cornell University, 1984.
    This dissertation contains an original composition by the author and a second seemingly unrelated section that consists of a detailed analysis of Frank Martin's most successful work, and concludes with "an assessment of the score in terms of both Martin's career and the broader context of twentieth-century musical development."

B272.   Ansermet, Ernest. "Frank Martin 'Petite symphonie concertante' 1944-1945." Orchestre de la Suisse Romande [program notes] (May 2, 1986)
    The program notes of a 1986 concert conducted by Erich Leinsdorf include a brief essay from 1946 by Ernest Ansermet who introduced the work to most of the world outside of Switzerland. This, in effect, established Martin as an international composer. Ansermet acknowledges the slow and careful mastery of Martin's craft which has led to this extraordinary work. What the conductor finds new and unique in Martin's music is the harmony and melody, and the way in which the composer employs the twelve-tone system while retaining a harmonic feeling. This results in a long and breathless melody

expressed through an original sonority of harp, harpsichord, and piano with string orchestra.

B273.   "Editorial Notes." Strad 64 (September 1953): 131.
        Frank Martin's Petite symphonie concertante is described as the most interesting novelty at the fifty-ninth season of the "Proms." Although it employs a conventional tone row at the outset, one discovers this usage to be a melodic device in writing traditional music with an extended tonality. "Schoenberg's abolition of harmony is itself superceded and the composer's lively rhythmical invention has produced a piece which in spite of its strong intellectual bias may well make a wide appeal."

B274.   "Frank Martin und seine 'Petite symphonie concertante.'" [program notes] Internationale Juni-Festwochen-Zürich Kammerorchester (June 23, 1985).
        In a revival of the Petite symphonie concertante a decade after the composer's death, and some forty years after its first performances in the same city, the annotator describes the unique tonal qualities of the work with its three soloists that interact with one another as a trio and with the double string orchestra which both accompanies and contributes independently. The composer's professional life and his works are surveyed in a summary that concludes the article.

B275.   Jacobson, Bernard. "Visiting Orchestras: Suisse Romande and Bath." High Fidelity/Musical America 17 (September 1967): MA16-17.
        Ernest Ansermet, founder of the Suisse Romande Orchestra, presents the Swiss orchestra for the first time in New York on the eve of his final season as its permanent conductor. Highlighting one of the programs is Frank Martin's Petite symphonie concertante. The combination of tonal and twelve-tone elements is described as masterly. "This work is one of the finest achievements of twentieth-century music, compelling in form, constantly fascinating in sound."

B276.   Kisselgoff, Anna. "The Dance: Shadows Premiere." New York Times November 21, 1985): 11.
        The first performance of Shadows, a ballet choreographed by Jean-Pierre Bonnefoux to Frank Martin's Petite symphonie concertante, was first presented by the New York City Ballet on November 21, 1985. The score is seen as a particularly good choice to convey and augment the psychological conflict which the dancers attempt to portray in this difficult dance piece.

B277.   Maskey, Jacqueline. "The Dance." High Fidelity/Musical America (March 1986): MA10-11.
        New York City Ballet opened its 1985 season with Shadows, a ballet choreographed by Jean-Pierre Bonnefoux and set to the music of Frank Martin's Petite symphonie concertante. The new dance on

the subject of lovers who can neither live with or without one another harkens back to the "psychological ballets" of Anthony Tudor. Martin's "somberly seething" music is seen as particularly appropriate for this work.

B278. "Martin, Frank 'Zur Petite symphonie concertante.'" Bayerischer Rundfunk (October 14-15, 1965). [program notes] Symphonie Konzerte 1965-66.

In a performance by the Bavarian Radio Orchestra conducted by Carl Böhm, the program annotator draws from Frank Martin's own description of the work in which he describes the circumstances which brought about its creation and outlines its formal structure. The composer also comments on an alternate version prepared for full orchestra without soloists. This version, which was intended to give the piece more opportunities for performance, proved to be a false judgment, as the Petite symphonie concertante has been performed worldwide, but always in its original version. The article concludes with a brief paragraph drawn from a radio interview in which the composer explains how he has utilized the twelve-tone system of Schoenberg in his own works.

B279. Martin-Boeke, Maria. "Martin: 'Petite symphonie concertante.'" [in Dutch] Radio Filharmonisch Orkest January 23, 1971.

The widow of Frank Martin is likely the most qualified of any living person to write about the composer and his most celebrated work. Here she briefly outlines the main events of the composer's early formative years and explains the nature of the commission from Paul Sacher which was the germinal idea of writing a solo work for harp, harpsichord, and piano with double string orchestra. The reader is then given a brief introduction to the structure of the piece, and the article concludes with a description of Martin's alternate version for large orchestra without soloists. This was composed almost simultaneously to protect the work from the perceived obscurity that would be the result of its unusual instrumentation. This precaution proved to be without merit because the piece has been performed worldwide but always in its original format.

B280. Menasce, Jacques de. "Frank Martin and his Petite symphonie concertante." Musical Quarterly 34 (1948): 271-278.

Here another composer pays tribute to the remarkable success of Martin's Petite symphonie concertante and of his increasing stature as a composer to be recognized worldwide. Martin's music is a unique development by a composer emerging from the ultra-conservative Suisse Romande, but who is among the first composers of a French cultural background to assimilate and modify for his own purposes the twelve-tone system of Arnold Schoenberg. Martin's mature works are "characterized by broad melodic lines of a chromatic nature, subtle harmonic and rhythmic patterns, and a sustained contrapuntal texture." If a stylistic handle is necessary, the

author calls the piece neo-classic with strong romantic feeling, but
with little kinship to either Stravinsky and Hindemith or Viennese
expressionism.

B281. Mooser, Robert-Aloys. "Petite symphonie concertante (for harp,
harpsichord, piano and two string orchestras) Zürich, 17 May
1946)." Regards sur le musique contemporaine 1921-1946, 442-
446. Lausanne: F. Rouge, 1946.

This enthusiastic review of Petite symphonie concertante at its
premiere (see W68.) indicates that Martin's most successful, most
often performed, and most popular composition was from its very first
performance a "hit." The reviewer is fascinated by the unusual
combination of instruments and the success with which the composer
achieves an interplay of soloists alone, with the strings, and in
combination with each other in a manner that seizes and sustains the
attention of the listener throughout. The author defines two distinctive
characteristics: the conciseness of its form and the sobriety present in
its development. "En vérité, exception faite de celles d'Arthur
Honegger, la musique suisse n'a pas produit, à ce jour, beaucoup
d'oeuvres aussi significatives et aussi accomplies au fond été à la
forme." "Only in the work of Arthur Honegger has a Swiss composer
produced a work so masterful and significant in its essence and
form."

B282. Mooser, Robert-Aloys. "Petite symphonie concertante pour piano,
clavecin, harpe et deux orchestres à cordes (1945)." In Aspects de
la musique contemporaine 1953-57, 156-160. Genève: Labor et
Fides, 1957.

After a ten-year span of years from its premiere, the listener
and/or analyst can better appreciate and evaluate the remarkable
achievement of the composer in this his most celebrated work. The
passage of time and rapidly changing styles and taste have not
diminished either its freshness nor the appeal of its unique
instrumental colors and melodic charm. When the composer chose
this unusual combination of solo instruments with double string
orchestra, he seemed to be unaware to what extent the choice of
instruments would dictate the shape of the work and force him to
conform to the internal demands of the music which he had created.
The composer's uncertainty about the experimental nature of the
scoring led him to prepare a second version for full orchestra,
eliminating the soloists, but in so doing, the essence of its constant
polychrony is lost. It is this parallel development and the alternation
of its five tonal levels that makes the Petite symphonie concertante so
unique in all the literature for stringed instruments. Further
investigation reveals still other marvels. The risk of writing a concerto
for two solo instruments with the limited sonic carrying power of the
harp and harpsichord is further compounded by adding the piano
whose sound intensity is many times greater than that of the harp and
harpsichord. So skillfully has Martin employed these combinations of

instruments that all of the parts can be heard both singularly and in combination. The work is further enhanced by its harmonic resources. Beginning with a twelve-tone melody of unusual beauty in the slow introduction, the piece moves into an allegro movement that introduces passages, both singularly and in combinations, and develops gradually into a lively march which provides a rousing bravura finale.

B283.   Schuh, Willi. "Frank Martins Petite symphonie concertante." Schweizerische Musikzeitung. Revue musicale suisse 86 (1946): 301-302.

In a perceptive review of the premiere of Frank Martin's Petite symphonie concertante, Professor Schuh provides an analysis of the composer's best known and most often performed work. At the premiere, the author acknowledges the prior success of Le Vin herbé, Jedermann, Der Cornet, and the oratorio In terra pax as major works representing an expressive and stylistic breakthrough for the composer in musical works that are settings of words to music. The Petite symphonie concertante is perceived to be the composer's breakthrough into his mature style in the area of purely instrumental writing. "Ja, die <<Petite symphonie concertante>> geniesst sogar den Vorzug einer breiteren geistig-seelischen Basis; sie gibt sich, vom Wort abgelöst, noch <<musikhaltiger>>, reicher und strömender, und dies trotz der äusserersten Strenge der thematischen und formalen Gestaltung und der gegenüber den Vokalwerken noch gesteigerten Bedeutung der eigentümlich <<gehärteten>> Rhythmik." "Indeed Petite symphonie concertante enjoys the advantage of a broader intellectual-spiritual basis; detached from the word, it reveals itself as even more 'Musikhaltiger' (music-containing), richer and more flowing, and that despite the utmost structures of the thematic and formal organization and the meaning of the peculiar (hardened) rhythm which compared with the vocal works is intensified and heightened. The unity of the thematic-constructive elements and the extraordinary handling of the three solo instruments are the elements calculated to make this piece a unique achievement."

B284.   Schuh, Willi. "Petite symphonie concertante." In Schweizer Musik der Gegenwart, 142-145. Zürich: Atlantis, 1948.

In this essay the author, after careful analysis of Martin's preceding vocal works: Der Cornet, Le Vin herbé, and Sechs Monologe aus Jedermann, finds the Petite symphonie concertante to be not simply a purely instrumental equivalent to the above-mentioned works, but one which is on an even higher level of intellectual-spiritual inspiration. In this work Martin is able to apply an even greater stylistic control over the thematic material employed, and a unique formal structure displays to the greatest advantage the unusual sound combination of solo harp, harpsichord, and piano against double string orchestra. The work contains a slow introductory section to each of two faster movements in which the concertante instruments are heard singularly and in combination with the string orchestra. The twelve-tone melody which begins the work contains the main material on which the entire piece is based. It is not difficult to understand the immediate success of this piece, for few contemporary works stand on the same level in terms of originality, vitality, or spirituality.

B285.   Stähli, Margrith. "Petite symphonie concertante." Basel, S.S.P.M., 1982. See: B223

Pilate

B286.   "Frank Martin - Pilate." [program notes] Radio Televisione Italiana Settimana mondiale della Radio concerto Sinfonico. November 14, 1964.

Pilate is perhaps the least known of Martin's choral works, but one for which the composer expressed a particular fondness. This article describes the premiere given as the opening work of the worldwide week of radio sponsored by the European Radio Union which commissioned the piece for this occasion. Pilate is a half-hour-long cantata drawn from Arnoul Gréban's four-day Nativity play, Le Mystère de la passion, from which Martin had previously extracted the text for his oratorio Le Mystère de la Nativité. Pilate is unique in that it focuses on the person of Pilate and his role in the passion story, and secondly, that Jesus does not take part although he is nevertheless always present, always the center of attention. The cantata uses a men's chorus to represent the crowd and a women's chorus to represent the Virgin and the daughters of Jerusalem whose function is not unlike the chorus in ancient Greek plays; that is, a collective voice that provides a commentary on the unfolding drama. The work is in eight short sections separated by pauses. The passion events center around the figure of Pilate, with the addition of Satan and Lucifer, two devils who foresee the loss of their satanic power through the resurrection of Christ and try unsuccessfully to intervene. The work concludes with a chorale section expressing the exultation of the redemption.

Poèmes de la mort

B287.   "CMS: Martin Premiere." High Fidelity/Musical America 22 (March 1972) MA18.

The world premiere of Frank Martin's Poèmes de la mort took place at Alice Tully Hall on Dec. 12, 1971, a commission by the Chamber Music Society of Lincoln Center. The eighty-one-year-old composer conducted the first performance of this unique work which consists of three poems on the subject of death by François Villon and set to music for three male voices and three electric guitars. "The rich modal harmonies for the voices evoke the renaissance mileau of the poetry, while the death-rattle twanging of the electric guitar lends the music a strong contemporary flavor. Whether the novel setting of the music can overcome the extreme gloom of the death poems in terms of public favor and acceptance remains to be seen."

B288. Soria, Dorle J. "Frank Martin, Master of all Trades." High Fidelity/Musical America 22 (March 1972): MA11-13.

Frank Martin and his wife Maria were interviewed in New York during the occasion of the world premiere of his Poèmes de la mort for three male voices and three electric guitars. The composer came to New York to rehearse and conduct the first performance of this new work which was commissioned for the opening of Alice Tully Hall. The author summarizes Martin's long career and includes personal notes and anecdotes on the composer's personal life, his family, his various interests, and hobbies, including being handy man at fixing things around the house.

Polyptyque

B289. "Menuhin Festival Orchestra." High Fidelity/Musical America 26 (February 1976): MA27.

Yehudi Menuhin as violin soloist and as conductor of his London based Festival Orchestra is the subject of this review of a Carnegie Hall concert in which the celebrated violinist plays Frank Martin's Polyptyque for violin and strings, a work commissioned by Mr. Menuhin. "The music is a sterling example of Martin's austere but deeply felt conservative idiom and makes its points with telling but economical strokes."

B290. Vranken, Toon. "'Polyptyque' van Frank Martin in Nederland première." De Tijd [Amsterdam] 17 December 1973.

The Holland premiere of Frank Martin's Polyptyque was to have had the composer conducting with Yehudi Menuhin, for whom the piece was written as soloist. Martin's illness required a replacement, but Menuhin was present to introduce the new work, which, rather than a traditional concerto, is a suite of seven sections which represent various stages in the passion of Christ. This concept and indeed the title is derived from the composer's response to a thirteenth-century polyptych by Duccio which he had seen in Siena. The music projects a strong touching power and evokes a feeling for the timeless and eternal. Whether heard and experienced in terms of scenes from the Passion, or only as instrumental concert music, the listener senses that this is music of a noble spirit.

Pseaumes de Genève

B291.   Paap, Wouter. "'Pseaumes de Genève' van Frank Martin." Mens en
        melodie 24 (July 1969): 215-216.
            In this review of a performance by the Roman Catholic Capitol
        Choir conducted by Jan de Hoog, the author describes the
        background of the work. Written as a response to a commission
        from Radio Geneva for a work to be used in ceremonies observing
        the four-hundredth anniversary of the founding of the University of
        Geneva by Calvin, Frank Martin has fashioned a work utilizing psalm
        melodies and texts from the Geneva Psalter. The work makes
        settings of six psalms and employs mixed choir, children's choir,
        organ, and small orchestra. In the first psalm (no. 127), the composer
        makes an allusion to the spiritual atmosphere in which the university
        was founded. Using psalm tunes as a base, Martin employs a free
        counterpoint with modern harmonies to construct an oratorio uniquely
        suited to the occasion for which it was written.

Les Quatre éléments

B292.   Bunge, Sas. "Frank Martin: Les Quatre éléments." [in Dutch]
        Preludium (December 1965): 55.
            Writing in the official publication of the Concertgebouw, the
        author discusses The Four Elements commissioned to celebrate the
        eightieth birthday of Ernest Ansermet by his Orchestre de la Suisse
        Romande. The author, drawing from the composer's program notes
        at a Hamburg performance, states that the pieces were written in an
        impressionistic manner to evoke the composer's response to the
        appearance of natural elements, as experienced during a vacation
        cruise along the Norwegian coast, and were not intended to be
        metaphysical. The Four Elements and their subtitles Earth, Water, Air,
        and Fire must necessarily serve only as a kind of guidepost for the
        listener. The author concludes that for the composer, the titles
        represent only a sounding board offered to the listener, in order that
        each listener in his own individual way may create his own "four
        elements" in sound imagery.

B293.   "Chicago Symphony Orchestra." Musical Leader 98 (December 1966):
        16.
            In this briefest review of Les Quatre éléments, in first
        performances by Jean Martinon and the Chicago Symphony, the
        author finds it to be "an interesting work of modern impressionism
        characterized by meaningful melody, undergirded by dynamic fresh
        harmony, colorful instrumentation, and grandiose climaxes."

B294. Degens, R.N. "In Gesprek met Frank Martin." Intermezzo 10
(September 1965): 4-6.
     In this interview article on the occasion of the Netherlands
premiere of Les Quatre éléments, a conversation with Frank and Maria
Martin is summarized and commented upon, rather than presented in
direct question and answer form. From this discussion we first gain
some insights into why the Swiss composer settled in Holland, his
feelings about mountains and the sea, and his steady and methodical
development as a composer over a span of forty-four years at the
time of this article. Martin reflects on his own work and that of his
peers, in which he finds new and experimental music being written
that is lacking in human contact and that fails to touch the soul of
listeners. Finally, the composer describes the composition of his Les
Quatre éléments to honor the eightieth birthday of Ernest Ansermet.
The elements of earth, water, air, and fire are seen as subjects that
musically call for colorful impressionistic writing for a large orchestra,
and thus lend themselves to Ansermet's temperament and musical
strengths. Although music cannot impersonate nature, the Les Quatre
éléments are intended to represent the feelings that these elements
invoke, however subjectively, rather than the projection of a more
abstract philosophical musical metaphor.

B295. Laderman, Ezra. "Two by the Pittsburgh." High Fidelity/Music
America 22 (March 1972): MA139, 145.
     The Pittsburgh Symphony, conducted by William Steinberg,
presents the first New York performance of Frank Martin's Les Quatre
éléments. This reviewer finds the work disappointing and says it
shows "obvious, impressionistic, inadventurous late-nineteenth-century
techniques."

B296. Muller, H.J.M. "Frank Martin's 'de Vier Elementen' ovationeel begroet."
Telegraaf [Amsterdam] 13 December 1965.
     In a review that is for the most part negative in its attitude
toward the conductor (Haitink), his handling of the orchestra (the
Concertgebouw) and the other musical interpretations (Sibelius and
Roussel), the one high point is the Holland premiere of Frank Martin's
The Four Elements. This performance, which received a standing
ovation for the composer and the performers, is an indication of the
high esteem that Concertgebouw audiences hold for Frank Martin.
The author finds that the composer succeeds in translating into
musical terms what he sees and feels about the elements of earth,
water, air, and fire. "Respectievelijk hoort men de Aarde in al zijn
onverzettelijkheid en kracht, het Water in zijn zwaarteloosheid en
dreiging tevens, vervolgens de Lucht en ten slotte het Vuur dat in zijn
puntige klankfiguren herinneringen wekt aan de 'Feuerzauber' uit de
'Walküre' van Wagner." "Respectively we can hear Earth in all its
immovability and power, the Water in its lightness, but also
threatening, the Air, and last, the Fire, which, because of its pointed

sound figures, reminds us of the 'Magic Fire Music' from the Walküre by Wagner."

B297.   Parsons, Arrand. "The Four Elements." Chicago Symphony Program Notes (November 24-25, 1966): 2-3, 5-7.

Arrand Parsons quotes extensively from Frank Martin's own words, in which the composer describes the piece written for and dedicated to his old friend and chief advocate, Ernest Ansermet. The choice was deliberate in selecting a subject that could best be expressed musically through impressionistic writing, and in this case for large orchestra. Ernest Ansermet as a conductor has over the years demonstrated his skill and affinity for interpreting impressionistic works, and The Four Elements is thus custom-made for Ansermet's particular musical strengths. The author reviews Martin's development as a composer and concludes with a brief description of each of the four elements: earth, water, air, and fire.

B298.   Walter, Franz. "Une nouvelle création de Frank Martin par Ansermet und concerto de Burkhard par H. Schneeberger." Journal de Genève 8 October 1964.

Frank Martin's work, Les Quatre éléments (The Four Elements), was composed for the eightieth birthday of Ernest Ansermet, who performs the premiere on the occasion of this review. These four "symphonic studies" are designed both to challenge the famed conductor but also to provide him with the kind of musical composition that he excels in most as an interpreter. This new work is seen to have two major characteristics: one that deals with the subject directly, that is, each element--earth, water, air, and fire--and secondly, a deeper reflection of the composer's intimate reactions to those elements which may account for a degree of austereness even in the "fire" section. The author discovers an astonishing instrumental virtuosity resulting from the composer's total mastery of orchestral writing and expressive elements that one associates with this composer: a chromatic contour, a rainbow effect formed by perfect harmony, and a playing of major-minor. "...c'est une oeuvre qui ne ressemble à aucune autre de Martin: et une fois de plus il a su trouver, avec une absolue sûreté de main, des solutions neuves à des problèmes nouveaux. Faisant fi des effets traditionnels, Martin, après avoir dnas la Terre évoqué les grands espaces et les grands amas, a trouvé aussi bien pour l'Eau que pour l'Air des irisations sonores et des reflets harmoniques aussi sensibles qu'originaux." "...this work resembles no other work by Frank Martin; and once again he has found with absolute sureness of the hand, new solutions to new problems. Rejecting traditional effects, Frank Martin, after evoking the grand spaces and masses of the Earth in that particular section, found sonorous rainbow effects and harmonious reflections, both sensitive and original, in his sections on water and air."

Quatre pièces brèves pour guitare

B299. Gilardino, Angelo. "Aspetti della musica per chitarra del secolo xx."
        Fronimo 1 (January 1973): 7-10.
        In an article entitled "Aspects of guitar music in the twentieth-
        century," the author asserts that the most important difference
        between guitar music of the classic period and that being written
        today is that, with the possible exception of Villa-Lobos, the
        composers of major works for the instrument in the twentieth century
        have been non-guitarists. In the past, music composed for the guitar
        was almost exclusively written by guitarists. Using Frank Martin's
        1933 Quatre pièces brèves as a starting point, the author briefly
        surveys the approach of Alexander Tansman, Benjamin Britten, Mario
        Castelnuovo-Tedesco, Hans Werner Henze, and Stephen Dodgson.
        Concerning Martin's guitar pieces, he says, "Frank Martin se ne è
        servito per rievocare, nei termini della sua pensosa spiritualità e delle
        sue scelte stilistiche, un clima preziosamente arcaico;..." "Frank Martin
        used the guitar to re-invoke a precious archaic climate in terms of his
        thoughtful spirituality and in regard to his stylistic choices;..."

B300. Kilvington, Chris. "Eliot Fisk plays Scarlatti, Martin, Ponce, Raffman,
        Paganini." Classical Guitar 3 (March 1985): 65-66.
        Kilvington enthusiastically reviews Eliot Fisk's Gitarre & Laute
        recording of a variety program which includes Frank Martin's Quatre
        pièces brèves. Most significant is that this recorded version is from a
        manuscript differing in some respects from the published score.

B301. Kozinn, Allan. "The Guitar Literature: Beyond Segovia's Influence."
        Guitar Review 58 (Summer 1984): 10-13.
        Here is a survey of the recent literature for guitar that moves
        beyond the repertoire performed by and /or endorsed and promoted
        by André Segovia and his followers. Frank Martin's Quatre pièces
        brèves from 1933, written for but rejected by Segovia, is seen as the
        pivotal work which has led composers and guitarists to search for
        expressive means outside of the obvious "Spanish" tonal idiom with
        which the instrument is so universally identified. The pioneering efforts
        of Julien Bream and others have born fruit with the creation of new
        works by major composers in a wide variety of styles, by such diverse
        talents as Michael Tippett, Elliott Carter, Roger Sessions, as well as
        Ned Rorem, and Andre Previn.

Quatre sonnets à Cassandre

B302. Mooser, Robert-Aloys. "Frank Martin Quatre sonnets de Ronsard,
        pour voix, flute, alto, et violoncelle." In Regards sur le musique
        contemporaine 1921-1946, 38-40. Lausanne: F. Rouge, 1946.
        In reviewing a concert of all new works sponsored annually by
        the Association of Swiss Musicians, the author singles out Martin's

work as an oasis amid a desert of aridity and mediocrity. With reference to works by Martin presented on these Festival programs in previous years, the reviewer sees a development of technical mastery and a disengagement from the obvious musical influences in his earlier works. "Sans perdre quoi que ce soit de la spontanéité que fait son plus grand charme, il a acquis du métier." "He is mastering his art without losing his spontaneity."

Quatuor à cordes

B303. Paap, Wouter. "Frank Martin: Strijkkwartet (1967)." Concertgebouw-Kamermuziek [program notes] (December 11-13, 1969).

   In program notes for the first performance in Holland of Frank Martin's only String Quartet by the Netherlands String Quartet, the author finds that Martin's instrumental "...verdiepte hij zich in het eigen karacter en in de eigen techniek van ieder instrument afzonderlijk." "...works seem steeped in the character of each individual instrument and seem uniquely suited to that instrument's technique...." The four-movement String Quartet of 1967 is "...een ernstig werk van diepe expressie, waarin een lang leven van creatieve ervaring is verdisconteerd." "...a serious work of deep feeling, wherein one can see the culmination of his creative experience."

B304. Schuh, Willi. "Frank Martin: 'Quatuor à cordes' (1967)." Schweizerische Musikzeitung. Revue musicale suisse 108 (July-August 1968): 278-279.

   Reviewing the premiere of Frank Martin's only string quartet which he had written in his seventy-seventh year for the Zürich Tonhalle Gesellschaft for its centennial, the author has only high praise for the new work and its performance by the Tonhalle Quartet. The four-movement quartet predictably eschews the classic-romantic quartet style in favor of the style of writing for strings employed in his Etudes and other works. Beginning with a solo passage for the viola, reminiscent of the Ballade and the Concerto for Cello, the movement contains thematic material based on a tone row. The second movement is a scherzo, followed by a larghetto movement in which the first violin assumes the melodic line most of the time. The final movement contains elegant counterpoint and vivacity to bring the work to a convincing conclusion.

B305. Seelmann-Eggebert, Ulrich. "Hundert Jahre Züricher Tonhalle: Uraufführung von Frank Martins Streichquartett in Zürich." Neue Zeitschrift für Musik 129 (September 1968): 378-379.

   With justifiable pride the city of Zürich celebrates the 100th anniversary of its concert hall, whose international reputation can be attributed largely to its last two conductors, Hans Rosbaud and Rudolf Kempe. Nevertheless, Zürich can include Richard Wagner, Ferruccio Busoni, and Richard Strauss among the notable musicians who have

lived and worked there.   In recent years the commissioning of new
works has become an important adjunct to Zürich's musical life, and
for its one-hundredth anniversary the new work was provided by the
nation's most distinguished composer, Frank Martin.   The String
Quartet is the composer's only work in this genre.   The four-
movement work begins with the solo cello, reminiscent of his concerto
for that instrument.   A succession of common chords and dissonant
sequences calls to mind still other works.   The final movement,
according to the composer, was inspired by a dream of dancing
figures, and this is reflected in music that produces a haunting effect.

Requiem

B306.   Badura-Skoda, Paul. "Für das Oeuvre Frank Martins." Neue Züricher
Zeitung 29 November 1979, No. 278 p. 39.
In a tribute to Frank Martin on the occasion of the fifth
anniversary of the composer's death, the Viennese pianist tries to
explain why Martin's music, being of such high quality, continues to
experience relative neglect in concert halls, the opera house, and on
recordings. He asserts that a major cause is that Martin created
music out of an inner conviction, without regard to current fashion,
and was not concerned with publicity or public relations. Further, he
experienced no scandals to attract public attention, but simply
continued to work quietly producing a succession of works of the
highest quality. The author continues with his own personal
relationship with the composer during which two important keyboard
works were written and an enduring friendship established. Badura-
Skoda considers the composer's Requiem as possibly his greatest
work and rejoices that a tape recording of its premiere, with Frank
Martin conducting, will become available as a recording, along with
some of the composer's performances of his piano works. This is a
result of the tireless work of Mme. Maria Martin and the Frank Martin
Society.

B307.   Böhm, Hans. "Frank Martins 'Requiem' in Meissner Dom." Musica 29
(November-December 1975): 506-507.
-----. "Frank Martin: 'Requiem' im Meissner Dom." Kirchenmusiker:
Mitteilungen der Zentralstelle für evangelische Kirkenmusik 6 (1975);
175-176.
"DDR-Erstaufführungen in Meissen." Musik und Gesellschaft 26
(February 1976): 124.
This performance of Frank Martin's Requiem, performed on the
eve of his eighty-fifth birthday at the cathedral of Meissen (Dresden),
was reviewed enthusiastically in most German language music
journals. This provides some indication of the importance attached to
this late work of the already deceased Swiss composer. The author
indicates that many of Martin's most important works are known from
performances in the Dresden area. The Requiem impresses by its

sound color in the orchestra, and by the skillful deployment of solo voices, solo ensemble, and full choir and orchestra effects in this succinct but powerful setting. As in earlier works, Martin has succeeded in reconciling opposite musical elements in a way that is technically expressive and yet lies within the grasp of sensitive listeners. The success of this performance creates the desire that the work be given additional performances.

B308.   Buffet, Daniel. "Frank Martin nous dit..." <u>Revue musicale de suisse romande</u> 26 (1973): 2-4.
   Daniel Buffet conducts an interview with Frank Martin on the day following the world premiere of Martin's <u>Requiem</u>. After being greeted warmly by the composer at his hotel, the author poses a series of questions under the general headings of "an act of faith" and "problems of language and expression." In the first group, the questions explore the motivation for writing a requiem, its elements of anguish, the composer's response to other requiems recognized as being masterworks, and the use of speaking chorus in the <u>Dies Irae</u>. The first series of questions concludes with some discussion of the solo artists and the actual performance. In response to further questions, the composer defines his position regarding dodecaphony, enharmonic writing in his music, his interest in writing for the voice, and, finally, a word about his newest composition, the <u>Polyptyque</u> to be premiered soon by Yehudi Menuhin.

B309.   Gradenwitz, Peter. "Uraufführung des Requiems von Frank Martin in Lausanne." <u>Österreichische Musikzeitschrift</u> 28 (July-August 1973): 351-352.
   In an enthusiastic review of the world premiere of Frank Martin's <u>Requiem</u>, conducted by the composer in the Lausanne cathedral on May 4, 1973, the reviewer finds that the piece does not leave a feeling of fear and resignation but rather one of strength and conviction in one's destiny through divine love. Some of the significant elements that make up each of the eight sections of the work are identified by the author. An overall characteristic is that the choir and soloists together make up eight-note chromatic melodies that sometimes expand to twelve-tone writing. The <u>Dies Irae</u> employs a whispering chorus in syncopated rhythms which creates a mysterious effect that is at the same time not frightening and is totally dissimilar to the <u>Tuba Mirum</u> atmosphere associated with classical and romantic settings of the text. Another unique element is the <u>Agnus Dei</u> section which is performed by a solo alto voice accompanied only by the organ. There is also a setting of the <u>In Paradisum</u> which is usually omitted in musical settings of the mass. In the final <u>Lux Aeterna</u> the atmosphere created is one of faith in eternal light, eternal love. The <u>Requiem</u>, conducted by Frank Martin with the Suisse Romande Orchestra, outstanding soloists and chorus prepared by Robert Mermoud, is seen as an outstanding musical event.

B310. Haefer, Viktoria. "Report from Switzerland." <u>American Choral Review</u>
21 (July 1979): 19-21.

In a review of Frank Martin's <u>Requiem</u> as performed by the
Tonhalle Gesellschaft Zürich during the 1978-79 season, the author
surveys Martin's creative life and works with emphasis on the
influences of his Swiss background. The <u>Requiem</u>, written at the end
of a long and creative life, employs dodecaphonic elements in a
"somber and utterly personal interpretation of the text's medieval
imagery."

B311. Hausammann, Rolf. "A propos du Requiem de Frank Martin." Ecole
Normale de Lausanne, 1979. <u>See</u> B223

B312. Horn, Wolfgang. "Tonale Basis als Fundament Frank Martins
'Requiem' unter Almut Rössler in Düsseldorf aufgeführt." <u>Musik und
Kirche</u> 55 (1985): 203.

This brief review pays tribute to the Director for undertaking an
important work of great dramatic intensity which has not had the
exposure of frequent performances in German-speaking countries, as
have had the composer's <u>Golgotha</u>, <u>Petite symphonie concertante</u>,
and other works. The author makes a point to emphasize that,
although this work employs serial devices, it skillfully retains a tonal
basis throughout.

B313. Martin, Bernard. "La genèse du Requiem." <u>Revue musicale de suisse
romande</u> 27 (1974) 3-4.

In anticipation of a performance in Switzerland, Bernard Martin,
nephew of the composer, writes about how the <u>Requiem</u> came to be
written. The idea of composing a requiem was a decision made in
mid-life, but it waited over twenty-five years to be brought to fruition.
Yet during this period, he continually returned to the theme of death,
beginning with his first fully mature work <u>Le Vin herbé</u>, followed by
<u>Der Cornet</u>, the <u>Jedermann</u> songs, the great passion oratorio
<u>Golgotha</u>, a <u>Stabat Mater</u>, and, finally, the <u>Poèmes de la mort</u>.
Despite this recurring theme in his musical works, Frank Martin was
never a victim of "morose contemplation or morbid anxiety," but
remained positive in his attitude toward life and his work up to and
including the last day of his life, despite several occasions when
accidents or illness brought him close to the edge of life. Despite the
composition of so many works that would seem to make him uniquely
qualified to compose a requiem, Martin spent a long soul-searching
period exploring various means of setting the requiem to music,
including the possibility of finding an alternate text. Even an approach
using some of the devices of pop music such as electric (amplified)
instruments and electronic manipulation of the voice were considered.
Finally, as in the case of the passion music <u>Golgotha</u>, the composer
could find no text whose imagery stimulated his imagination as that of
the Mass of the dead, and he chose traditional oratorio resources of
soloists, choir, organ, and orchestra to convey his message. The

result of his long labor produced a powerful, succinct setting that will speak to many in a contemporary voice for today, and is a work that "...qui vous saisit dès la première note, et que ne vous lâche pas jusqu'au dernier <<Quia pius es!>>." "...grabs you from the first note and does not let you go until the last 'quia pius es.'"

B314.   Seelmann-Eggebert, Ulrich. "Lausanne: Das Requiem von Frank Martin Uraufführung als Auftakt des internationalen Musikfestes." Neues Zeitschrift für Musik 134 (1973): 365-366.

   The eighty-two-year-old composer, Frank Martin, conducted the premiere of his Requiem to open the 1973 International Music Festival in Lausanne (see W135). By his own admission, Frank Martin had long planned to write a requiem, but the work required what is perhaps the longest gestation period of any work which he composed--nearly a lifetime. Using the traditional resources of oratorio, that is, a quartet of soloists, organ, chorus, and orchestra, the composer has fashioned a work that employs all of the accumulated technical skills of a long creative life in writing music that at times employs the full force of the whole ensemble, and at others, as in the Agnus Dei, a single solo voice accompanied only by the organ. This Requiem, stark and uncompromising in its concentrated fifty minutes, is without sentimentality, yet powerful and moving for the audience hearing this quintessential work for the first time.

B315.   Shaw, A.T. "Festival stages British Premiere." Worcester Evening News 27 August 197-.

   Frank Martin's Requiem, conducted by John Saunders on a program with Vaughan Williams' Sancta Civitas, is given its first performance in Britain at the Three Choirs Festival in Worcester Cathedral. The reviewer predicts that this highly successful performance will lead to the Requiem finding a secure place in the repertoire of the leading choral societies.

Roméo et Juliette

B316.   Mermoud, Robert. "La musique de scène de Frank Martin pour Roméo et Juliette." Revue musicale de suisse romande 30 (1947): 14-19.

   Robert Mermoud reports on his research leading to a revival and performance of the music from a 1929 production of Shakespeare's Romeo and Juliet. The score, obtained from Mme. Maria Martin, revealed that Martin had composed fourteen pieces of incidental music in addition to five interspersed choruses with texts by René Morax. The composer creates an Elizabethan atmosphere using an unusual combination of five instruments: flute, violin, double bass, basset horn, and viole de gamba. The music is of two types: dances which are pastiches that display an elegance of writing but are not particularly original; and dramatic music employed at key points in the drama: the prologue, the prologue of the second act (describing Romeo's love), and the theme of death which is expressed in the final chorus. The author finds this music, which has remained unheard for half a century, impressive in its craftsmanship and expressiveness and worthy of being heard again, with or without the play of Shakespeare.

Rythmes

B317.   Mooser, Robert-Aloys. "VIIe Festival de la Société Internationale de Musique Contemporaine (Genève, Avril 1929): Rythmes, trois mouvements symphoniques." In Regards sur la musique contemporaines 1921-1946, 75-79. Lausanne: F. Rouge, 1946.

In reviewing the more than twenty new works at the seventh Festival of Contemporary Music, the author indicates that it is not a succession of masterworks destined to make their mark on the musical world, but that one feels lucky to go away having heard two or three pieces that really have something to say and that say it in a very personal way. The Rythmes of Frank Martin displays a mature style of writing and the skillful handling of a large orchestra. The three movements containing some orientalisms are seen as rhythmic experiments that deserve the favorable attention of the jury.

Sechs Monologe aus Jedermann

B318.   Mengelberg, Karel. "Rehfuss en Martin in fraaie liederavond." Vrije Volk [Amsterdam] 13 November, 1957.

In an article called "Rehfuss and Martin in beautiful lieder evening," the author reviews a recital given in the Kleinezaal (the small recital hall at the Concertgebouw) in which the Swiss-German baritone, assisted by Frank Martin, performs songs by Debussy, Wolf, Schubert and Martin's Sechs Monologe aus Jedermann. The reviewer, who indicates some negative feelings about the monologues of von Hofmannsthal, which he finds are full of dread, fear of death, and guilt, nevertheless indicates that these are masterfully set to music by Frank Martin and that the composer's participation at the piano surpasses that of the vocalist. The capacity audience was richly rewarded by the music and performances of this recital.

B319.   Regamey, Constantin. "Sechs Monologe aus 'Jedermann' pour baryton et orchestre." In Musique du vingtième siècle presentation du 80 oeuvres per orchestre de chambre, 153-154. Lausanne: Editions du Cervin, 1966.

After an initial success with Le Vin herbé, Frank Martin turned to works of German inspiration, and there produced in rapid succession the two ballets, Das Märchen vom Aschenbrödel and Ein Totentanz zu Basel. These were then followed by two song cycles, Der Cornet on the famous prose poem by Rilke and Sechs Monologe aus

Jedermann on Hugo von Hofmannsthal's setting of the morality play Everyman. The Jedermann songs, because of the type and shape of the literary work, constitute a German language counterpart to Le Vin herbé. Using simple but concentrated means, Martin is able to convey the unique flavor of Rilke's German text with power and originality. "Comme la ligne mélodique du <<Vin Herbé>> semble avoir été créé par langue francaise, de même la déclamation vocale épouse dans <<Jedermann>> les nuances les plus subtiles des inflexions pourtant si différentes du texte allemand." "As the melodic trend of Le Vin herbé seems to have been created by the French language, so the vocal declamation in Jedermann follows the most subtle points of the inflection of the German text which are very different." In a subsequent orchestral version, which came in 1949, the composer used the resources of a full orchestra to illustrate the poetic text.

B320.   Schuh, Willi. "Jedermann - Monologe." In Schweizer Musik der Gegenwart, 134-135. Zürich: Atlantis, 1948.
As in the timeless medieval legend of Tristan to which Frank Martin gave new expression while faithfully retaining its links to original sources, so once again Martin's creative muse has been stimulated by the Everyman morality play as set in German by Hugo von Hofmannsthal. It is no small achievement that the French-speaking composer has been able to extract the monologues from the play and yet retain a unity that achieves its own fulfilled expressive whole in a song cycle, and to respond with such sensitivity to verse in the German language. Employing a declamatory style throughout, the composer uses both dissonant and consonant elements side by side to achieve the somber, spiritual, and powerful cumulative effect which this work evokes.

B321.   Taubman, Howard. "Music: Work by Martin." New York Times 6 November, 1956.
Dietrich Fischer-Dieskau with Thomas Scherman and the Little Orchestra Society present the first performance in America of Frank Martin's Six Monologues from Jedermann in its orchestral version (see W89). Derived from von Hofmannsthal's adaption of the English morality play, Martin's austere music matches the emotional content of these monologues, and the artistry of Fischer-Dieskau assures that "one was drawn into the emotional ambience of the work whether one liked it or not."

Sonata da Chiesa

B322.   "Sonata da Chiesa. Six Monologues from Hofmannsthal's Jedermann." Music and Letters 35 (January 1954): 70-71.
In brief reviews of the scores issued by Universal-Edition, the reviewer gives high marks to the Sonata da chiesa, especially for its

long flexible melodic lines, but is negative about the far more frequently performed <u>Jedermann</u> songs.

Der Sturm

B323. Fiechter, Helmut A. "Martins Zauberlustspiel Wiener Festwochen." <u>Melos</u> 23 (October 1956): 297.
 In writing about the premiere in Vienna of Martin's opera <u>Der Sturm</u>, the author refers to Martin's essay "Nécessité d'une musique contemporaine" (see M27) where the composer talks about the ideal of being able to compose what he really wants to write, while at the same time searching for the impossible perfect piece that is new and original and is immediately accepted and loved by audiences. In <u>Der Sturm</u>, the composer moves in this direction by choosing to set to music almost the entire text of Shakespeare's <u>Tempest</u> as a labor of love. In this first operatic venture, Martin employs his already widely known style of lyrical and arioso-like recitative. In addition, we experience a new Martin writing music full of good humor and charm in a lightweight idiom. There are jazz rhythms with piano and muted strings, contrasted with tone rows in Caliban's music, a quote out of Mendelssohn's <u>Midsummer Night's Dream</u>, even a passage where the orchestra members are required to clap to illustrate a slap in the face. Particularly unique was the part of Ariel, played by a solo dancer and his lines sung by a chamber choir. Missing are big arias and operatic theatricality. Using the resources of the Vienna State Opera and the Vienna Philharmonic Orchestra, the work achieved a stunning premiere and is enthusiastically received despite its lack of operatic convention and the greater demands placed on the audience.

B324. Fierz, Gerold. "Märchen und Shakespeare - Frank Martin's Der Sturm in neuer Fassung." <u>Opernwelt</u> 8 (August 1967): 36.
 Frank Martin's opera on Shakespeare's <u>Tempest</u> is given a positive and sympathetic review. In this revival presented in Geneva in the French language and revised slightly to strengthen its theatrical effectiveness, but at the possible loss of some of its poetic fantasy, the new setting concerns the role of Ariel which originally was a non-speaking dancing role. Ariel's lines are sung by an off-stage madrigal choir with a small instrumental accompaniment dominated by the harp and harpsichord, which reminds us of the composer's <u>Petite symphonie concertante</u>. In the new version, the role is both danced and spoken. This raises the question: is it better to understand the words of Ariel in a literal and theatrical sense, or to enjoy the fantasy created by the offstage sung but unintelligible lines? There is also high praise for the composer's orchestral delineation of characters and even groups of related characters, and for the sensitive controlled conducting of Ernest Ansermet. The author hopes that the Geneva performances will lead to other performances of a deserving work.

B325.   Goddard, Scott. "Swiss Music of this Century." Listener 62 (October 15, 1959): 653-654.

In a BBC broadcast performance [in English] of Frank Martin's opera on Shakespeare's Tempest, the reviewer concludes that the opera only partially succeeds, most often in the orchestral score. He found that there were long stretches where the music seemed to distance itself from the action and thus failed to sustain the interest of the listener.

B326.   Kern, Heinz. "Zürich: Harmloser Sturm." Die Bühne No. 188 (May 1974): 23-24.

A review entitled "Harmless Storm," as the title suggests, is a mostly negative view of the Zürich production of Frank Martin's opera on Shakespeare's Tempest. Unique in this performance is a modification of the original role of Ariel which is performed by a dancer while the lines are sung by a small chorus. In this revision the dancer also speaks the lines, and in Zürich the part was played by the composer's youngest daughter, Teresa Martin, a professional dancer. This reviewer, however, finds her deficient in vocal training and the dance not sufficiently characteristic of the airy spirit. He also faults the conductor, the manner of depicting the actual storm, and the role of Caliban. Finally, the author recognizes Frank Martin as one of the most important musicians of our time but concludes that Der Sturm is undramatic.

B327.   Klein, Rudolf. "Frank Martins erste Oper." Österreichische Musikzeitschrift 11 (February): 50-56.

In an article written just prior to the premiere of Der Sturm, the editor of Vienna's Österreichische Musikzeitschrift reviews the relationship of Frank Martin with the musical public of Vienna. The Viennese, he states, are forever classic-romantic conservative and seldom accept a musical style from a foreign source, least of all from French impressionism; yet for a decade the music of Frank Martin has received critical and popular acclaim. To account for this, the author cites the composer's stylistic affinity for pure chords, sensuous tones, and full homophonic orchestral and choral writing combined with a response to Martin's seriousness and honesty in writing. The attraction that Shakespeare's Tempest holds for musicians is well documented. The singular lack of success can also be demonstrated. Despite the risks, Frank Martin devoted two and a half years of his life to just this task. Using the German text of Schlegel and reducing the play to three acts, the composer has otherwise adhered strictly to the text. This is achieved by what Wagner called "unending melody." In Martin's Tempest, there are long melodies sounded by the orchestra while the recitative is most often represented by short phrases interrupted by pauses. Contrasting characters and situations are sometimes represented by dodecaphonic procedures, sometimes by speech alone, or even by using jazz elements. The pivotal role of Ariel is cast as a solo dancer, whose lines are assigned to a chamber chorus, thus raising the level of fantasy to its highest point. Whether a work so innovative and so far removed from traditional opera can survive remains to be seen. The composer, however, by his own admission, has no regrets, so great has been his pleasure in composing the work.

B328.   Klein, Rudolf. "Stil und Technik der Musik in Frank Martins Oper <<Der Sturm>>." "Style et technique musicale de l'opera <<La Tempête>> de Frank Martin." <u>Schweischerische Musikzeitung.</u> <u>Revue musicale suisse</u> 96 (June 1956): 238-240.
        In an article written shortly before the world premiere, and based on talks with the composer as well as an examination of the score, the author describes the elements of style and technique that are employed in <u>Der Sturm</u>. Based on his previous accomplishments, Martin is perceived to be especially well suited to attempt Shakespeare's elusive fantasy play. The parallel between Debussy's <u>Pelléas et Melisande</u> music and Martin's opera is so striking that the author believes that, in a sense, Frank Martin has revived impressionism now generally concluded to be long passed. The technical means to this end are the composer's use of pure chords especially minor chords that provide strong coloration, while at the same time avoiding strong progressions that lead into cadences. "...verzichtet, resultiert daraus ein kaleidoskopartig rascher Wechsel der Akkorde, ein dauerndes Irisieren der Klangflächen, ein Glitzern und Flimmern, das immer in Bewegung ist." "...this means that a rapid kaleidoscopic change in chords results, a constant iridescence of the sound planes, a glistening and scintillating, which is in constant motion; nevertheless the feeling of a tonal basis is never lost." The composer has written that he attempted to give formal coherence to the opera by writing music that holds its own through its own development. Only performance experience will determine the success of his effort. The major thrust of carrying forward the drama of Shakespeare is accomplished through a form of "eternal melody" if we may borrow Wagner's term. The author describes it as a double melody consisting of long flowing melodies in the orchestra and short conversational phrases from the singers. This device is used for the music of Prospero, Miranda, and Ferdinand, while music reminiscent of the jazz idiom depicts the usurpers. Character delineation is further expanded by still other orchestral and formal devices. Caliban is defined by the sounds of the lower instruments in parallel seconds, the drunkards by spoken lines, and Ariel by ethereal choral sounds. The twelve-tone technique is used to express pain and trouble. Frank Martin acknowledges both the appeal and the enormous challenge of setting to music a work of such great diversity, being so musical yet elusive in the dramatic force needed to sustain operatic treatment. Only the experience of performances will determine the success of this unique musical work.

B329. Koch, Heinz. "Frank Martins Sturm in Zürich." <u>Opernwelt</u> 15 (June
       1974): 43.
           Frank Martin's Shakespeare opera on <u>The Tempest</u> was revived
       at Zürich in April, 1974, some fifteen years after its original premiere.
       With due respect paid to the inspiration and the skill of the composer,
       the author concludes that this play, which "...das so sehr nach der
       Einkleidung in Musik zu verlangen scheint, durch Musik eben nicht zu
       erreichen ist." "...so much demands the engagement of music, just
       cannot be reached with music." He finds that even at its best the
       addition of music binds and limits, even diminishes Shakespeare's
       elusive play and fails to grasp the varying spheres of the magic tale.
       The part of Ariel danced and spoken by the composer's daughter fails
       to come across convincingly, and the role of Ariel seemed to be
       withdrawn from the remainder of the play. Despite a performance of
       considerable distinction, <u>Der Sturm</u> remains a problematic work.

B330. Lockspeiser, Edward. "A New Shakespeare Opera." <u>Listener</u> 62
       (October 1, 1959): 548.
           This is a preview of a forthcoming radio broadcast for which
       Frank Martin's opera <u>The Tempest</u> had been converted back into
       English from the German translation of Schlegel used by Martin in his
       opera. After acknowledging Martin's success in setting the text of
       significant literary works by Rilke and Bédier, the author sets forth the
       enormous problem confronting a composer in setting the <u>Tempest</u> to
       music, and concludes that Frank Martin is only partially successful.
       The most significant weakness is perceived to be the lack of vocal
       lines that are sufficiently interesting enough to sustain the lengthy
       work. Strengths are seen in orchestral characterizations and in the
       poetic symbolism of Ariel's music as realized by a small chorus.

B331. Martin, Bernard. "La Tempête Shakespeare-Frank Martin - Vienne."
       <u>Christianisme social</u> 64 (October 1956): 804-806.
           The author praises the elegant production of the world premiere
       of the <u>Tempest</u> by Vienna's Staatsoper and the Vienna Philharmonic,
       in which every effort was expended to make it a truly festival
       occasion. The composer, Frank Martin, is perceived to be a musical
       mind of great wit and individuality, whose musical language is
       especially appropriate for a musical setting of the <u>Tempest</u>. Despite
       its elements of comedy, even gross farce, the <u>Tempest</u> most of all
       conveys a fairy tale atmosphere which Frank Martin has so
       successfully achieved. Martin's music enriches without deforming the
       play, and much of this is achieved by the skillful and imaginative
       writing for the orchestra. "Enfin, l'épilogue, ou Prospero, resté seul
       sur l'immense scène chante sa faiblesse d'homme dépouillé de tout
       pouvoir magique a inspiré à Frank Martin une page d'une
       extraordinaire et émouvante grandeur." "In the epilogue, where
       Prospero alone on the stage sings of his weakness as a man now
       stripped of his magical powers, Frank Martin has produced a musical
       scene of extraordinary and moving grandeur."

B332. Mittag, Erwin von. "Vienna Tempests." <u>Opera News</u> 21 (October 22, 1956): 16-17.
  In this brief review of the 1956 world premiere of Frank Martin's <u>Tempest</u> the reviewer finds the piece unconvincing as an operatic work, with too much of the score having the character of oratorio and chamber music.

B333. Mooser, Robert-Aloys. "Frank Martin 'Der Sturm' ein Zauber-Lustpiel en 3 Actes (Vienne, 17 juin 1956)." In <u>Aspects de la musique contemporaine, 1953-1957</u>, 215-220. Genève: Labor et Fides, 1957.
  After acknowledging the unusual hybrid nature of Martin's stage work on Shakespeare's "Tempest," the author explores the history and difficulties in adapting this elusive play to the lyric theatre. At least twenty composers have tried and failed, even though there may have been a limited success as with Halévy in 1850. Despite the lack of a composer of genius in past attempts, the play itself creates a formidable challenge in that dramatic action is reduced to a minimum, thus robbing an operatic version of dramatic energy and motion to carry forward the necessarily reduced pace required by the addition of music. Despite this, the many diverse elements and characters and the musical nature of this fantasy play present a temptation and challenge that composers cannot resist. Thus it was with Frank Martin, who, as always, remains absolutely faithful to the text and who creates unique music for the various characters and elements, but permits Ariel to dominate the score despite the fact that the part is assigned to a dancer. Similarly, the role of Caliban is distinctly defined by using serialistic musical language. "M. Frank Martin s'est ingénié à tendre, sur le texte de Shakespeare, ..." "Frank Martin wanted to put a musical texture, a light and transparent web on to Shakespeare's text." The composer accomplished his goal with consummate skill. It remains to be seen if his concept will be able to transcend operatic convention to become a permanent success.

B334. Saathen, Friedrich. "Current Chronicle. Austria." <u>Musical Quarterly</u> 42 (October 1956): 533-535.
  Frank Martin's opera on Shakespeare's <u>Tempest</u> is a world premiere at the Vienna Festival and a major social event as well. This reviewer finds that the German language setting of the fantasy comedy falls short, both as a stage piece and as a musical setting, in spite of a feeling that Martin's style is well suited for the <u>Tempest</u>. The part of Ariel is seen as the dominant role in Martin's setting, but the part is for a dancer, with Ariel's lines sung by a chamber chorus. Despite its flaws, this unusual work in the hands of skilled singing actors played to enthusiastic capacity audiences.

B335. Sargeant, Winthrop. "Mild Tempest." <u>New Yorker</u> 32 (October 20, 1956): 170.
  The New York premiere of Frank Martin's opera, <u>The Tempest</u>, is assessed to have been a failure due to the character of Martin's

music which lacks passion and dramatic momentum, and which ultimately creates an obstacle to the comprehension of Shakespeare's lines. This is most notable in the songs of Ariel assigned to a small chorus and portrayed by a dancer during which the text becomes nearly unintelligible.

B336. Schuh, Willi. "Frank Martin: 'Der Sturm' Uraufführung an der wiener Staatsoper." Schweizerische Musikzeitung. Revue musicale suisse 96 (July 1956): 316-319.

This extended and thoughtful essay goes considerably in depth beyond what one usually finds in the review of a new work. Martin's attraction to the Tempest is seen in terms of the correlation between the magic and poetic elements in the figure of Prospero, together with the mutual penetration of the lyrical and epic elements of the play over the dramatic. These qualities exerted a longtime attraction for the composer and ultimately resulted in his setting the entire play to music rather than in composing incidental music or a derivative concert hall piece. The result of Martin's musical fantasy is an esoteric work for the stage "...sein <<Sturm>> ist keine Oper (und will es gar nicht sein)..." "...that is not an opera and doesn't want to be one." What does emerge is a theatre piece that makes unusual demands on the audience and presupposes a thorough knowledge of Shakespeare's play (in the German translation by Schlegel) which will permit the listener to be drawn into the elements of fantasy and yet be able to follow the play simultaneously. The fantasy element that is most enlarged through musical means is the role of Ariel, the airy spirit creature, which is divided into a role for solo dancer whose lines are spoken through a backstage chamber choir and ensemble. Musically, the composer envelopes the characters and the play with a spiritual fundamental sound while employing a wide variety of musical devices to delineate various characters, moods, and situations. These include jazz elements and twelve-tone melodies, with narrative and dialogue sections employing the utmost non-operatic restraint. The complex and elusive fantasy play is not without problem areas. The addition of music necessarily adds weight and time and at times greater complexity, with the universal problem of the words versus the music ever present. The Vienna State Opera has given this new and innovative work its best in a production that reflects credit on all concerned.

B337. Walter, Franz. "A propos de la 'Tempete' de Frank Martin." Schweizerische Musikzeitung. Revue musicale suisse 96 (July 1956): 319-320.

In an enthusiastic response to the Vienna premiere of Frank Martin's opera on Shakespeare's Tempest, the author asserts that Martin has magnified Shakespeare's play, transcending it without alteration or simplification. Martin has achieved a nonrealistic and supernatural level which only his music could create. The author then attempts to explain how Martin has achieved this success in terms of the unique development of his musical style which has proceeded from simple sequences of perfect chords and modalities to atonal indetermination. In his attempt to escape the limitations of traditional keys and cadences, the composer explored a form of atonality that "...qui se meut, lui, dans ce monde intérmediaire qui est au-dessus de terre, qui flotte insaisissable, dans une région qu'on n'arrive pas à délimiter mais que certaines fibres de notre imagination et de notre sensibilité la plus profonde sont à même d'atteindre." "...moves about in an intermediary world, which floats above the earth and cannot be grasped, in a region that cannot be defined, yet our imagination and sensitivity can experience it." It is through this language, especially in the role of Prospero, that one experiences this power and fascination. Similarly, the originality of presenting the character of Ariel as a dancing role, whose lines are assigned to a chamber chorus, reinforces still further the magical atmosphere of the entire work. The review concludes with a tribute to the collective forces that took part in this stunning performance.

Symphonie pour grand orchestre

B338.   Ansermet, Ernest. "Frank Martin: 'Eerste symfonie' Holland Festival 1974." Concertgebouworkest June 18, 1974.
         In program notes from a 1974 Holland Festival concert, with Ernest Bour conducting the Concertgebouw Orchestra, in which Frank Martin's 1936 Symphony was revived, Ansermet's commentary from performances given during 1938 was also revived. First, the literary sources from which the composer drew inspiration are explored. These are the Apocalypse and Shakespeare's Tempest. Ansermet finds only the opening storm music of the Symphony and the end of this section to have an identifiable relationship to the Shakespeare play and feels that any further attempts to establish relationships would be misleading for the listener. Then, there is a brief summary of the movements in purely musical terms, and an attempt to label the work's musical style as Schoenbergian, but not atonal; instead, it is better defined as "harmonic polytonal."

B339.   Mooser, Robert Aloys. "Symphonie pour grand orchestre." Regard sur la musique contemporains 303-307. (March 10, 1938) Lausanne: F. Rouge.
         The compositions of Frank Martin during a span of twenty-five years, beginning with the First Violin Sonata, are briefly summarized to indicate the path followed by the composer in searching for his own musical style. The Symphony is perceived to have retained Martin's melodic gifts, even though the composer attempted to employ the principles of the twelve-tone system uncompromisingly. This four-movement symphony, despite its richness and intensity of feeling, is flawed by its excessive complexity both rhythmically and in its polyphonic lines, creating a confusion even for the most cultivated and

experienced ear. The Symphony makes an uncommonly strong statement from a young Swiss composer.

B340. Schönberger, Elmer. "Frank Martin componist von een onbekend gebleven symphonie." Preludium 32 (June - July 1974): 224-226.

In this article with the unusual title of "--composer of a symphony that remained unknown," the author previews a revival of Frank Martin's 1936 Symphony which was to be performed at the 1974 Holland Festival. The author carefully documents the background of the composer's environment, describing French-speaking Geneva as being totally Germanic in its musical culture until after World War I. It was the formation of the Orchestre de la Suisse Romande by Ernest Ansermet, and his subsequent programing of French and Russian contemporary music, that first exposed Martin to the new directions that early twentieth-century music was taking. After a period of living and studying in Paris, Martin first moved away from his late romantic formative style by attempting to embrace a manner of writing like that of Ravel. Finding this unsatisfactory, Martin undertook a through study of Schoenberg's system of composing with twelve equal tones. It is during this period and before he discovered his own unique style that Martin attempted to follow the system of Schoenberg in the strictest sense without becoming atonal. The large and complex Symphony has had few performances since its premiere by Ernest Ansermet in 1937.

Ein Totentanz zu Basel im Jahre 1943

B341. "Ein Totentanz zu Basel im Jahre 1943." Jubilaümskonzert der VKB (September 7-8, 1984): 23-24.

In program notes for a revival of A Death Dance in Basel in the Year 1943, the author recalls the impersonal "massdeath" that miraculously stopped at the borders of Switzerland in each of the two world wars. In this outdoor pageant, the figure of death confronts young and old, rich and poor, those awaiting death as a welcome friend, as well as the unexpecting and the terrified. It is a mimic play, utilizing strong dramatic music with chorus and orchestra, with the voice of death assigned to the drums. In 1943, Frank Martin composed new music using "old tunes" from the region of Basel.

Trio sur des mélodies populaires irlandaises

B342. Eeden, Hugo van. "Grondioos." De Tijd [Amsterdam] 11 December 1972.

In a review of Amsterdam's Guarneri Trio, the author comments on a program of Beethoven's E-flat Trio (Op. 70, no. 2), Frank Martin's Trio on Irish Folksongs and Tchaikovsky's sprawling A minor Trio, a combination described as "peculiar." For this reviewer, the

high point of the evening was the Martin work which he found to be
lighthearted, transparent and very original, demanding the greatest
skill and artistry from the players due to its complex polyrhythmic
structure. This music from 1925 remains fresh, and is only beginning
to find its rightful place in the active repertory.

Trois danses

B343.   Aprahamian, Felix. "Mellow Martin." London Sunday Times 13
        December, 1970, p. 24.
            In reviewing the British premiere of Frank Martin's Trois danses,
        a concertante piece commissioned by Paul Sacher for oboist Heinz
        Holliger and his wife, harpist Ursula Holliger, the author indicates how,
        in this new work from the eighty-year-old composer, Martin continues
        to write in his instantly recognizable style, regardless of other outside
        influences which he may have assimilated. Just as in the past, Martin
        adapted the twelve-tone technique of Schoenberg to his own style, so
        in the Trois danses elements of flamenco rhythm have been
        incorporated into this new work which remains totally in the idiom of
        Martin.

B344.   Hyatt, Willard. "Journal Reviews. Los Angeles." Music Journal 31
        (February 1973): 60.
            The American premiere of Trois danses was presented by
        Mitchell Lurie, clarinet, and Suzanne Balderston, harp, with Neville
        Marriner conducting the Los Angeles Chamber Orchestra. This was
        the first performance substituting clarinet for the original oboe for
        which the piece was written.

B345.   Martin, Maria. "Frank Martin 'Trois danses voor hobo, harp,
        strijkkwintet en strijkorkest.'" Preludium Nr. 6 (February 1975): 12-
        13.
            In a brief article written for the Concertgebouw subscription
        concerts, Maria Martin describes the Trois danses as a portrait of
        traditional flamenco music, written in the spirit of this art form, rather
        than an attempt to produce it literally. Borrowing from Frank Martin's
        own comments, we learn of his interest and motivation in writing this
        piece and a brief description of the rhythmic structure of the three
        dances.

B346.   Reich, Willi. "Ein neues Werk von Frank Martin." Schweizerische
        Musikzeitung. Revue musicale suisse 110 (November-December
        1970): 375-376.
            This is an account of the world premiere of Frank Martin's Trois
        danses, dedicated to Paul Sacher and his Collegium Musicum, Zürich.
        Sacher commissioned the work for the celebrated Swiss oboist, Hans
        Holliger. Martin responded with a work for both Holliger and his wife,
        harpist Ursula Holliger. As a tribute to the fine work of the Collegium

Musicum, he also included a part for solo string quintet. The piece was written at a time when the composer was intensely interested in the rhythmic aspects of flamenco music, and he created a work in which each of the three movements explores a different flamenco rhythmic figure. The reviewer finds in this new work musical developments which very strongly showed "...seine originelle thematische Erfindung, seine kühnen polyphonen Führungen, sein feines Formgefühl..." "...his unique thematical invention, his adventurous polyphonic voicings and his exquisite feeling of form...."

B347. Seelmann-Eggebert, Ulrich. "Zürich/Basel: Uraufführung der Trois danses von Frank Martin." Neue Zeitschrift für Musik 132 (January 1971): 132-134.

In its world premiere less than one month after the composer's 80th birthday, the Trois danses is seen as a reciprocal honor: the composer's gift of a new piece to the world, and its first presentation by Paul Sacher's Baseler Kammerorchester and the Zürich Collegium Musicum with whom the composer has had a long and cordial association, with several commissions by and dedications to the conductor and his orchestras. The Trois danses, written for Heinz and Ursula Holliger, was premiered by these artists along with the Petite symphonie concertante, commissioned and dedicated to Paul Sacher some 25 years earlier. The new three-movement work reflects Martin's recent interest in flamenco music, but it is never a folkloristic imitation of Spanish flamenco, either harmonically or melodically. Rather, the composer incorporates rhythmic and stylistic elements borrowed from flamenco into his own unique style.

B348. Swift, Richard. "Frank Martin Trois danses pour hautbois, harpe, quintette solo, et orchestre à cordes." Notes 24 (June 1973): 809-811.

Martin's Trois danses is reviewed along with George Perle's Serenade No. 2 and Eugene Kirtz's Conversations pour 12 instruments with top marks going to Mr. Perle. The reviewer describes the use of flamenco rhythms in each of the three movements of Martin's Danses, but faults the work for it's "plodding earnestness."

Le Vin herbé

B349. Arruga, Lorenzo. "Le Vin herbé." [program notes] Teatro alla Scala. alla piccola Scala (April 19, 1977): 7-10.

In program notes for a performance sung in Italian, we learn nothing of the particulars of this production of Il Vino stregato, but rather, the author examines the life and work and the stylistic evolution of Frank Martin in terms of those traits of character that have contributed to this unique setting of the Tristan legend. "Le Vin herbé è una rievocazione, come una vetrate moderna che rifaccia a suo modo quelle antiche di Chartres, del mondo medievale di Tristano ed Isotta." "Le Vin herbé is a re-evocation, like a modern stained-glass window, that refashions in its own way the ancient ones at Chartres, from the medieval world of Tristan and Isolde." Despite the influence of Debussy's Pelléas et Melisande, the extreme chromaticism--inherited from Wagner--but carried beyond into the dodecaphonic school of Schoenberg, Martin has succeeded in creating a work that speaks with the medieval voice of Joseph Bédier's noble prose, on which the work is based. This achievement is all the more remarkable for having been brought to fruition at a time when the greatest human catastrophe was beginning to take place in Europe and worldwide.

B350. Bernheimer, Martin. "Current Chronicle: Munich." Musical Quarterly 48 (October): 525-528.
    The evolution of Le Vin herbé is summarized, from its beginnings as a half-hour-long commission for a chamber choir and instruments, through its subsequent additions to create an evening-long three-part work, to its final format as a staged opera. The reviewer suggests that the work is not enhanced by staging, and lacks the dramatic impulse to succeed as a theatre piece. In addition, he finds that the work suffers from vocal, harmonic, and orchestral monotony.

B351. Cremers, Adrienne. "De legende vom Tristan en Isolde bej Richard Wagner en Frank Martin." Ph.D. diss., Leiden, 1963.
    This is believed to be the first in a series of formal papers on the musical works of Frank Martin that now number over two dozen. This early work, in the Dutch language, compares and contrasts the sources and the approach to the Tristan legend as employed by Wagner in his Tristan und Isolde and by Frank Martin in his Le Vin herbé.

B352. Daniel, Oliver. "Antiquity Updated." Saturday Review 45 (March 31, 1962): 39.
    Reviewed with the recording of Carl Orff's Antigone, Frank Martin's Le Vin herbé "updates" the Tristan legend based on three chapters of the novel by Joseph Bédier. In the greatest possible contrast to Wagner's monumental setting, Martin's score is for only twelve singers and eight instrumentalists. Its French text setting is stylistically far closer to Debussy than to Wagner. This recording, issued twenty years after the premiere, utilizes principal players from the Winterthur Orchestra, with the composer playing the piano part and with Victor Desarzens conducting.

B353. Fierz, Gerold. "Tragodie und Satyrspiel." Opernwelt 23 (May 1982): 42-43.
    Despite the extreme dramatic contrast in offering a double bill of Frank Martin's Le Vin herbé with Puccini's Gianni Schicchi, the risk of one work overshadowing the effectiveness of the other has been avoided and the interest and excitement of the contrast between the

two works is achieved, not only by the musical and dramatic skills of the artists, but by the skillful scenic designs and costumes. Both works were in the hands of the same creative designers. Le Vin herbé was especially successful in overcoming its oratorio conception, and proved to be a convincing theatre work in the imaginative productive in Genf (Switzerland). See: D229

B354. Frankenstein, Alfred. "Le Vin herbé: What Debussy planned now consummately achieved." High Fidelity 12 (May 1962): 66.
    In reviewing the Westminster recording of Le Vin herbé, the author asserts that Debussy's plan to write a Tristan opera in order to restore the legend to its original French ambience has now been successfully achieved by Frank Martin. The analogy to Debussy is not to specific impressionism, but rather to Martin's use of short themes that weave in and out, and his particular sensitivity to the rhythms, colors and intonation of the French language. "Every now and then, in the concert hall or on records, you will hear a new work so beautiful that for a while you do not want to hear any more music, wishing only to go back in memory and savor the loveliness of what has just been revealed. One such work is Le Vin herbé."

B355. Gugliemo, Edoardo. "Le Vin herbé." Academia musicale Chigiana, Siena. Estate musicale Chigiana (August 21, 1986)
    In the program notes for a 1986 performance in Siena, the author compares and contrasts the work of Martin with that of Wagner and Debussy. While comparisons with Wagner's grand epic are inevitable, Martin's piece is inspired by that of Debussy, and by his Pelléas and Melisande in particular. In the work of Frank Martin, elements of twelve-tone writing are fused with an undeniably impressionistic flavor to create a unique language that expresses a sort of archaism that brings to mind stained glass windows and early tapestry. The three-part work is drawn from chapters of the Roman de Tristan et Iseult by Joseph Bédier. Unlike Wagner's massive setting of the Tristan legend, Martin uses a small chorus from which solo voices emerge. A small chamber ensemble of instruments serves as the orchestra. Le Vin herbé, despite its twelve-tone elements, is fundamentally French. It is neither gaudy nor showy, rather it is formal, detached, stylized and very faithful to the legend of Tristan and Isolde.

B356. Hunziker, Andre. "Geneva." Opera 33 (August 1982): 852-853.
    This is a brief review of a double bill pairing Martin's Le Vin herbé with Puccini's Gianni Schicchi. This reviewer sees Martin's work as a combination of opera, oratorio, and mystery play. He praises both the theatrical skills employed, and the high artistry of the musicians in making a successful stage work of a piece conceived as oratorio which is basically static and severe in content. For another reaction to this same production see B353.

B357.   Jacobi, Peter. "Review of Recorded Music: Non Wagnerian Tristan, non ..." Music Magazine 164 (July 1962): 48.

In reviewing the Westminster recording of Le Vin herbé (see D229), the reviewer pays tribute to Frank Martin in having the courage to risk direct comparisons with Wagner's monumental work. In fact, the Swiss composer ignores the Wagnerian setting and approaches the Tristan legend in his own way. "Call it a cantata or a dramatic oratorio or a chamber opera, it is poetry of immense subtlety and refinement. It is less a drama unfolding directly than a tale told through the veils of third persons, story tellers, minstrels - a story more told about than told."

B358.   Kessler, Giovanna. "Keine Ruhmesblätter. Martins Zaubertrank und Debussys Pelléas und Melisande in Mailand." Opernwelt 18 (July 1977): 34-35.

Although it is gratifying that the season at La Scala contains a generous number of modern works, these new works do not assure an artistic success. Frank Martin's Le Vin herbé (Zaubertrank), conceived as an oratorio, but now being presented as a staged operatic production, provided great difficulty for Director Lamberto Poggelli. It seemed as if "...Dirigent, Musiker und Solisten vermummt und geduckt, wie nach einem Bombenangriff aus dem Keller kommen..." "...conductor, musicians and soloists mummified and crouched like after a bomb attack come out of the cellar." Musically the chamber ensemble of musicians performed the uncommonly attractive score with all of its subjectivity. The singers, though uneven, gave it their best.

B359.   Lewinski, Wolf-Eberhard von. "Wiesbadener Beiträge." Opernwelt 26 (July 1985): 11.

An unusual double bill at Wiesbaden's State Theatre paired Dvořák's Geisterbraut with Frank Martin's Le Vin herbé (Zaubertrank). The almost undramatic oratorio is presented choreographically with the singers placed on the side of the stage. Unfortunately, the choreographic action is not sufficiently convincing, and the work proved to be less exciting than thirty years ago when it was new.

B360.   "Martin's 'Le Vin herbé' has impressive U.S. Premiere." Musical Courier 163 (April 1961): 9,12.

The first performance in New York of Le Vin herbé by Hugh Ross and the Schola Cantorum, some twenty years after it was written, is seen as an impressive success. The reviewer finds the handling of the solo voices, the striking use of the chorus as an active participant in the setting forth of the story, and the effective use of the small ensemble who make up the orchestra all add up to an effective setting of the Tristan legend. Only its consistent and unrelieved sadness is seen as a weakness in the score.

B361.   Martin-Boeke, Maria. "Frank Martin: 'Le Vin herbé.'" [in Dutch]
        Holland Festival 1957 June 24, 1957.

        In program notes for the 1957 Holland Festival, the composer's
wife describes the circumstances of the work, and how it was
commissioned for a madrigal choir in Zürich, consisting of only twelve
voices in which the piece was to be "custom-tailored" for each of the
singers, and was to be of a half hour duration. Martin's solution was
to adapt one chapter from Joseph Bédier's Le Roman de Tristan et
Iseult for the chorus of twelve singers and an ensemble of seven
strings and piano. Both solo roles and the choral parts were sung by
the madrigal choir. The success of the performance led the
composer to expand the work to three chapters from the Tristan
legend, and for it to subsequently be staged as an operatic
production. Mme. Martin concludes with a detailed description of the
story.

B362.   Miller, Philip L. "The Most Famous Work of Frank Martin." American
        Record Guide 28 (April 1960): 643.

        This is a review of the Westminster recording of Le Vin herbé
(see D229), in which the composer takes part by playing the
important piano part. As any setting of the Tristan legend invites
comparisons with Wagner's monumental opera, Martin's setting is in
sharpest contrast to that of Wagner, employing chamber oratorio
resources and using them in a way totally removed from the idiom of
Wagner and of traditional opera. The reviewer applauds and predicts
a wide appeal for Martin's work.

B363.   Mooser, Robert Aloys. "Frank Martin Le Vin herbé." In Regards sur la
        musique contemporaine 1921-1946, 351-354. Lausanne: F. Rouge,
        1946.

        In an article written when Le Vin herbé was a new and
unorthodox conception of the Tristan legend, the author praises the
composer for his belief that art forms cannot remain the same, but
that each generation must seek new forms of expression. He
recognizes the value of Martin's assimilation of the twelve-tone system
and his skillful and personal use of it in this work. Using three
chapters from the novel by Joseph Bédier, the composer has
fashioned chamber music which is in the greatest possible contrast to
Wagner's grandiose conception. Martin, using only twelve voices
singing in French and assisted by an ensemble of only eight
instruments, tells the tragic story. He uses the singers as the chorus
of an ancient tragedy, but also to portray the action of the drama
from which the solo roles are drawn. The result is a work, though
stylized and detached, which nevertheless speaks in true and
experienced emotions that constitute its subtle force and power.

B364.   Paap, Wouter. "Le Vin herbé van Frank Martin." <u>Mens en melodie</u> 20
(September 1946): 303-306.

In a preview of the Netherlands premiere of <u>Le Vin herbé</u>, the
author reviews the composer's background and achievements and
presents a detailed list of his works up to the point of <u>Golgotha</u>,
which had not yet been completed. Focusing on <u>Le Vin herbé</u>, the
structure of the work is discussed, including the use of a prologue
and epilogue. The twelve voices employed achieve their expressive
ends by sometimes singing all together, while at other times the music
passes back and forth between sections and also is used to support
solo voices that are at other places heard with only the instrumental
ensemble. The music is written in a recitative style in which the
descending third interval is used to great effect in the melodic line to
enhance the expression of words. There is a discernible similarity
between Martin's motifs and those of Schoenberg, although Martin's
sense of stylistic freedom and independence links him more closely to
the aesthetic of Alban Berg. The author concludes that "...het
twaalftonensysteem heeft gehanteerd, hem niet verhinderd een sterk
geïnspireerd, plastisch, teeder en op sommige plaatsen aangrijpend
kunstwerk te scheppen, dat van een zeer oorspronkelijke visie op de
bekende litteraire stof getuigt." " ...the twelve-tone system has not
hindered him in exhibiting surprising, flexible (plastic), tender and in
some places gripping artistry that gives witness to a truly original
vision of the literary material."

B365.   Ponse, Luctor. "Frank Martin Le Vin herbé." [in Dutch] <u>Preludium</u> No.
9 (June 1957): 178-179.

In this article, the author describes how <u>Le Vin herbé</u> came to be
written as a commission for a twelve-voice madrigal choir in Zürich.
The composer selected a favorite story of his, the Tristan legend as it
appears in the novel by Joseph Bédier, setting to music the fourth
chapter of this book for twelve singers, accompanied by a chamber
ensemble of only seven strings and piano. Subsequent to its
successful premiere, Martin enlarged the work with two additional
chapters from Bédier plus a prologue and an epilogue. Using the
singers as both soloist and chorus, the composer was able to fashion
a work of great subtlety and emotion using minimal performing
resources to accomplish his purpose. By writing in a monodic style,
the words can be heard and understood at all times. "Bij het
beluisteren van Le Vin herbé, kan men niet onverschillig blijven voor
de gevoelens van het menselijk hart. Ze zijn getransponeerd in
muziek met een zuiver lyrisme, en met gebruik van zeer gevoelige
harmonieen, hetgeen typerend is voor de kunst van Frank Martin."
"When listening to <u>Le Vin herbé</u>, one cannot remain unmoved by the
feelings of the human heart. They are brought out in the music by a
very pure lyricism through the use of very emotional harmonies full of
feeling, which is typical of the art of Frank Martin."

B366. Rasponi, Lanfranco. "Geneva." <u>Opera News</u> 47 (August 1982): 34.
Le Vin herbé, as presented in German as a double bill with
Puccini's <u>Gianni Schicchi</u>, is seen as more oratorio than opera. The
author faults the staging, costumes, and lighting as "senseless and
ugly," while the whole production is mostly lost in darkness. The
director is perceived to have failed in "not allowing the tender, elegiac
quality of the text and music to transpire on stage." For another view
of this same production see B353.

B367. Regamey, Constantin. "'Le Vin herbé.'" In <u>Musique du vingtième siècle
presentation de 80 oeuvres pour orchestre de chambre</u>, 150-153.
Lausanne: Editions du Cervin, 1966.
Essentially the same essay was used as program notes on two
previous occasions (see B368).

B368. Regamey, Constantin. "Frank Martin 'Le Vin herbé.'" <u>Orchestre de
Chambre de Lausanne</u> [program notes] (March 11, 1968).
In program notes for a performance at Lausanne's Théâtre
Municipal in 1968, the author's essay from a similar performance on
28 January 1957 is reprinted. In writing about Le Vin herbé, Regamey
states that the dominant characteristics of this work are its equilibrium
and sense of moderation. He further asserts that the characteristic
which is common to all of Martin's great works is the search for
artistic achievement which results from finding, to some degree,
solutions to problems both technical and of a human and artistic
nature. In Le Vin herbé, one such problem was the existence of
Wagner's monumental opera on the Tristan legend. In this instance,
the composer followed the path of the author Joseph Bédier, and
attempted to create a musical "Latin" version with no attempt to
compete with Wagner on operatic terms. In so doing, Le Vin herbé
became a secular oratorio without theatrical effect or operatic
convention, which makes its points using the absolute minimum of
musical resources, only a chorus of twelve voices supported by seven
strings and piano. Uniquely, the argument is set forth by the chorus
in stylized language like a monotone. From this, individuals emerge
from the group to become the principal soloists whose music, in
contrast, is dramatic, expressing sometimes violent emotions. It is the
stylized reserve in moments such as the lover's kiss and Tristan's
death that represent the greatest contrast with Wagner's opera.
Martin's technical devices include music that is not essentially
polyphonic, but tonal. At other times twelve-tone procedures are
employed, in which the melody is tonal while the accompanying
harmony is dodecaphonic. This is a procedure which reverses the
composer's more common practice of composing melodies on the
twelve-tone principle while undergirding them with a tonal framework.
Finally, there is a prologue and epilogue differing from the remaining
music, which is deliberately archaic and serves as a frame which
encloses the triptych to create a unified whole.

B369.   Rothon, Greville. "Le Vin herbé." Opera 13 (Autumn 1962): 86-87.
        This is a review of Le Vin herbé presented at the Munich Opera
        Festival in 1962, in which this reviewer found that, despite some good
        singing, the work fails as both a convincing musical score and
        particularly as a stage work. The result [for him] is thus a complete
        bore.

B370.   Sabin, Robert. "New York Premier of Martin's Vin Herbé." Musical
        America 81 (April 1961): 24.
        Some twenty years after its premiere Frank Martin's Le Vin herbé
        received its first New York performance by Hugh Ross and the Schola
        Cantorum. Martin's music is perceived to be not very "advanced," yet
        his very free but complex harmonic structure creates a tenderness
        especially appropriate for the Joseph Bédier setting of the Tristan
        legend.

B371.   Sams, Jeremy. "College and other performances- Le Vin herbé."
        Opera 33 (July 1982): 767.
        At the first staged performance in Britain of Frank Martin's
        oratorio Le Vin herbé, the reviewer sees the work as a masterpiece
        but not an operatic one when he states: "Martin's distant, stylized
        music can only make sense in an unoperatic presentation."

B372.   Schuh, Willi. "Frank Martin 'Le Vin herbé.'" In Schweizer Musik der
        Gegenwart, 131-134. Zürich: Atlantis, 1948.
        This is an elegant essay that defines Frank Martin's musical work
        in terms of its relationship to both Joseph Bédier's Roman de Tristan
        et Iseult and Wagner's Tristan und Isolde. Martin succeeds in his
        setting of the Tristan legend by a strict adherence to the text of
        Bédier's novel, in which the writer draws from the oldest sources and
        never mixes modern conceptions with the old forms of thinking and
        feeling. The composer began with a single chapter (le Philtre), but
        soon expanded his work to embrace three chapters from Bédier's
        novel, with a few lines borrowed from other parts of the book to
        create the necessary continuity. These chapters are then divided into
        several tableau, which are masterful in form, and permit the tragic tale
        to unfold. By using the greatest economy of singers and
        instrumentalists in a modern oratorio style, he is able to transform the
        current tragedy into a feeling of timelessness. Le Vin herbé is a piece
        of highly creative uniqueness, and is the "Tristan" of our times.
        Martin's work succeeds, just as Wagner's Tristan succeeded, because
        love becomes a tragic and unavoidable destiny which is developed
        through a highly personal tonal language of great seriousness, with
        dark and painful beauty which keeps its unique original-archaic
        character despite its modern setting.

B373. Tappolet, Willy. "Musique contemporaine suisse." Schweizerische
Musikzeitung. Revue musicale suisse 81 (February 1941): 29-30.
This review describes Martin's Le Vin herbé as originally
conceived as a commission for the Madrigal-Choir of Zürich, and
containing only the musical setting of Joseph Bédier's "Le Philtre,"
chapter four of his Roman de Tristan et Iseult. The author finds most
noteworthy the extreme economy of means which achieves so much.
The vocal resources consist of only twelve voices which include the
title roles, and an even smaller instrumental ensemble. The resulting
work is perpetually somber, employing twelve-tone devices to achieve
a remarkable sonorous richness. The article begins by asking the
question of whether Le Vin herbé is an oratorio, a dramatic cantata, a
ballad, or music to accompany a drama. It concludes by calling it an
extraordinary piece of chamber music.

B374. Trilling, Ossia. "Frank Martin und Betty Roe beim Winterfestival."
Operwelt 24 (March 1983): 47-48.
The English port city of Camden is the setting for Frank Martin's
Le Vin herbé (The Magic Potion), staged here for the first time in
English, and performed alternately with a newly commissioned work,
Betty Roe's Gaslight. Martin's work, described as "thrilling music
drama," is well sung and well played with imaginative lighting and
direction. The piece was conducted with inspiration and sensitivity by
Timothy Dean.

B375. "Le Vin herbé Der Zaubertrank." [in German and English] Saltzburger
Festspiele [program notes] (1948): 59-62.
Despite, or perhaps because, of the great success of Wagner's
opera on the Tristan legend, the Latin peoples of Europe have long
desired and felt the need of a setting more faithful to the early legend
and in a Latin language. This idea is now realized by Frank Martin in
a setting of Joseph Bédier's Tristan novel using a chamber ensemble
of voices and instruments in sharp contrast to Wagner's mammoth
work, and which is set in the French language. "The music,
developed out of a few clearly profiled principal tunes, is marked by
strong colour and great inner motion."

Appendix I: Alphabetical List of Compositions

The "W" numbers following each title in Appendices I and II refer to the "Works and Performances" section of this volume.

A la Foire d'amour	W77
A la Fontaine	W77
Agnus Dei (Messe)	W125
Agnus Dei (Requiem)	W136
Amour de moy	W75
Ariel	W92
Armide	W18
Athalie	W82
Au clair de la lune	W101
Ballade des pendus	W132
Ballade pour alto et orchestre à vent	W137
Ballade pour flûte et grand orchestre	W47
Ballade pour flûte et piano	W47
Ballade pour flûte et orchestre à cordes	W52
Ballade pour piano et orchestre	W48
Ballade pour saxophone et orchestre à cordes	W43
Ballade pour trombone et petit orchestre	W53
Ballade pour trombone et piano	W49
Ballade pour violoncelle et piano	W87
Blaue Blume, Die	W38

Campagnarde (Eho! Eho!)	W71
Canon pour Werner Reinhart	W66
Cantate pour le 1er août	W54
Cantate sur la Nativité	W26
C'était Anne de Bretagne	W72
Chaconne (from Second Violin Sonata)	W105
Chanson (le petite village)	W30
Chanson des jours de pluie	W77
Chanson des Metamorphoses	W90
Chanson du Mezzetin	W16
Chanson en canon	W32
Chanson satirique	W70
18 Chansons (from La Nique à Satan)	W24
Chantons, je vous en prie	W10
Clair de lune	W95
Concert pour clavecin et petit orchestre	W94
Concert pour instruments à vent et piano	W19
Concerto I pour piano et orchestre	W35
Concerto II pour piano et orchestre	W129
Concerto pour sept instruments à vent et orchestre	W88
Concerto pour violon et orchestre	W93
Concerto pour violoncelle et orchestre	W124
Cornet, Der	W60
Coucou, Le	W31
Danse de la peur (from Die blaue Blume)	W39
Danse grave (from Das Märchen vom Aschenbrödel)	W57
Dédicace	W78
Dithyrambes, Les	W7
Divorce, Le	W22
Drei Fragmente auf Der Sturm	W99
Drey Minnelieder	W113
Du Rhône au Rhin	W46
Eho! Eho! (Campagnarde)	W71
Eléments, Les Quatre	W120
En revenant d'Auvergne	W72
Entr'acte	W19
Erasmi monumentum	W131
Es ist ein Schnitter, heisst der Tod	W36
Esquisse pour orchestre	W11
Esquisse pour piano	W123
Et la vie l'emporta	W141
Etude de lecture	W123
Etude rythmique	W122
Etudes pour orchestre à cordes	W102
Etudes pour deux pianos	W104

Fantaisie sur des rythmes flamenco	W139
Faut partir pour l'angleterre, II	W91
Five Ariel Songs	W92
Golgotha	W80
Grenouilles, le rossignol et la pluie, Les	W42
Guitare pour orchestre	W34
Guitare pour piano	W34
Huit préludes pour piano	W86
In dulci jubilo	W112
Inter arma caritas	W118
In terra pax	W68
Janeton	W62
Jeux du Rhône	W27
Joli tambour	W71
Luzerner Festival Ouvertüre (Ouverture en rondeau)	W108
Ma belle	W70
Magnificat	W127
Mai, Le	W70
Marche de Genava	W59
Marche des 22 cantons	W59
Märchen vom Aschenbrödel, Das	W55
Maria-Triptychon	W130
Meine Stimme klinge	W74
Messe	W15
Monsieur de Pourceaugnac	W114
Mystère de la Nativité, Le	W106
Nique à Satan, La	W23
Noël de Praetorius	W70
Notre Père (In terra pax)	W69
Nous sommes trois souverains princes	W119
Ode à la musique	W115
Ode et sonnet	W3
O Dieu, c'est dans ta Sion sainte	W128
Oedipe à Colone	W17
Oedipe-Roi	W14
O Nuit, heureuse nuit	W70
Ouverture en hommage à Mozart	W103
Ouverture en rondeau	W108
Ouverture et foxtrot	W19
Ouverture pour Athalie	W83

Passacaille pour grand orchestre	W117
Passacaille pour orchestre à cordes	W97
Passacaille pour orgue	W67
Pavane couleur du temps	W12
Petite complainte (from Das Märchen vom Aschenbrödel)	W56
Petite eglise	W65
Petite fanfare	W79
Petite marche blanche et trio noir	W42
Petite symphonie concertante	W76
Pièce brève (from Mystère de la Nativité)	W107
Pilate	W121
Poèmes de la mort	W133
Polyptyque	W138
Psaume 42	W70
Psaume 104	W70
Pseaumes de Genève	W110
Quant n'ont assez fait do-do	W84
Quatre pièces brèves pour guitare	W34
Quatre sonnets à Cassandre	W13
Quatuor à cordes	W126
Que Dieu se montre seulement	W109
Quintette avec piano	W9
Requiem	W135
Rhapsodie	W37
Roméo et Juliette	W25
Roy a fait battre tambour, Le	W8
Rythmes	W21
Sechs Monologe aus Jedermann	W64, 89
Si Charlotte avait voulu	W63
Sonata da chiesa pour flûte et orchestre à cordes	W111
Sonata da chiesa pour flûte et orgue	W51
Sonata da chiesa pour viole d'amour et orchestre à cordes	W96
Sonata da chiesa pour viole d'amour et orgue	W45
Sonate en La majeur d'Henrico Albicastro	W28
Sonate en Mi mineur de Gaspard Fritz	W29
Sonate en Mi mineur d'Henrico Albicastro	W28
Sonate I pour violon et piano	W5
Sonate II pour violon et piano	W33
So wünsch ich ihr eine gute Nacht	W73
Sturm, Der	W98
Suite pour orchestre	W4
Symphonie concertante	W81
Symphonie pour grand orchestre	W41
Symphonie pour orchestre burlesque	W6

Tête de Linotte	W1
Totentanz zu Basel im Jahre 1943, Ein	W61
Trimousette (Le Mai)	W71
Trio à cordes	W40
Trio sur des mélodies populaires irlandaises	W20
Trois Chants de Noël	W85
Trois Danses	W134
Trois Poèmes païens	W2
Verse à boire	W116
Vin herbé, Le	W44, 50
Voix des siècles, La	W58
Wach auf, Wach auf	W73
Wer jetzig Zeiten leben will	W74
Wohl auf, wer bass will wandern	W74
Zaubertrank, Der	W44, 50

Appendix II: Classified List of Compositions

STAGE

Athalie	W82
Die blaue Blume	W38
Le Divorce	W22
Das Märchen vom Aschenbrödel	W55
Monsieur de Pourceaugnac	W114
Mystère de la Nativité	W106
La Nique à Satan	W23
Oedipe à Colone	W17
Oedipe-Roi	W14
Roméo et Juliette	W25
Der Sturm	W98
Ein Totentanz zu Basel im Jahre 1943	W61
Le Vin herbé	W44, 50
La voix des siècles	W58
Der Zaubertrank (Le Vin herbé)	W44, 50

ORCHESTRAL

Ballade pour alto et instruments à vent	W137
Ballade pour flûte et grand orchestre	W47
Ballade pour piano et orchestre	W48
Ballade pour trombone et petit orchestre	W53
Ballade pour violoncelle et petit orchestre	W87
Chamber Fox Trot	W19
Concert pour clavecin	W94
Concert pour instruments à vent et piano	W19
Concerto I pour piano	W35

Concerto II pour piano	W129
Concerto pour sept instruments à Vent	W88
Concerto pour violon et orchestre	W93
Concerto pour violoncelle et orchestre	W124
Danse de la peur pour deux pianos et orchestre	W39
Du Rhône au Rhin (band, arr. also for orchestra)	W46
Entr'acte pour orchestre	W19
Erasmi monumentum pour orgue et grand orchestre	W131
Esquisse pour orchestre	W11
Guitare (version for orchestra)	W34
Inter arma caritas	W118
Luzerner Festival Ouverture	W108
Ouverture en hommage à Mozart	W103
Ouverture en rondeau	W108
Ouverture pour Athalie	W83
Passacaille pour grand orchestre	W117
Pavane couleur du temps pour petit orchestre	W97
Les Quatre eléments pour grand orchestre	W120
Rythmes pour orchestre	W21
Suite pour orchestre	W4
Symphonie concertante	W81
Symphonie pour grand orchestre	W41
Symphonie pour orchestre burlesque	W6

WORKS FOR STRING ORCHESTRA

Ballade pour flûte et orchestre à cordes	W52
Ballade pour saxophone et orchestre à cordes	W43
Etudes pour orchestre à cordes	W102
Petite symphonie concertante	W76
Polyptyque pour violon solo et 2 orchestres à cordes	W138
Sonata da chiesa pour viole d'amour et orchestre à cordes	W96
Trois danses pour hautbois, harpe et orchestre à cordes	W134

CHAMBER AND INSTRUMENTAL

Agnus Dei pour orgue	W125
Ballade pour flûte et piano	W47
Ballade pour saxophone et piano	W43
Ballade pour trombone et piano	W49
Ballade pour violoncelle et piano	W87
Chaconne pour violoncelle et piano	W105
Pavane couleur du temps	W12
Petite complainte	W56

Petite fanfare	W79
Piece brève pour flûte, hautbois et harpe	W107
Quatre pièces brèves pour guitare	W34
Quatuor à cordes	W126
Quintette pour piano et quatuor à cordes	W9
Rhapsodie pour 2 violons, 2 altos, et contrebasse	W37
Sonate I pour violon et piano	W5
Sonate II pour violon et piano	W33
Sonata da chiesa pour flûte et orgue	W51
Sonata da chiesa pour viole d'amore et orgue	W45
Trio à cordes	W40
Trio sur des melodies populaires irlandaises	W20

KEYBOARD WORKS

Agnus Dei pour orgue	W125
Au clair de lune	W101
Clair de lune	W95
Danse grave	W57
Drei leichte Klavierstücke	W42, 101
Esquisse	W123
Etude rythmique	W122
Etudes (2 pianos)	W104
Fantaisie sur les rythmes flamenco	W139
Les grenouilles, le rossignol et la pluie petit nocturne [2 pianos]	W42
Guitare: quatre pièces brèves	W34
Huit préludes	W86
Ouverture et foxtrot [2 pianos]	W19
Passacaille pour orgue	W67
Pavane couleur du temps [2 pianos]	W12
Petite marche blanche et trio noir [2 pianos]	W42

VOCAL WORKS WITH ORCHESTRA

Der Cornet	W60
Drei Fragmente aus der Sturm	W99
Maria-Triptychon	W130
Le Roy a fait battre tambour	W8
Sechs Monologe aus Jedermann	W89
Trois poèmes païens	W2
Le Vin herbé	W44, 50

VOCAL WORKS WITH KEYBOARD ACCOMPANIMENT

Agnus Dei (Requiem)	W136
Dédicace	W78
Drey Minnelieder	W113
Faut partir pour l'angleterre, II	W91
Sechs Monologe aus Jedermann	W89
Tête de Linotte	W1

VOCAL WORKS WITH VARIOUS INSTRUMENTS

Ballade des pendus	W132
Chanson du mezzetin	W16
Drey Minnelieder	W113
Poèmes de la mort	W133
Quant n'ont assez fait do-do	W84
Quatre sonnets à Cassandre	W13
Trois chants de Noël	W85

CHORAL WORKS WITH ORCHESTRA

Les Dithyrambes	W7
Et la vie l'emporta	W141
Golgotha	W80
In terra pax	W68
Jeux du Rhône	W27
Mystère de la Nativité	W106
Ode à la musique	W115
Pilate	W121
Pseaumes de Genève	W110
Requiem	W135

CHORAL WORKS WITH VARIOUS INSTRUMENTS

Cantate pour 1er Août	W54
Chantons, je vous en prie	W10
Notre Père	W69

CHORAL WORKS UNACCOMPANIED
MIXED CHORUS

Canon pour Werner Reinhart	W66
Chanson en canon	W32
Five Ariel Songs	W92
Messe pour double choeur	W15
Verse à boire	W116

Arrangements

Es ist ein Schnitter, heisst der Tod	W36
So wünsch ich ihr eine gute Nacht	W73
Wach auf, wach auf	W73

MEN'S CHORUS

A la faire d'amour	W77
A la fontaine	W77
Chanson des jours de pluie	W77
Janeton	W62
Petite église	W65
Si Charlotte avait voulu	W63

Arrangements

Chanson satirique	W70
Eho! eho! (Campagnarde)	W70
Ma belle	W70
Le Mai (Trimousette)	W70
Noël Praetorius	W70
Psaume 42	W70
Psaume 104	W70
O nuit, heureuse nuit	W70

WOMEN'S CHORUS

Campagnarde (eho! eho!)	W71
C'était Anne de Bretagne	W72
Joli tambour	W71
Trimousette (Le Mai)	W71

Arrangements

Chanson, le petite village	W30
Le coucou	W31
Ode et sonnet	W3
Petite église	W65

CHILDREN'S VOICES

Arrangements

Meine Stimme klinge	W74
Wer jetzig Zeiten leben will	W74
Wohl auf, wer bass will wandern	W74

REALIZATIONS, INSTRUMENTATIONS AND ARRANGEMENTS

Stage

Armide pour Jean-Baptiste Lully	W18

Chamber and instrumental

Sonate en la majeur, pour violon et piano pour Henrico Albicastro	W28
Sonate en mi mineur, pour violon et piano pour Henrico Albicastro	W28
Sonate in mi mineur pour flûte ou violon et piano de Gaspard Fritz	W29

CHRISTMAS MUSIC ARRANGED FOR PRIVATE USE BY THE MARTIN FAMILY

In dulci jubilo	W112
Nous sommes trois souverains princes	W119
O Dieu, c'est dans ta sion sainte	W128
Que Dieu se montre seulement	W109

Index

W = Works and Performances, D = Discography, B = Bibliography, M = Writings by Martin.

A la Foire d'Amour, W77
A la Fontaine, W77
A propos du Vin herbé, M8; B20
Abbey, Lynne, D225
Abendroth, Walter, B1
Academy of St. Martin-in-the-Fields, D161
Adam, Theo, D195
Adams, Byron, B271
Adcock, Don, D217
Agnus Dei, W125, W136
Agostini, Gloria, D157
Aiello, Theresa, D224
Aitkin, Robert, D219
Alain, Marie Claire, D198
Albicastro, Henrico, W28
Amati Quartett, Zürich, D186
Ameling, Elly, D67, D71, D218; B73, B80, B238
Amerongen, Alex von, B166
Amour de Moy L', W75; D1
Andreae, Hans, W76; D158
Andreae, Volkmar, W46
Andrews, Mitchell, D157
Angelico, Fra, B165

Ansermet, Ernest, W7, W11, W21, W34-W35, W41, W47-W48, W53, W68, W81, W98-W99, W103, W106, W108, W110, W114, W118, W120; D24, D56, D59, D83, D120, D155; B3-B7, B25, B118, B126, B135, B140, B150-B151, B169, B214, B272, B275, B292, B297, B324, B338, B340
Antigone, B352
Antonioli, Jean-François, D26, D51, D54; B125
Apocalypse, M23; B338
Appia, Edmond, W39; B8, B177
Aprahamian, Felix, B262, B343
Arcidiacomo, Aurelio, W96
Ariel, B155, B323-B324, B326-B327, B329-B330, B333-B334, B336-B337
Ariel songs see Five Ariel Songs
Armide, W18
Arnold, Johanna, D1, D41, D68, D90, D191, D224
Arruga, Lorenzo, B349

Ars Laeta Groupe Vocale, D43, D185, D227
Arseguet, Lise, D121
Association of Swiss Musicians, W2, W4-W5, W7, W13; B68, B302Athalie, W82
Au clair de la lune, W101
Auberson, Jean-Marie, D32
Augustine, St., M22; B179, B186, B188-B191
Aussenseiter der neuen Musik, B14
Austin, William W., B9-B10
Ave Maria, W130; B216, B218
Bach Chor, Gütersloh, D131
Bach, Hans-Elmar, B11
Bach, J. S., M22; B7, B14, B25, B37-B38, B43, B55, B69, B132, B135, B151, B177, B179, B188-B189, B191, B194-B196, B200, B206-B207
Bach, Rudolf Am, W76; D158
Badura-Skoda, Paul, W129, W139; D52; M20; B12, B62, B66, B125, B128, B130-B133, B174, B306
Bahr, Gunilla von, D200-D221
Balderston, Suzanne, B344
Baldwin, Dalton, D71
Balissat, Jean, B44
Ball, Andrew, D223
Ballade des pendus, W132; D107, D189; B16, B86
Ballade pour alto et orchestre à vent, W137; D2-D3
Ballade pour flûte (flute & string orchestra), W52; D19-D23
Ballade pour flûte et orchestre, D24; B118
Ballade pour flûte et piano, W47; D4-D18
Ballade pour piano et orchestre, W48; D25-D26; M10; B104, B119, B125
Ballade pour saxophone, W43; B104, B120
Ballade pour saxophone et orchestre, D27-D28
Ballade pour trombone, W49, W53
Ballade pour trombone (tenor saxophone & piano), D33-D34

Ballade pour trombone (trombone & orchestra), D31-D32
Ballade pour trombone et piano, D29-D30
Ballade pour violoncelle et orchestre, D38; B94, B117, B121-B122, B154, B304
Ballade pour violoncelle et piano, W87; D35-D37
Balmer, Hans, W45
Balmer, Luc, W88
Barblan, E., W7
Bargen, Martina von, D96
Barker, George, B249
Bartók, Béla, B10, B46, B92, B206
Baseler Kammerorchester, W76; D19, D226; M5, M17, M23; B2, B161, B172, B347
Basle Chamber Orchestra see Baseler Kammerorchester
Baud-Bovy, Samuel, W80; B102, B178
Baumann, Max, B184
Bavarian Radio Orchestra, B278
BBC Chorus and Orchestra, B183, B191
Beattie, Herbert, W133
Beckett, Edward, D201
Bediér, Joseph, M8; B19, B68, B79, B330, B349, B352, B355, B365, B368, B370, B372, B375
Beethoven, Ludwig van, B152, B180, B204, B342
Benary, Peter, B174
Benda, Sebastian, D25
Benkö, Zoltan, D10
Benoit, Jean-Christophe, W121
Bensmann, Detlef, D33
Berg, Alban, B10, B100, B364
Berlin Philharmonic, W117; D196, D207; B29, B234, B243
Berlioz, Hector, B185
Berner Liederheft, W73
Bernheimer, Martin, B233, B350
Best, Martin, W133
Bettens, Etienne, D165
Beze, Theodore, W110
Bidal, Denise, W86; D114

Billeter, Bernhard, D144; B13-B17, B201, B240, B263
Binkley, Paul, D164
Bizet, Georges, B43
Blaser, Corina, W76
Blaser, Pierre-André, D165
Blasius, Martin, D96
blaue Blume, Die, W38-W39
Blum, Robert, W44, W50
Boepple, Paul, W80; B18, B186
Bogdan, Thomas, D66, D167
Böhm, Hans, B307
Böhm, Karl, B278
Bollen, Ria, W135; D188-D189
Bolton, Ivor, D147
Bonaventura, Mario di, W108
Bonnefoux, Jean-Pierre, B276
Bonte, Hans Georg, B19
Bopp, Joseph, W52; D19
Bornand, Suzanne, W37
Borowski, Felix, B136
Bossler, Andreas, D199
Bour, Ernest, B338
Bourquin, Francis, W77
Boyden, John, D193
Brancaleone, Francis, D167
Brandt, Maarten, B20
Brashovanova-Stancheva, Lada, B21
Bream, Julien, D168; B301
Breitmeyer, Maggy, W5
Brevet, Francoise Pulfer, B220
Britten, Benjamin, B214, B299
Bruckner, Anton, B107, B139, B152, B256
Brückner-Rüggeberg, Wilhelm, B197
Brun, Virgilio, W96
Brunelle, Philippe, W110
Brunner, Gerhard, B234
Brunnert, Franz, W15; B224
Brusilow, Anshel, W135
Bruyr, Jose, B179
Bucher, Josef, D146
Buckel, Ursula, D120
Budapest Symphony Orchestra, D38
Buffet, Daniel, B308
Bunge, Sas, B292
Burge, David, B202
Bugenhagen-Kantorei, W15; B224

Burkhard, Willy, B101, B161, B195, B298
Busoni, Ferruccio, B203, B305
Buttolph, David, W130
C'etait Anne de Bretagne, W72
Cadieu, Martine, B22
Caliban, B326, B328, B333
Calvin, John, B102, B291
Campagnarde, W71
Campbell, Susan, D214
Canin, Stuart, W40
Canon pour Werner Reinhart, W66
Cantata misericordium, B214
Cantate pour 1er août, W54
Cantate sur la Nativité, W26; M12; B38
Canterbury Cathedral Choir, D123
Cantiones sacraes, B189
Cariven, E., D154
Carnegie Hall, B252, B289
Carner, Mosco, B23
Carter, Elliott, B301
Casey, Ethel, D70, D217
Castelnuovo-Tedesco, Mario, B299
Castleman, Charles, D209, D212
Catala, Eugénia, B42, B97, B113
Cavelti, Elsa, W60, W89; D63
Cellérier, B., W7
Chaconne, W105; D40
Chamber Music Society of Lincoln Center, W133
Chamber Orchestra of Lausanne, D25, D31-D32, D50, D154
Chanson, W30
Chanson des jour de pluie, W77
Chanson des métamorphoses, W90; D41
Chanson du mezzetin, W16
Chanson en canon, W32; D43-D44
Chanson le petite village, D42
Chanson satirique, W70
Chansons, W18, W24
Chansons de "la Nique a Satan", D45
Chantons, Je vous en prie, W10
Chapallaz, Gilbert, B24
Charles d'Orleans, W84
Charlston, Elsa, D69, D185

Cherechewski, Leon, W37
Chicago Symphony Orchestra, D57;
  B136, B293
Choir of All Saints Church, D39, D42,
  D44, D75, D94, D136, D138, D228
Choir und Orchester
  Johannes-Kantorei, D122
Chopin, Frederic, B43, B107, B173,
  B201
Chor der Erlöserkirche, Bad
  Homburg, D96
Christ lag in Todesbanden, B164
Christmann, Max, W64
Chronicles of My Life, M19
Cincinnati Symphony Orchestra,
  W129; B132
Cinderella, W55
Clair de lune, W95; D46, D47
Clark, Andrew, B235
Claudel, Paul, B190
Clavier Trio Francais, Le, D214
Clement, Andries, D133
Clément, Marianne, W111
Cleveland Symphony Orchestra,
  W124; B153
Cohn, Ed, D164
Collegium Musicum, Zürich, W76,
  W87, W134; D24, D63, D158;
  B117, B161, B346, B347
Combat, B164
Comedie de Genève, W14, W17
Compositeur moderne et les textes
  sacrés, Le, B187
Concert pour clavecin et petit
  orchestre, W94; D49-D50; B104,
  B123-B124
Concert pour instruments à vent et
  piano, W19
Concertgebouw Orchestra, B27, B93,
  B154, B218-B219, B264, B292,
  B296, B345
Concerto I pour piano et orchestre,
  W35; D51; B38, B119, B125-B126
Concerto II pour piano et orchestre,
  W129; D52-D54; B12, B66, B125,
  B127, B128-B134
Concerto pour sept instruments à
  vent, W88; D55-D58; M13; B29,
  B51, B89, B135-B139, B186

Concerto pour violon et orchestre,
  W93; D59-D61; M3; B24, B46,
  B71, B94, B106, B140-B149,
  B155, B175
Concerto pour violoncelle et
  orchestre, W124; D62; B93, B100,
  B150-B155, B304
Concours de Composition in
  "Carillon", W37
Concours National Suisse
  d'Exécution Musicale, W47, W49,
  W56
Confessions, B179, B191
Consort for Strings, B155
Contemporains, Les, W95
Conversations pour 12 instruments,
  B348
Corboz, Michel, W141; B164
Corena, Fernando, W68
Corleonis, Adrian, B203
Cornell, Klaus, D150
Cornet, Der, W60; D63-D65; M5;
  B23, B35, B45, B74-B75, B94,
  B156-B162, B283-B284, B313,
  B319
Cornil, Dominique, D53, D117
Coucou, Le, W31; D48
Cowell, Henry, B180, B198
Cremers, Adrienne, B351
Cruz-Froelich, Louis de la, W2
Cuenod, Hugues, W78, W84
Czech Philharmonic, D162
D'Adario, Tony, D165
Dalcroze, Jacques, W78, W122; M30;
  B38, B68, B86, B99
Dale, S.S., B151
Daneels, François, D28
Daniel, Oliver, B352
Danse de la peur, W39
Danse grave, W57
Dartmouth College, W40, W108
Dartmouth Symphony Orchestra,
  W108
Debogis-Bohy, M.-L., W7
Debussy, Claude, B1, B7, B34, B37,
  B46, B55, B58, B75, B92, B108,
  B132, B140, B160, B173, B182,
  B188, B206, B318, B328, B349,
  B352, B354

Decker, Friedhelm, D96
Decroos, Jean, B93, B152, B154
Dédicace, W78; D66
Defraiteur, Renée, W80
Defrancesco, Edmond, W107
Degens, R. N., B294
Delaney, Charles, D4
Delden, Lex van, B152, B216
Delman, Jacqueline, D221
Dennington, Arthur, B143
Dean, Timothy, B374
Deroubaix, Jeanne, W121
Desarzens, Victor, W111, W129; D55,
    D154, D229; B46, B352
Dessoff Choirs, W80; B18, B185-
    B186, B198
Deutsch, Helmut, D14
Devain, Henri, W65
Devos, Louis, W121
Di Tullio, Louise, D21
Dies Irae, B86, B308-B309
Dietmar von Eist, W113
Dingfelder, Ingrid, D12
Dinkel, Philippe, D215
dissertations see theses
Distler, Hugo, B263
Dithyrambes, Les, W7
Dittmer, Petronella, D223
Divorce, Le, W22
Dobson, Michael, D2
Dodgson, Stephen, B299
Doktor, Paul, D209
Doneyne, Désiré, D73-D74
Dornya, Maria, W130
Douglas, Basil, B191
Dovaz, Rene, B25
Downes, Edward, B236-B237
Drei Fragmente aus Der Sturm see
    Sturm, Der, W99
Drey Minnelieder, W113; D67-D68;
    B73, B80, B163
Drey Minnelieder (with Flute, Violin &
    Cello), D69
Du Rhône au Rhin, W46; D72-D74
Dubuis, Madeleine, W68
Duck, Leonard, B26
Dull, Ben, B27
Dunckel, Rudolf, D195

Dutilleux, Henri, B151
Dvořák, Antonin, B359
E la vie l'emporta, W141; D79; M2;
    B16, B78, B81, B164-B165
Eby, Anders, D135
Eder, Helmut, W137
Edinburgh Festival, B148, B204
Eeden, Hugo von, B342
Egel, Martin, D197
Ehinger, Hans, B28, B214, B226
Eho! Eho!, W70
Einhovens Kamerkoor, D133
Ellis, Osian, D161
En Revenant d'Auvergne, W72
Engel, Karl, D109
English Chamber Orchestra, D21
Ensemble de l'Oiseau-Lyre, D49
Entr'acte pour grand orchestre, W19
Epstein, David, D3, D204
Epstein, Rhea S., B30
Erasmi monumentum, W131; B166-
    B168
Erasmus, W130-W131; B66, B166-
    B168
Erickson, Eric, D93, D127
Erickson, Karle, D132
Es ist ein Schnitter, heisst der Tod,
    W36; D75
Esquisse, W11
Esquisse pour piano, W123; D76-
    D78
Etcheverry, H.B., W80
Etude de lecture see Esquisse pour
    piano
Etude rythmique, W122; D80-D82
Etudes pour deux pianos, W104;
    D86-D87
Etudes pour orchestre à cordes,
    W102; D83-D85; M13, M17; B46,
    B169-B173, B304
European Radio Union, B286
Evans, Peter, B31
Evers, Reinbert, D175
Exhibition Band, D72
Exsultet, B194
Fagius, Hans, D200
Faller, Charles, W51
Faller, Robert, D95

Fantaisie sur des rythmes flamenco,
  W139; D88-D89; M2, M20; B27,
  B62, B86, B174
Fauré, Gabriel, B26, B108, B148
Faut partir pour l'angleterre, Il, W91;
  D90
Ferdinand, B328
Festival of Besançon, B77
Festival of Contemporary Music,
  B317
Festival of the SIMC, W94
Fêtes du Rhône, B68
Fiechtner, Helmut, B33-B34, B323
Fierz, Gerold, B324, B353
Fischer, Edith, D6
Fischer, Kurt von, B35-B38
Fischer-Dieskau, Dietrich, W89, W99;
  D196, D207; B29, B321
Fisk, Eliot, D177; B300
Five Ariel Songs, W92; D91-D94; M3;
  B103, B144-B146, B175-B176
flamenco, M20; B27, B343, B345-
  B347
Fleury, A., W7
Flower, Edward, W133
Flügel, Gertrud, W45
Forbes, Colin, D160
Forte, Allen, B129
Fournet, Jean, W130-W131; D124;
  B168
Fournier, Pierre, W124; B151, B153-
  B155
Francesco, M.G. de, D154
Franck, César, B14, B26, B46, B90,
  B107, B197, B256
Frank Martin sein Leben und Werk,
  B208
Frank, Alan, B39
Frankenstein, Alfred, B354
Frankfurter Bläservereinigung, D96
Frankhauser, Max, W107
Frey, Walter, W35, W48
Frias, Leopoldo, B238
Fricsay, Ferenc, W50; D156
Fritschel, James, D125-D126
Fritz, Gaspard, W29
Froment, Louis, D49
Fryba, Hans, W37
Fuller, Albert, D157

Funiculi-funicula, B228
Gabbi, Mario, D165
Gaillard, Paul Andre, B43
Gaillard, Roger, B257
Gardner, Bennitt, B240
Garth, Eliza, D87, D97, D140, D152-
  D153
Gaslight, B374
Gatti, Guido M., B182
Gaudibut, Eric, B44
Gebhardt, Joachim, D96
Geisterbraut, B359
Geller, Doris, D203
Genet, Patrick, D215
Geneva Psalter, B291
Genuit, Werner, D110, D212
Georges, Richard, B89
Geraedts, Jaap, M36; B175
Gerber, Steven, D224
Gesellschaft der Musikfreunde, B131
Gianni Schicchi, B6, B353, B356,
  B366
Gieseking, Walter, W35
Gilardino, Angelo, B299
Gilles, Marie-Louise, D121
Gino, Bobbio, D165
Glassman, Robert V., B221
Goddard, Scott, B325
Goering, Jean, W33, W37
Goethe, Johann Wolfgang von, B160
Golan, Ron, W137; D3
Goldberg, Bernard Z., D183
Goldron, Romain, B44
Golgotha, W80; D95-D96; M12; B18,
  B19, B33-B34, B36, B38, B50,
  B68-B69, B72, B77, B102, B158,
  B177-B200, B255-B256, B312-
  B313, B364
Gordon, Anita, D12
Gradenwitz, Peter, B45, B309
Gradmann-Lüscher, Marguerite, W55
Graf, Kathrin, D222
Graf, Peter-Lukas, D6, D222
Gréban, Arnoul, W10, W26, W106,
  W121; B65, B242, B245, B249-
  B250, B253, B255-B256, B286
Greene, David Mason, B47
Grenouilles, le rossignol et la pluie,
  Les, D97

Grétillat, Nelly, W68, W80
Grier, Christopher, B204
Grimanig Tod mit seinen Pfeil, B164
Grimm, Jacob and Wilhelm, W55;
    B74
Grinke, Frederick, B143
Guarneri Trio, B342
Gugliemo, Edoardo, B355
Gui, Vittorio, B148
Guillaume de Machaut, W115; B261
Guitare - quatre pièces brèves pour
    piano, D98-D100
Gunther, Siegfried, B48
Gurley, Barbara, D184
Gutscher, Manfred, B49
Haberlen, John B., B176
Haefer, Viktoria, B310
Haefliger, Ernst, W68, W80; D120
Hager, Adr., B222
Haitink, Bernard, W127; B152
Halévy, Jacques, B333
Haller, Charles, B261
Halter, Mary Frances, B50
Hambro, Leonid, D29
Hamilton, Iain, B51
Handel, George Frideric, B55, B189
Harden, Wolf, D216
Hari, Machiko, D86, D139
Harpur College Orchestra, W130
Harvard Glee Club, W106; B252
Harvard Orchestra, W106
Hausammann, Rolf, B311
Haydn, Joseph, M31; B37, B127
Heitz, Klaus, D35
Helm, Everett, B227, B241
Helmis, Irmgard, D156
Hempfling, Volker, D130
Henke, Rosel-Maria, B223
Hensley, Douglas, D164, D178
Herchenröder, Martin, B52
Hersh, Ralph, W40
Herzog, Gerty, D7, D156
Hindemith, Paul, B9, B15, B125,
    B206, B225, B263, B280
Hindermann, Franz, D210
Hirayama, Masayuki, D171
Hirst, Grayson, W133
Hodges, Craig, B53-B54
Höffgen, Marga, D120

Hofmann, Monica, D9, D35, D80,
    D86, D98, D108, D139, D194
Hofmannsthal, Hugo von, W64; M4;
    B29, B74, B318-B322
Holbein, Hans, B190
Holland Festival, B338, B340
Holliger, Heinz, W134; D226; B25,
    B343, B346-B347
Holliger, Ursula, W134; D226; B25,
    B343, B346-B347
Homo pro se, B166-B168
Honegger, Arthur, B35, B51, B108,
    B185, B190, B281
Honegger, Henri, D36; B201
Hoog, Jan de, B291
Hoover, Katherine, D202
Hoppstock, Tilman, D179
Horn, Wolfgang, B312
Houtmann, Jacques, D225
Howarth, Elgar, D21
Hugli, Pierre, B56
Huit préludes pour le piano, W86;
    D101-D103, D105-D119; B62,
    B71, B73, B201-B206
Hungerbühler, Margit, D96
Hunziker, Andre, B58, B356
Hürlimann, Emmy, D158
Hutchinson, Joyce, D160
Hutchinson, Robert Joseph Jr., B184
Huttenlocher, Philippe, W141; D79,
    D95; B164
Hyatt, Willard, B344
Ikon Foundation, B80
In Praise of Folly see Laus stultiae
In terra pax, W26, W68, W140; D120-
    D123; M12, M23; B38-B39, B50,
    B102, B158, B199, B207-B213,
    B256, B283
Incarnation, M19, M26
Indermühle, Heidi, D220
Institut Jacques Dalcroze, W31
Inter arma caritas, W118; B214-B215
International Music Council, W138
International Society for
    Contemporary Music, W35
Internationaler Musikwettbewerb,
    W123
Iseler, Elmer, D134
Iseler, Elmer Singers, D134

Jaccottet, Christiane, D50; B104
Jackson, Nicolas, D201
Jacobi, Peter, B357
Jacobson, Bernard, B275
Jacopone da Todi, W130
Jaermann, Marc, D215
Jäggin, Christoph, D176
Jamet, Pierre, D155
Janáček, Leoš, B107
Janeton, W62
Jarocinski, Stefan, B59
Jaton, Henri, B60
Jelden, Georg, D121
Jesus, B19, B65, B179, B194
Jochum, Eugen, B218-B219, B264
Jochum, Veronica, D119
Johnson, Louise, D160
Joli Tambour, W71
Jungend-Sinfonie-Orchester, D150
Kagel, Mauricio, B263
Kägi, Walter, D210
Kaiser, Hans-JÜrgen, D203
Kammertrio Bern, D220
Kapp, Richard, D5, D8
Kates, Stephen, D62
Kaye, Milton, D13
Kazandjiev, Vasil, D53, D85
Keijzer, Arie, W131; B168
Keller, Marianne, D11
Kelterborn, Rudolph, B44
Kempe, Rudolf, B305
Kern, Heinz, B326
Kessler, Giovanna, B358
Kilvington, Chris, B300
Kimball, Carol, D184
Kind, Silvia, D156
King David, B102
King, Charles W., B61
Kirtz, Eugene, B348
Kisselgoff, Anna, B276
Klein, Rudolf, B14, B63-B66, B131,
    B163, B208, B242-B243, B327-
    B328
Kleine geistliche Konzerte, B200
Kletzki, Paul, B108
Kling, Paul, D60
Kobayashi, Michio, D222
Koch, Heinz, B329
Kodadová, Renata, D162

Koelliker, Andrée, B67
Kölner Kantorei, D130
Kolodin, Irving, B185
Kozinn, Allan, B301
Krapp, Edgar, D145
Kreis, Marie-Eve, W55
Krenek, Ernst, B263
Kreutz, Hermann, D131
Krips, Joseph, B130
Krombholc, Jaroslav, B249
Kromer, Oskar, W40
Kubilik, Rafael, W89
Kuhn, Hansjörg, D220
Kuhn-Indermühle, Brigitte, D220
Kunz-Aubert, Willy, W37
Kurz, Sigfried, D22
La Brecque, Rebecca, D77, D81,
    D88, D99
La Psallette de Genève, D128, D137
Lacroix, Jules, W14
Laderman, Ezra, B295
Lagger, Peter, W135; D188-D189
Lambert, Meinrado, B68
Lambrechts, Jean, B69
Lamke, Jürgen, D163
Lancelot, James, D148
Lang, Walter, D210
Lang, Walter Trio, D210
Langham, Jennifer, D209, D212
Langmeir, Samuel, D211
Lauber, Joseph, W5; B33-B34, B36,
    B75
Laus stultiae, B166, B168
Lausanne Chamber Orchestra see
    Chamber orchestra of Lausanne
Lawrence University Concert Choir,
    D132
League of Swiss Musicians, B34
Ledger, Philip, D161
Leeb, Hermann, W84
Lehel, György, D38
Leinsdorf, Erich, W98; B272
Leppard Orchestra, B124
Lewinski, Wolf-Eberhard von, B70,
    B359
Lewis, Eric, W130
Liepa, Yolanda, D1, D18, D34, D37,
    D40-D41, D68, D87, D90, D97,

Liepa, Yolanda, cont.
  D118, D140, D152-D153, D191,
  D205-D206
Ligeti, György, B263
Lindberg, Christian, D30
Lindtberg, Susanne, D9
Lipatti, Dinu, W39, W86; M1, M10;
  B62, B205
Lipatti, Madeleine, W39, W84
Lipovšek, Marjana, D65
Lisle, Leconte de, W2
Liszt, Franz, B173
Litschauer, Franz, B71
Little Orchestra Society, W87; B122,
  B321
Lockspeiser, Edward, B330
London Chamber Orchestra, D159
London Philharmonic and Chorus,
  B244, B246, B249
Los Angeles Chamber Orchestra,
  B344
Louisville Orchestra, D60, D62
Loup, Francois, D165
Lucerne International Music Festival,
  M20, M33; B89, B174
Lucke, Annegret, D17
Lully, Jean-Baptiste, W18
Lurie, Mitchell, B344
Luther, Martin, W127, W130; B164-
  B165, B216-B217
Lutoslawski, Witold, B215
Lüttwitz, Heinrich von, B228
Luy, André, W135; D95, D188-D189
Lyle, Andrew, D123
Lyric Arts Trio, D219
M.I.T. Symphony Orchestra, D3,
  D204
Ma Belle, W70
Maeterlinck, Maurice, B160
Magic Fire Music, B296
Magnificat, W127, W130; B216-B219
Mai, Le, W70
Malcolm, George, B124
Malno, Kras, D183
Marche de Genève, W59
Marche des 22 Cantons, W59
Märchen vom Aschenbrödel, Das,
  W55-W57; B74, B319
Marcus, Michael, B244

Maria-Triptychon, W127, W130;
  D124; B66, B89, B216-B219
Marot, Clément, W110
Marriner, Neville, D161; B344
Martin, Bernard, B72, B313, B331
Martin, Frank (conductor), W13-W14,
  W17, W23, W25, W115, W117,
  W133, W135; D31, D52, D61,
  D64, D165, D188-D189, D196,
  D207; B46, B309
Martin, Frank (pianist), W9, W20,
  W33, W64, W78, W84, W85,
  W104; D16, D36, D67, D106-
  D107, D192, D218, D229-D230;
  B354, B362
Martin, Maria, W51; M2; B12-B13,
  B42, B73, B80, B97, B113, B165,
  B200, B224, B279, B288, B294,
  B306, B316, B345, B361
Martin, Pauline, W10; B255, B258
Martin, Teresa, W139; M20; B27,
  B62, B86, B174, B326
Martinon, Jean, D57; B293
Maskey, Jacqueline, B277
Mason, John, D159
Massenkeil, Günther, D194
Mathis, Edith, D124
Matuz, Istvàn, D10
Mauppin, Bernard, D214
Mayer-Reinach, Ursula, D64; B157
McLarin, Lyn, D223
Meditations, B179, B191
Meester, Magda de, B156
Meili, Max, W55
Meine Stimme Klinge, W74
Melroy, Mardia, B187
Menasce, Jacques de, B280
Mendelssohn, Felix, B107, B323
Mengelberg, Karl, B73, B264, B318
Menuhin Festival Orchestra, D2,
  D166
Menuhin, Yehudi, W138; D2, D166;
  B25, B289-B290, B308
Mermoud, Robert, D43, D188, D227;
  B258, B309, B316
Messe pour double choeur a
  cappella, W15; D125-D135; M12;
  B38, B102, B220-B225
Messiaen, Olivier, B263

Messiah, B102
Mester, Jorge, D62
Meyer von Bremen, Alexander, W104
Meyer, Christina, D111
Meyer, J. William, D167
Meylan, Frank, B157
Meylan, Pierre, B74, B158, B188
Micheelsen, Hans Friedrich, B263
Michno, Dennis G, D39, D42, D44,
    D66, D75, D94, D136-D137, D167,
    D202, D228
Midsummer Night's Dream, B323
Mikaeli Kammarkör, D135
Mila, Massimo, B209
Miller, Philip, B362
Mills, John, D174
Miranda, B328
Missa solemnis, B102
Mitchell, Marjorie, D105
Mitropoulos, Dimitri, W93; B144
Mittag, Erwin von, B332
Modern Symphony Orchestra, B143
Moeschinger, Albert, B155
Mohr, Ernst, B17, B75
Möhring, Susanne, B76
Molière, W114; M9; B226-B232
Mollet, Pierre, D95, D120; B77
Monsieur de Pourceaugnac, W114;
    M9; B65, B155, B226-B232
Montegazzi, G.C., D72
Monteverdi, Claudio, B132
Montmollin, Marie-Lise de, D95
Mook, Ted, D69, D185
Moore, David W., B125
Mooser, Robert-Aloys, B118-B119,
    B126, B159, B281-B282, B302,
    B317, B333, B339, B363
Morax, René, W25; B316
Morehen, John, B265
Moret, Norbert, B44
Morley, Thomas, W53
Morrison, Mary, D219
Mose, Marlis, D213
Moser, Hans Joachim, B189
Mozart, W. A., B43, B107, B139,
    B180, B204
Mozarteum of Salzburg, W137
Mücke, Michael, D216
Muller, H.J.M., B296

Muller, Paul, B161
Munchinger, Karl, W97; D149
Munich Opera Festival, B369
Murray, Bain, B153
Musici, I, D84
Musique des Gardiens de la Paix de
    Paris, D73-D74
Mussorgsky, Modest, B55
Muster, Ludmila, D163
Mystère de la Nativité, W106; B50,
    B60, B64, B77, B98, B102, B163,
    B232-B256, B286
Mystère de la passion, W10, W121;
    B242, B256, B286
Nagano, Kent, D164
NCRV Vocal Ensemble, B222
Nécessité d'une musique
    contemporaine, B323
Nederlands Kamerkoor, W92, W116;
    D91, D92, D134; B222
Nef, Isabel, W94; D49, D154; B123
Negro, Lucia, D76, D113, D221
Netherlands String Quartet, B303
Neuhaus, Wilhelm, D163
Neukirchen, Alfons, B229
Neuman, Maxine, D18, D37, D40
New String Trio, D209, D212
New York City Ballet, B276-B277
New York City Center Opera, W98
New York Philharmonic, W88, W93;
    B136, B142
Newmark, John, D193
Nicolet, Aurèle, D7, D20
Nique à Satan, Le, W23; B226,
    B257-B260
Nitsche, Paul, D121
Nobel, Felix de, W116; D91-D92
Noël de Praetorius, W70
North Texas State University, W135
Notre Père, W69, W140
Nous sommes trois souverains
    princes, W119; D135
Nun ist das Heil und die Kraft, B207
Nürnberg Symphonie Orchester,
    D197
O Dieu, c'est dans ta Sion Sainte,
    W128
O nuit, heureuse nuit, W70
Ochsenbein, Walter, D208

Ode à la musique, W115; B261
Ode et sonnet, W3; D137-D138
Odé, Pieter, D218; B73, B80
Oedipe à Colone, W17
Oedipe-Roi, W14
Offenbacher Kammerorchester, D96
Offrande, B164
Ogle, Alex, D69, D185
Olefsky, Paul, W40
Olsen, Derrik, W121; B238
Orchestre Symphonique National de la Radio Bulgare, D53
Orchester der Kantonschule Stadelhofen, D208
Orchestra della Radio Svizzera, D64
Orchestre de la Suisse Romande, W120; D56, D59, D83, D120, D155, D188-D189; B110, B123, B275, B292, B340
Orchestre Philharmonique de la BRT, D28
ORF - Sinfonia Orchestra, D65
Orff, Carl, B352
Oster, Otto, B79
Österreichische Musikzeitschrift, B327
Otterloo, Willem van, D160
Our Father see Notre Père
Ouverture en hommage à Mozart, W103
Ouverture en rondeau, W108
Ouverture et foxtrot, W19; D139-D140
Ouverture pour Athalie, W83
Overeem, H.M.J., B80
Paap, Wouter, B81, B190, B210, B291, B303, B364
Paganini, Nicolo, B300
Page, Tim, B82
Páleniček, Josef, D162
Parsons, Arrand, B297
Passacaille, B29, B112, B262-B270
Passacaille (orchestra), W117
Passacaille (string orchestra), W97; D149
Passacaille pour orgue, W67; D141-D148
Passion (1969), B184
Passionsbericht des Matthäus, B184

Pavane couleur du temps (chamber orchestra), W100; D150
Pavane couleur du temps (string quintet), W12
Pavane couleur du temps (2 pianos), D152
Pavane couleur du temps (string orchestra), D151
Paychère, Albert, W18, W82; B211
Pearson, Leslie, D159
Pekinel, Güher, D17
Pelikan, Tina, D69, D182
Pelléas et Melisande, B160, B206, B328, B349, B355, B358
Penderecki, Krzysztof, B184
Peoples, Baker, D164
Pépin, André, W47
Pepping, Ernst, B184, B189, B263
Perényi, Miklós, D38
Perle, George, B348
Pernaud, Pierre, D128, D137
Perret, Claudine, W141; D79; B164
Perrin, Jean, B44
Peterson, John David, B267
Petit Village, Le, W30, W32
Petite Complainte, W56
Petite eglise, W65
Petite fanfare, W79
Petite marche blanche et trio Noir, W42; D153
Petite symphonie concertante, W76; D154-D163; B1, B34, B45-B46, B51, B68, B70, B75, B78, B91, B94, B100, B106-B107, B117, B137-B138, B178, B186, B206, B270-B285, B312, B324, B347
Petrou, Nicholas, D181
Peyser, Herbert, B136, B144
Piachaud, René-Louis, W27
Piano Quintet, B89, B100
Pièce brève, W107
Pijnenburg, Piet, B218
Pilate, W121; B65, B286
Piquet, Jean-Claude, M16; B83
Pittsburgh Symphony, B295
Plymouth Music Series, W110
Poèmes de la mort, W133; D164-D165; B16, B86, B287-B288, B313

Poggelli, Lamberto, B358
Polonsky, Larry, D164
Polyptyque, W138; D166; B25, B30, B86, B289-B290, B308
Ponce, Alberto, D170
Ponce, Manuel, B300
Ponelle, Pierre-Dominique, D197
Ponse, Luctor, B365
Pontinen, Roland, D30
Pope, George, D15
Porter, Andrew, B248
Posthuma, Klaas, B230
Postludes, B214
Potrei, Yves, D214
Poulenc, Francis, B225
Pour une mise en scène du Mystère de la Nativité, B242
Preston, Simon, D161
Previn, André, D103; B301
Previtali, Fernando, W94
Proms, B273
Prospero, B328, B331, B336-B337
Psalm 65, W128
Psaume 104, W70
Psaume 42, W70
Pseaumes de Genève, W110; B102, B291
Puccini, Giacomo, B6, B353, B356
Purcell, Henry, B73
Quant n'ont assez fait do-do, W84; D166
Quartet de Boer, W9
Quatre eléments, Les, W120; M28; B65, B81, B292-B298
Quatre pièces brèves pour guitare, W34; D168-D182; B299-B301
Quatre sonnets à Cassandre, W13; D180-D182; B100, B302
Quatuor à Cordes, W126; D186; B57, B303-B305
Querela pacis, B166-B168
Quintette en re mineur, W9; D187
R., J.-L., B84
Radcliffe Choral Society, W106; B252
Radio Geneva, M23
Raffman, Relly, B300
Rameau, Jean Philippe, B73
Rampal, Jean-Pierre, D198
Ramuz, C.F., W30, W32

Rankin, Nell, D183
Rapt, Kurt, D24
Rascher, Sigurd, W43
Rasponi, Lanfranco, B366
Ravel, Maurice, M25; B1, B9, B14, B34, B46, B58, B75, B90, B232, B340
Rayment, Malcolm, B249
Reardon, John, W133
Reda, Siegfried, B263
Redditi, Amedea, W107
Reeves, Michael, D159
Regamey, Constantin, B85-B87, B121, B137, B145, B171, B268, B367-B368
Regnard, Jean Francois, W22
Rehfuss, Heinz, W80; D192; B318
Reich, Willi, B88, B172, B346
Reichel, Bernard, W141; B16
Rembrandt, B190, B200
Requiem, W135-W136; D185, D188-D189; M7; B16, B50, B86-B87, B103, B306-B315
Responsabilité du compositeur, B95, B154, B178
Rhapsodie, W37-B38
RIAS, W113
RIAS Sinfonietta, D33
RIAS Symphony, D156
Richmond Sinfonia, D225
Rilke, Rainer Maria, W60; M5; B74, B158-B161, B319, B330
Robertson, Alec, B191
Robson, Mark, D15
Rochester, Mark, B192
Roe, Betty, B374
Rogg, Lionel, D143
Roman Catholic Capitol Choir, B291
Roman de Tristan et Iseult, Le, B355, B361, B372-B373
Roméo et Juliette, W25; B316
Ronsard, Pierre de, W3, W13, W66; B302
Röntgen, Joachim, W40
Rorem, Ned, B301
Rosbaud, Hans, B305
Rosen, Armin, D31
Rosenkavalier, Der, B228, B232
Rosove, Lewis, D184

Ross, Hugh, B360, B370
Ross, Marion, D219
Rossiaud, Doris, D155
Rossignol, Le, W42
Rössler, Almut, D122; B312
Rost, Monika, D180
Rostand, Claude, B193
Rothon, Greville, B369
Rotterdam Philharmonic, W130-W131;
    B166, B168
Rouse, John, D163
Roussel, Albert, B148, B296
Roy a fait battre tambour, Le, W8;
    D191
Royal Festival Hall, B169
Royal Philharmonic, B148
Ruck, Jürgen, D182
Rudhardt, Albert, W23, W85; B257-
    B259
Rudolf, Karl, B120
Runnett, Brian, D142
Růžičková, Zuzana, D162
Rythmes, W21; B68, B317
Saathen, Friedrich, B334
Sabbe, Hermann, B90
Sabin, Robert, B370
Sacher, Paul, W52, W55, W60, W76,
    W87, W93, W102, W124, W134;
    D19, D63, D158, D226; M5, M17,
    M23; B2, B94, B116-B117, B161,
    B172, B279, B343, B346-B347
Sadowski, Carol, D205-D206
Sagmaster, Joseph, B132
Saint-Céré, Choeur et Orchestre,
    D121
Saltzburg Music Festival, W50; B199,
    B253
Salzer, Felix, B15
Salzman, Theo, D183
Samama, Leo, B154
Sams, Jeremy, B371
Sanchez, Raùl, D169
Sancta Civitas, B315
Sandoz, Paul, W68
Sargeant, Winthrop, B183, B191,
    B335
Sattler Trio, D211
Sattler, Gerty, D211
Sattler, Klaus, D211

Saunders, John, B315
Scarlatti, Alessandro, B127
Scarlatti, Domenico, B300
Schenker, Heinrich, B15
Scherman, Thomas, W87, W89;
    B122, B321
Schibler, Armin, B44, B92
Schippers, Thomas, W129; B132
Schlegel, Wilhelm von, W98; B74,
    B327, B330, B336
Schmidt, Niklas, D216
Schneeberger, Hansheinz, W93
Schneiderhan, Wolfgang, W127,
    W130; D59, D61, D124; B66,
    B216, B218-B219
Schoenberg, Arnold, M6, M11, M33;
    B1, B6, B14, B26, B33-B34, B46,
    B50, B58, B64, B68, B75, B90,
    B100, B115, B140, B256, B263,
    B273, B278, B280, B340, B349,
    B364
Schola Cantorum, New York, B360,
    B370
Schönberger, Elmer, B93, B340
Schroder, Helmut, D199
Schubert, Franz, B160, B318
Schuh, Willi, B94, B146, B160-B161,
    B194, B283-B284, B304, B320,
    B336, B372
Schulz, Wolfgang, D14
Schuman, Davis, D29
Schumann, Peter, D190
Schumann, Robert, B55
Schütz, Heinrich, B179, B189
Schweizerische
    Tonkunstlerverein, B195
Schweizerisches Festspielorchester,
    D124
Sebestyén, Janos, D104
Sechs Monologe aus Jedermann,
    W64, W89; D192-D195; M4; B23,
    B29, B39, B74-B75, B78, B160,
    B162, B216, B283-B284, B313,
    B318-B322
Sechs Monologe aus Jedermann
    (with orchestra), D196-D197
Secretan, André, W17
Secretan, Pierre, W6

Seefried, Irmgard, W127, W130; B66,
  B163, B216, B218-B219
Seelmann-Eggebert, Ulrich, B155,
  B305, B314, B347
Segovia, Andrés, W34; B301
Semkow, Jerzy, W129
Sénéchaud, Marcel, B231
Senn, Kurt Wolfgang, W67
Serenade No. 2, B348
Serkin, Rudolph, B138
Sessions, Roger, B301
Seven Short Pieces for the
  Cultivation of Polyphonic Playing,
  B203
Shadows, B276-B277
Schäffer, Boguslaw, B91
Shakespeare, William, W25, W92,
  W98; B74, B145-B146, B316,
  B323-B329, B333, B335, B337-
  B338
Shallon, David, D33
Shaw, A.T., B315
Shaw-Taylor, Desmond, B147-B148
Shigihara, Susanne, B212
Shostakovich, Dmitrii, B9
Si Charlotte avait voulu, W63
Sibelius, Jean, B296
Sidell, Bill, D217
Siemans, Hayko, D96
Siirala, Seppo, D172
Silverman, Robert, D115
Silvermann, Stanley, W133
Simmons, Walter, B205
Sinfonia concertante, K.297b, B139
Sinfonia für Streichorchester, B161
Sinfonie Orchester des
  Norddeutscher Rundfunks, D163
Singbuch für die Oberstufe der
  Volksschule, W74
Sjökvist, Gustaf, D129
Skulsky, Abraham, B95, B136
Slokar, Branimir, D32
Slonimsky, Nicolas, B96
Smith, Tim, D34
Snook, Paul, B162
So Wünsch Ich eine gute Nacht,
  W73
Société de Chant Sacré, W80, W110
Sofia Chamber Orchestra, D85

Solistes de L'ensemble vocal, Les,
  D79
Solisti di Zagreb, D151
Sonata da Chiesa, W45, W51, W96,
  W111; B39, B322
Sonata da Chiesa (flute and organ),
  D198-D203
Sonata da Chiesa (viola d'amore &
  St. Orchestra), D204
Sonate en la Majeur, W28
Sonate en mi Mineur, W28-W29
Sonate I pour piano et violon, W5;
  D205; B30, B339
Sonate II pour piano et violon, W33;
  D206
Sophocles, W14, W17
Soria, Dorle J., B288
Soule, Richard, D184
Southwick, Janet, D70
Speiser, Elizabeth, W135; D188-D189
Speiser, Peter, D101
Sperber, Roswitha, D190
Spivakovsky, Tossy, B142
St. Luke's Passion, B184
Staatskapelle, Dresden, D22
Stabat Mater, B216, B219, B313
Stadelmann, Arlette, W122
Stähli, Margrith, B285
Stähli, Roland, W62-W63, W77
Staempfli, Wally, D95
Stämpfli, Jakob, D120
Stevens, David, B251
Stockhausen, Karlheinz, B10
Stockholm Kammerchor, D93
Stockholm Radio Choir, D127
Stokowski, Leopold, D157
Storkyrkans Kör, D129
Storrer, William Allin, B252
Stoutz, Edmond de, W138; D20,
  D166; B25, B207
Strategier, Herman, B224
Strauss, Richard, B228, B232, B305
Stravinsky, Igor, M19; B7, B26, B34,
  B46, B92, B206, B225, B232,
  B280
Stubin, Blanche, B97
Stuckenschmitt, H. H., B98, B195
Stucki, Hans Walter, D11
Studio d'Arts Dramatique, W22

Sturm, Der, W98; B7, B28-B29, B66, B72, B74, B155, B232, B323-B324, B326-B329, B332-B333, B336
Sturm, Der - 3 Fragmente aus der Oper, D207
Stuttgart Chamber Orchestra, D149
Suite pour orchestre, W4
Suter, Louis-Marc, B99
Suter-Moser, Hélène, W55
Swift, Richard, B348
Swiss Authors and Musicians Festival, M24
Swiss National Exposition, W46
Swoboda, Henry, W106
Swol, Els von, B100
Sydney Symphony Orchestra, D159
Symphony Orchestra and Chorus of the University of Lausanne, D95
Symphonie Concertante, W81
Symphonie pour orchestre burlesque, W6; D153; M2
Symphony, W41; B34, B38, B119, B338-B340
Symphony of Psalms, B102
Symphony Orchestra of Radio Luxembourg, D52, D61
Szell, George, W88, W124; B138, B153
Szigeti, Joseph, W93; B140, B144, B148-B149
Tanner, Andre, B206
Tanner-Egyedi, Klära, D213
Tansman, Alexander, B299
Tappolet, Walter, B101
Tappolet, Willy, B102, B196, B232, B253, B259
Tappy, Eric, W135; D95, D188-D189; B238
Taubman, Howard, B321
Tchaikovsky, Peter, B342
Teachey, Philip, D225
Teatro Colón, B238
Tempest, W92, W98; B145-B146, B226, B323-B327, B329-B338
Terby, Fernand, D28
Terzian, Alicia, B197
Tête de Linotte, W1
Thayer, Edwin, D4
Théâtre du Jurat, B257

Théâtre municipal, Lausanne, B368
theses, B15, B30, B50, B52-B53, B67, B76, B99, B105, B109, B129, B134, B156, B187, B192, B220-B221, B223, B225, B260, B271, B285, B311, B351
Thijsse, Wim, B103
Thomas, Ernst, B254
Thompson, Marcus, D204
Thomson, Virgil, B186, B198
Three Choirs Festival, B213, B315
Three Crosses, The, M2; B190, B199-B200
Timme, Tragott, D141
Tonhalle Gesellschaft, Zürich, W126, B310
Tonhalle-Quartett, W126
Tortelier, Paul, W87; D159; B122
Totentanz zu Basel im Jahre 1943, W61; B319, B341
Toulet, J.-P., W31
Trilling, Ossia, B374
Trimble, Lester, B104
Trimousette, W71
Trio à cordes, W40; D209; B38
Trio Fontenay, D216
Trio Montavo, D213
Trio Musiviva, D215
Trio Röntgen, W40
Trio sur des mélodies populaires irlandaises, W20; D210-D216; B342
Trio, Op. 70, No. 2, B342
Tristan legend, B320, B349, B351-B352, B354-B355, B357, B360-B361, B363, B365, B368, B370, B372, B375
Trois Chants de Noël, W85; D217-D224; B73, B80
Trois danses pour hautbois, harpe et orchestre, W134; D225-D226; B25, B27, B86, B343-B348
Trois poèmes païens, W2; B38
True, Nelita, D112
Tschupp, Räto, B116
Tudor, Anthony, B277
Tully, Alice, B287-B288
Tupper, Janet Eloise, B105
Tusa, Antonio, W40

twelve-tone system, B6, B8, B10,
B18, B26, B31, B33-B34, B36,
B38, B48-B49, B51, B64, B68,
B70, B74-B75, B100, B106-B108,
B110, B112, B131, B150, B188,
B191, B197, B199, B209, B211,
B253, B256, B275, B278, B309,
B328, B336, B339, B355, B363-
B364, B373
Union Chorale et Choeur des Dames
de, D119, D188-D189
University of Geneva, B291
University of Lausanne, B85
Unterweisung in Tonsatz, B15
Vajnar, František, D162
Valery, Paul, M18
Vantine, Bruce Lynn, B225
Varendonck, Dirk, D58
Vaucher-Clerc, Germaine, D155
Vaughan Williams, Ralph, B315
Verlaine, Paul, W16
Vermeulen, Ernst, B133
Verse à boire, W116; D227-D228
Vessieres, Andre, B238
Vestdijk, Simon, B106-B107
Vicuña, Magdalena, B108
Vienna Philharmonic, B323, B331
Vienna State Opera, B323, B331,
B336
Villa-Lobos, Heitor, B299
Villisech, Jacques, D121
Villon, Francois, W133; B16, B287
Vin herbé, Le, W44, W50; D229-
D230; M8, M10; B4, B6, B19, B23,
B33, B35, B38, B46, B56, B60, B68,
B75, B79, B95, B110, B116, B160,
B256, B268, B313, B319, B349-B375
Vink, Fija, B109
Vintschger, Jürg, D102
Violinkonzert, B161
Viotti, Marcello, D26, D51, D54
Vlad, Roman, B10, B110-B112, B270
Voix des siècles, La, W58-W59
Voorberg, Marinus, B222
Vranken, Toon, B219, B290
Wach auf, Wach auf, W73
Wagner, Richard, M25; B19, B43,
B46, B79, B107-B108, B256, B296,

Wagner, Richard, cont.
B305, B327, B351-B352, B355,
B357, B362, B368, B375
Wakamoto, Takeshi, D121
Walcha, Helmut, B263
Wallberg, Heinz, W106; B234
Walter, Franz, B255, B298, B337
Walter, Johannes, D22
Walter von der Vogelweide, W113
Wanansell, Camillo, D24
Wand, Günter, D163
Wartburg College Choir, D125-D126
Watson, William, D5, D8
Weber, Carl Maria von, B108
Webern, Anton, B7
Webster, Elizabeth, B213
Weinrich, Hans, B120
Weise von Liebe und Tod des
Cornet Ch. Rilke, Die, see Cornet,
Der
Welbourne, Todd G., B134
Wellner, Christa, D122
Wenziger, August, W87
Wer Jetzig Zeiten Leben Will, W74
Werba, Eric, B163
Werker, Gerard, B167
Westflämisches Orchester, D58
Whitney, Robert, D60
Whittall, Arnold, B115
Wickihalder, Nicole, D78, D82, D89,
D100, D116
Wicks, Alan, D123
Widmer-Hoch, Pauline, W55
Willoughby,Robert, D16
Wilson, Ransom, B82
Winkler, Gerhard E., B199
Winterthur Symphony Orchestra,
D55, D230; B352
Wissmer, Pierre, M14
Witteman, Wim, B256
Wohl Auf, Wer Bass Will Wandern,
W74
Wolf, Hugo, B318
Wolf, Jan, D173
Wolfensberger, Rita, D213
Wolff, Charles de, B210
Wolvekamp, W. H., B168
Wouters, Jos., B173
Wyss, Colette, W13

Zagrosek, Lothar, D65
Zarou, Jeannette, D122
Zaubertrank, Der see Vin Herbé, Le
Zundel, Maurice, W141; B164-B165
Zürich Kammerorchester, D20, D166;
    B25, B207
Zürich Piano Quintet, D187
Züricher Madrigalchor, W44, W50
Zwol, Cornelis van, B200
Zyma/Nyon, W141

About the Compiler

CHARLES W. KING is Assistant Music Librarian at the University of Arizona Library. His previous published articles include "Arizona's State Song(s)," "A Discography of the Music of Frank Martin," and "Music for Flute and Harp."

**Recent Titles in
Bio-Bibliographies in Music**

Vincent Persichetti: A Bio-Bibliography
Donald L. Patterson and Janet L. Patterson

Robert Ward: A Bio-Bibliography
Kenneth Kreitner

William Walton: A Bio-Bibliography
Carolyn J. Smith

Albert Roussel: A Bio-Bibliography
Robert Follet

Anthony Milner: A Bio-Bibliography
James Siddons

Edward Burlingame Hill: A Bio-Bibliography
Linda L. Tyler

Alexander Tcherepnin: A Bio-Bibliography
Enrique Alberto Arias

Ernst Krenek: A Bio-Bibliography
Garrett H. Bowles, compiler

Ned Rorem: A Bio-Bibliography
Arlys L. McDonald

Richard Rodney Bennett: A Bio-Bibliography
Stewart R. Craggs, compiler

Radie Britain: A Bio-Bibliography
Walter B. Bailey and Nancy Gisbrecht Bailey